RELATIONSHIP
FUNDRAISING

Other books by the same author

Advertising by Charities
Charity Annual Reports

RELATIONSHIP FUNDRAISING

A DONOR-BASED APPROACH TO THE BUSINESS OF RAISING MONEY

KEN BURNETT

The White Lion Press Limited London

in association with The International Fund Raising Group London

Published by
The White Lion Press Limited
White Lion Court
7 Garrett Street
London EC1Y 0TY

In association with
The International Fund
Raising Group
352 Kennington Road
London SE11 4LD

First printed 1992
Reprinted 1993

Printed and bound in the United
Kingdom by Page Brothers Limited
Norwich NR6 6SA, England

Contents

Motives and background – 15 years of change –
fundraising professionals – introducing relationship
fundraising – making friends with your donor –
investing in the future – what is a donor? – what
fundraising is all about – action points.

DONOR PROFILE – MARY TEWSON

Coming out at parties – challenging public prejudice –
pride in the profession – scale and opportunity – putting
the world's troubles to right – value for money –
fundraiser role models – initiating new recruits –
action points.

DONOR PROFILE – FRED AND ELEANOR SYKES

Ten principles of fundraising – why people give – what
makes a successful fundraiser – commitment and
involvement – action points.

DONOR PROFILE – ROSE LISTER

making clinics – the one-per-cent club – action points.

DONOR PROFILE – ALICE JENKS

Crystal ball gazing – some crises – short-term thinking – consumerism – how to change your board – the technique take-over – getting the right people – predictions – wishful thinking – a happy ending – action points.

DONOR PROFILE – MR AND MRS CHRISTISEN

Acknowledgements

The ideas and efforts of a large number of people have helped in the preparation of this book and I owe them all a considerable debt. Lack of space prevents me from listing everyone.

I am grateful particularly to the International Fund Raising Group for having faith in my idea and for providing the encouragement and the means to enable it to see the light of day.

I am indebted to all my colleagues at Burnett Associates who made it possible for me to disappear for weeks on end to work on this book, although I confess to being slightly alarmed to see that they managed to do so well without me.

I am grateful to all our clients, who have allowed me to work on so many interesting projects over the years and at whose hands I have learned more lessons than I care to remember. Through them I have been able to meet a large number of donors, members and supporters, those endlessly fascinating people who are the lifeblood of all the organisations for which I work. I have tried to give a fleeting introduction to some of these people through the donor profiles which appear at the end of each chapter. But I should explain that these are composite images, not based on any particular individual. Their purpose is only to remind you that donors are all different and that each represents an opportunity. Make of them what you will.

Specifically, I would like to thank a number of authors, many of whom I have never met, whose published works have played an important part in my research for this book.

It amazes me how many people I meet in fundraising and direct marketing who have never read any of the many great textbooks that have been published recently in our business area, both in this country and abroad. I have been in the marketing business for more than 20 years and I still couldn't exist without them. My company keeps a well-stocked reference library which everyone uses and we are continually adding to it. Some of these books, such as Harold Evans' *Pictures on a Page* and Drayton Bird's *Commonsense Direct Marketing*, are in almost constant use.

In preparing this publication on relationship fundraising I have been inspired and guided by several works and I owe their authors a tremendous debt of gratitude. I have always advocated plagiarism and consider it the most sincere form of flattery, so I hope they will be flattered if they find some of their ideas (always properly acknowledged, of course) reproduced in my pages. True creativity is borrowing someone else's idea and adding to it, rather like the sparrow who climbed on the eagle's back so he could fly just a little higher. In such ways is knowledge advanced. I would like to pay tribute here to the following eagles: Stan Rapp and Tom Collins for *MaxiMarketing*, Drayton Bird for *Commonsense Direct Marketing*, Robert Leiderman for *The Telephone Book*, Judith E Nichols for *Changing Demographics: Fund Raising in the 1990s*, Graeme McCorkell for *Advertising that Pulls Response*, James Gregory Lord for *The Raising of Money*, and Peter F Drucker for *Managing the Non-profit Organization*. I also owe a lot to *Professional Fundraising* (UK) and *Fund*

Raising Management (USA), two indispensable journals on fundraising. A fuller list of relevant publications can be found in the bibliography.

Specific chapters have been read and commented on at manuscript stage by several acknowledged experts and I am grateful to them for their time and commitment. Thanks to Anne Wrangham of Crossbow Research, Rich Fox of telemarketing specialists Facter Fox International and David Ford of Smee and Ford Limited, the world's leading authority on wills and legacies.

Others whose ideas also shaped my thoughts include Guy Stringer, John Groman, John Hambley, Roger Millington, Ian Ventham, Redmond Mullin, Michael Downes, Gavin Grant and, of course, Harold Sumption. You each might recognise a little bit of what I learned from you in this book.

Cary Goode and Sanchi Heesom both cast their professional eyes over the final manuscript and made valuable suggestions. Theresa Lloyd and Annie Moreton also provided help in the final stages.

Giles Pegram has been an indispensable source of ideas, guidance and encouragement through all the manuscript stages and ranks in the quality of his contribution alongside George Smith, who read the draft twice making useful comments at each pass and still survived to write a masterly foreword. What more can I say?

I must also credit Roy Williams' striking cover design and contributions from my colleagues Ernst Goetschi, Susan Kay, Derek Humphries, Celia Cole and Jackie Fowler. The hands on the jacket belong to Jane Sowerby and Graham Curd. Marie Burnett supervised research, production and the editing of the text. Felicity Ford deciphered my hieroglyphics, typed and retyped all the text, edited my appalling grammar and punctuation and even assisted with designing the text pages.

Whatever value this book has, it wouldn't have been as good without any of you. Thanks.

Ken Burnett
London
March 1992

Foreword

I have always been leery of experts. It seems to me that the twentieth century has paid a significant price for idle worship of what we too freely think of as expertise and which so often turns out to be institutional fashion. The M25 and tower blocks were planned by experts, the British economy has been forever run by experts. Need I say more?

Wherever you turn, there is expertise. Wine experts tell you what best to drink, football experts predict results, politicians have answers for everything and the expertise of the marketing wallahs continues complacent and smug in the face of all negative experience. About ten years ago, there came to be fundraising experts.

Of course, there is value in experience, there is value in common sense, there is often value in opportunism and the best value always lies in original clear-cut thinking. But the extent to which these humble virtues aggregate to expertise is highly questionable. For fundraising experts should be able to offer predictive success each campaign out. Rather obviously, they cannot. The man who mends your washing machine is a better expert.

Ken Burnett's book accidentally proceeds from a certain suspicion of fundraising expertise and it's one of the reasons I value it. This is not a book where the author tells you how precisely to raise funds cost-effectively. This is a book that tries to wave goodbye to formulaic practice in favour of vivid reporting of the author's considerable experience, some very diligent translation of other people's experience and offering fundraisers a great big fat Point of View.

The Point of View may sound obvious but it badly needs restating. It says that we've all become too obsessed with technique and too forgetful about the personal and human relationships which lie at the heart of true fundraising. This, I can assure you, is no sentimental bromide but a highly functional and usable observation. And it has never been better explored and developed than in this new book of Ken's.

It could be that, in publishing it, we might have created a new and fashionable theology of Relationship Fundraising. That is not the intention of either the author or the publishers. If you are anxious about the early dominance of technology in fundraising, you need not swing into a facile counter-revolutionary stance that condemns database management as heresy and the silicon chip as the root of all evil. And this is not a Luddite book, far from it.

Indeed, I've just written some of the longest and most pompous words you'll find between these covers. For this book is actually fun. The many anecdotes are entertaining as well as instructive, the case histories amusing as well as revealing, the statistics are always selected for relevance and not just for bulk. But underpinning them all is that Point of View – fundraising is to do with people, not technology. It's actually a passionate Point of View.

For Ken Burnett is actually a passionate kind of bloke. If I called him that in public he'd cringe. But it's true. And it's relevant. For that most un-British virtue of passion lies at the heart of all fundraising and I am delighted to see it stalking its proud way through these pages. Ken tells you to care about raising money and to resist all temptation to see that noble and altruistic craft as a matter of buttons pressed and files shuffled.

Relationship Fundraising is likely to be the most important book in British fundraising for some time to come. That's why I'm glad that Ken has made it more than a mere textbook. If he'd done that, he would have postured as Expert. As it is, he's done something superior. He's made all of us think.

We should be grateful for the difference.

George Smith
Chief Executive, International Fund Raising Group
March 1992

Why this book?

'He urged us to work for their freedom, not to despise even the small help that each of us can give. He told us where their courage comes from. It comes from you.'

Reporting the words of released hostage Terry Waite in an advertisement for Amnesty International, *Where does their courage come from?*

I think I actually decided to write this book on a train, coming back from Bristol to London in November 1990 after the Institute of Charity Fundraising Managers* Wales and West Region's annual conference. I was with ICFM's director, Stephen Lee, and we were discussing the shortage of good British books on the subject of fundraising. At the same time we were trying to listen to the crackly radio on Stephen's personal stereo which he held against the train's window to improve reception as we rumbled across the West Country. This was not normal commuter practice. Our interest in the radio that day was the promised announcement of the results of the first ballot in the election of a leader for Britain's Conservative party which was then going through internecine strife, much to the glee of most Parliament-watchers at the time.

I remember the occasion well. Not just because we discussed the gap in good books on fundraising, but

---

* The Institute of Charity Fundraising Managers (ICFM) is the professional association that provides training and standards for fundraisers in the United Kingdom.

I feel a growing unease about some aspects of the direct marketing explosion in fundraising.

because, on Stephen's insistence, I was wearing the headphones and describing events from Westminster to an expectant gathering of fellow commuters. The tension was considerable. The high point of the occasion, obviously, was to be the announcement of the actual votes cast and we had breathlessly built up to that climactic moment. As I relayed the broken words of the announcer saying, 'And here it is, ladies and gentlemen, the votes cast in this leadership election are ...,' the train entered a tunnel. Our slender radio link with the outside world was instantly and completely severed. We were, literally, left in the dark.

The tunnel just outside Bristol is one of the longest in Britain. When we emerged it was all over. I think *Gardeners' Question Time* might have been on but I really can't remember.

Life on the train returned to normal and Stephen and I returned to discussing the lack of any good up-to-the-minute book on fundraising.

A unique business area

Of course, none of this has anything to do with *why* I decided to write this book. The real reason has more to do with lessons learned from the wide variety and large number of fundraising organisations I have worked with during 15 years as a fundraiser. It's also to do with a growing unease I feel about some aspects of the direct marketing explosion in fundraising and the way that the onset of 'professionalism' is leaving a sour taste in the mouths of many of the donors I meet. The scale of advance in training and technique in fundraising has been spectacular. But, not surprisingly, amidst all the excitement some of the fundamentals of fundraising have been neglected, if not overlooked entirely, in the rush to professionalise.

I'm astonished at how rapidly and, in some cases, how completely the naïve and often counter-productive amateurism of the past has given way to professionalism in strategy, materials and approach.

In recent years, fundraisers have seen some remarkable changes. Although very many of the old ways and prejudices still exist, the new fundraiser coming in for professional training now will see a very different career area to the one I joined. I keep telling myself that 15 years is not a long time, but 15 years ago even some of the biggest charities had barely heard of marketing, or training, or even professionalism.

Looking back, I'm astonished at how rapidly and, in some cases, how completely the naïve and often counter-productive amateurism of the past has given way to professionalism in strategy, materials and approach from charities. Charities are now better managed, more clearly focused and stronger as a result. In general, increased professionalism has been a great blessing for both charity and donor, but there has been a downside because most donors don't understand professionalism in charities. Many are suspicious of it and don't like it.

Nowhere has the increase in professionalism been more evident than in charity marketing, particularly in the growth of direct mail and other printed communication. The 1980s were a boom time for charity marketing in Britain. It wasn't a time of much new invention. It was rather a time for learning the lessons already understood by our brothers and sisters in more 'commercial' trade, taking what has been proven to work for them and applying it to the business of raising money.

But raising money for a cause is a unique business area. It benefits from many of the highest human emotions and is lucky enough not to be burdened by some of the basest. One thing is certain, a fundraising transaction is fundamentally different to a

... they will commit a fatal, suicidal, error if they embrace commercial practices too enthusiastically.

commercial business transaction and while fundraisers have much to learn from commercial practice they will commit a fatal, suicidal, error if they embrace commercial practices too enthusiastically.

Charity marketing professionals have certainly appeared in numbers in recent years, but I suspect that their short and unglamorous career is coming to an end.

A new breed of professional will have to emerge to take their place. I hope that this new breed will be what I call 'the relationship fundraiser'.

The relationship fundraiser will have learned all the lessons of commercial marketing that the old-style charity marketer had learned. But he or she will have something else – he will have a deep commitment to his chosen profession of fundraising and a clear understanding of all the important aspects that mark fundraising out from other commercial applications.

He or she will, of course, be a supremely skilled and well-trained professional in every aspect of his trade. But he will realise that to succeed in fundraising marketing he has to *adapt* commercial marketing methods, not simply *adopt* them. Above all he will understand his donor – his version of 'the customer'.

He or she will study and appreciate the unique bond, the relationship, that exists between donors and the cause that they support. And preserving, developing and extending that relationship will be the relationship fundraiser's primary goal.

What is a donor?
Donors are people who actively support your work through their sustained financial contributions. Charities don't depend by any means on donors for all their income, but donors do provide a large and

vitally important part. They also have many other valuable uses.

Your donors are your organisation's friends. With friends you can share good news and bad, keep in touch and develop a long-term relationship that brings benefits to both sides. Your donors benefit from their role in the work you do, from sharing in your successes and achievements and from the satisfaction of knowing their contribution has been effective. You benefit, of course, from the level and frequency of their donations, but also because they will often be the most enthusiastic ambassadors of your cause. They will recruit their friends, they will enable you to undertake reciprocal mailings with other charities, they will purchase your mail order products and will respond to your crises, your emergency and special appeals. They will tell you what your organisation is doing right and what they don't believe in. They'll help you lobby for change. They will involve their families, will support your events, will help you build a network of local activity, will fundraise for you, will volunteer for all sorts of unpaid work, will provide free public relations, will introduce you to valuable business contacts and much more besides. They will also, in the fullness of time, make their largest contribution to your cause by leaving you a legacy in their will.

Two quite different anecdotes illustrate the value of committed donors. Several years ago a major British children's organisation became involved in a scandal. A social worker employed by the charity had falsified records to show that a child at risk had received supervisory visits, when no such visits had been made. Later the child had died at the hands of its own parent. The news was carried in the press and

Donors applauded this sincere and honest action and responded accordingly.

caused a national uproar. The charity involved wisely made no attempt to disguise its responsibility. Instead it wrote a detailed account to all donors, explaining what had happened and outlining the action it proposed taking to ensure nothing similar could happen in the future. Donors applauded this admission of failure and responded accordingly. They were asked to renew their support at this difficult time and money came flooding in spontaneously, for these people really cared.

During the Ethiopian famine of 1984 Oxfam learned that already weakened children were dying of cold. They wrote to volunteers and donors, asking them to knit woollen sweaters which could be airlifted out. The response was overwhelming. Donors were placed in the front line of disaster relief and willingly did what they could. Oxfam flew literally millions of knitted jumpers into Ethiopia to meet that need immediately.

In *Managing the Non-profit Organization* management guru Peter Drucker says, 'We can no longer hope to get more money from the donor, they have to become contributors.'

I suspect his definition of a donor may be narrower than mine but I believe that really to thrive in the future we have to *involve* donors even more: to make them more than donors and more than contributors. We have to be genuinely accountable to them.

Some years ago one of Oxfam's small overseas programmes failed because the responsible individual on the spot was ill. As a result, Oxfam's investment was a complete flop. One particular donor, a bank, had put up a sizeable part of the money. Oxfam went to see the bank and explained exactly what had happened. That bank still supports

Every fundraiser has a responsibility to the donor, to satisfy himself that the organisation's programmes are sound and to report back to the donor that they are.

Oxfam in many ways.

You have to share disappointments as well as achievements.

In developing donor relationships we are seeking ways to enable our donors to participate actively in the work we do through their giving. We have to see donors as co-owners of the organisation, partners in a common aim. And we have to enable them to feel that sense of co-ownership too.

In return for all this contribution and commitment from donors the fundraiser has to ensure that the donor's money is well spent and his or her trust is not misplaced. Every fundraiser has a responsibility to the donor, to satisfy himself that the organisation's programmes are sound and to report back to the donor that they are. This often means the fundraiser has to ask awkward questions of the programme managers and to insist on full answers. That's the fundraiser's job.

Fundraising is important

The fundraising role is crucial. Each one of the service organisations for which fundraisers work can only succeed if it receives the voluntary financial support that pays for the work it does. It is up to fundraisers to make this happen. They have to work on many fronts, across an enormous range of commercial marketing disciplines – from managing a local and regional network to national press advertising, from retailing and catalogue trading to publications design and pro-duction, from press and public relations to organising large-scale public events and including every aspect of direct marketing, television and radio appeals, managing volunteers, corporate campaigns and a host of other promotional specialisations to boot.

Few professions offer such variety as fundraising ... If you think selling a product is difficult, try getting someone to give you money for nothing.

Few professions offer such variety as fundraising – and, of course, the overstretched fundraiser also has to ensure that the needed funds are raised ultra-efficiently and cost-effectively. If you think selling a product is difficult, try getting someone to give you money for nothing.

Also, because there is no tangible product or service in most fundraising transactions, the fundraiser has to meet and satisfy a range of complex emotions and conditions in the donor. To do this over a sustained period of time – the donor's life cycle – requires consummate skill and understanding at the highest professional level.

I start from the conviction that the relationship fundraiser must be one of the most skilful, most proficient and most versatile marketing professionals to be found anywhere in the world.

Anyone who has any doubts about the high commercial standards of fundraisers should look closely at the 1,000+ entries submitted each year for the annual British Direct Marketing Awards, about 50 of which will be entered for the fundraising category. Recently I was asked to be one of the judges for these prestigious awards, which are the highest accolades awarded by Britain's thriving direct marketing industry. I not only learned a lot through looking at the best submissions in 22 different categories of direct marketing activity, I was also immensely impressed by the high standard of the fundraising entries. I was proud beyond measure to hear my fellow judges overwhelmingly agree that the most outstanding category of all, the category with the highest overall quality in creativity, strategy and performance, was – fundraising.

This will come as a surprise to many but it

The techniques, approaches and systems have similarities with other areas of marketing endeavour but, essentially, they are quite unique to fundraising.

shouldn't. In fact, anything else would be something of a failure. Fundraising should be the best area of marketing. We should set the standard others follow. Why? Because we have the best stories, the best case histories and the best reasons why people should buy our product. And the best incentive to present our case distinctively.

Confusion with a commercial marketing career should swiftly be put to rest. Fundraisers are not selling products such as baked beans or razor blades and there is little similarity in the underlying motivations fundraisers invoke. We simply share a few of the processes. What fundraisers do is *they make caring service possible* by enabling donors to realise their capacity and potential to support good works.

The techniques, approaches and systems that will achieve this have similarities with other areas of marketing endeavour but, essentially, they are quite unique to fundraising.

That is relationship fundraising.

Fundraisers are members of a profession that is one of the world's most powerful catalysts for change. Because without the money raised by fundraisers there are no good works. Deprived of the funds that fuel their every activity the aims and objectives of the organisations that employ us would simply fail.

But when fundraisers are successful and increase the resources that enable these organisations to go on to do *new work* then there is literally no limit to what we can achieve and to the good we can do.

Voluntary agencies lead the way in the welfare sector. It is fundraisers who provide the means that let them do it.

This is a dreadful indictment of the state of our profession, but it's true.

Spot the difference

What difference will it make if fundraisers become more donor-oriented? Will charities, in time, present a different image and identity to their audiences than the image and identity they present today?

I think they will. Imagine if television advertising, for example, were to be consumer-oriented rather than sales-oriented. It's a radical thought.

I'm not suggesting that anyone takes relationship fundraising to that extreme, or at least not immediately and without fully considering all the consequences. But, despite its risks and its costs, consumerism has done a lot to improve the public acceptability of a range of industries and, along with the rest of society, those industries themselves have ultimately benefited. Our society and our employers can similarly benefit from relationship fundraising.

Something special

If this book can convey something of why fundraising is such a special field of work then it will have achieved one of its objectives. If it can encourage fundraisers to active concern for their donors and their donors' feelings and thereby avoid shooting themselves in the foot through inappropriate promotion then it will have achieved another objective.

And if it can find its way into the hands of charity trustees and senior management and help them to appreciate some of the complexities and importance of the donor/fundraiser relationship then I'll be satisfied. The most common problem voiced at fundraising seminars I attend is the comment 'that's a great idea, but how on earth can I get it past my trustees?' This is a dreadful indictment of the state of our profession, but it's true.

It seems to me to be ridiculous for any charity to have large investments in property or in stocks and shares if it hasn't invested in the development of its donor list.

I have one other important aim for this book. It is to encourage fundraising organisations to invest for the future, not in stocks and shares, but in building a body of committed supporters and in developing and extending the commitment of these donors through relationship fundraising. This is the most important investment any fundraising organisation can make. In fact, it seems to me to be entirely ridiculous for any charity to have large investments in property or in stocks and shares if it hasn't invested in the development of its donor list.

Please note

This is not intended to be an expert work. I am not an expert and I am rather anxious not to become one since I realised that Noah's Ark was designed by an amateur and the Titanic was designed by an expert.

Fundraising is delightfully free of experts. Most people in fundraising, even those who are very long in the tooth, are only too ready to admit they haven't seen it all.

I am lucky enough to have been involved in the business of fundraising for a comparatively long time. I am further fortunate, thanks to the clients of my company, to have worked alongside many of Britain's best and most experienced fundraisers on a wide range of promotional projects for virtually every type and shade of fundraising organisation. I have had at least as many dismal failures as spectacular successes and the majority of the rest have been somewhere in between – quiet, unspectacular little money-earners.

So this book is also not a scholarly work. It is a practitioner's observations. Parts of it may be contentious. You may disagree with some of what I say. If so, please let me know.

Here again there is a two-way relationship where both volunteer and cause can benefit.

It is also not complete. My fundraising experience does not include much that's worth saying about several specialist areas of fundraising including special events, corporate fundraising, local activities and volunteers. That's why you won't find much about these areas in this book – it's not because I don't think they are important.

I wish I did know more about volunteers, because that seems to me to be an area of enormous potential for the organisations we work for and for the good work they support. People who give their time are in every way as important as people who give their money. Their gift of time can achieve every bit as much as a financial donation. I was a volunteer myself once and I found it a richly rewarding experience. So I know that here again there is a two-way relationship where both volunteer and cause can benefit.

I hope that some of what I say in this book will also apply to volunteers and that those people whose job it is to encourage and coordinate the efforts of volunteers will find at least some parts of it useful.

Inevitably there is a large amount of overlap between chapters although I have tried my best to limit it. The subjects I am writing about – donors, research, marketing, communications, dangers, opportunities, and so on – are not isolated compartments and each in some way or other inextricably involves most of the other subjects. Consequently, editing out duplication is not only difficult it is often impossible. I have tried to remove the more obvious areas, save those where a bit of repetition is justified by the importance of the subject.

Also, of necessity, I have assumed that you, the reader, have a reasonable knowledge of the major areas of fundraising so I haven't, for example, sought to describe the basics of fundraising marketing, such as direct mail or press advertising, in absolute detail.

One word or two?

One of the great fundraising mysteries, still unsolved, is to do with the very word 'fundraising' itself. How should it be spelled? Is it 'fundraising' or 'fund raising'? Or is it hyphenated?

I think it is one word to describe one area of activity and that is the style I shall use in this book. Many others hold an alternative view (for example, the International Fund Raising Group). There is no obvious solution so not surprisingly a further group, no doubt confused, uses all three forms with seeming abandon. The *Oxford English Dictionary*, source of arbitration in such matters, is not much help. Until recently it didn't even mention us. Now it does, but as two words, hyphenated.

Some closing remarks

For the last few years the closing remarks at the International Fund Raising Workshop (the gathering of professional fundraisers from around the world which takes place each year in the Netherlands) have been delivered by Guy Stringer, formerly director of Oxfam, one-time senior executive with a major manufacturing company, and now one of fundraising's most eminent and respected gentlemen. He has more experience of and insight into the power and potential of fundraising than most of us are likely to achieve in a lifetime. For several years Guy has fulfilled a unique role for fundraisers as Chairman of the International Fund Raising Group (IFRG).

Guy has a single purpose in the few minutes he occupies on the platform at the end of each year's

Workshop. As he addresses the several hundred delegates, who have just survived three intensive days learning at the frontiers of the art and science of their profession, he seeks to remind them of the larger purpose of being there. Techniques and skills are limited without a clear purpose, he tells them. To remind fundraisers of what it's really all about Guy tells some stories from his own long experience. His purpose is to send them off with spirits soaring and sights set high. He invariably succeeds, because he knows what makes good fundraisers tick.

With Guy's permission I'll relate two of his stories.

Who am I?
'Surat is a town in western India and the last time that I was there I arrived by train. You come out of the station and walk across a square, up a long hill and down a lane, where at the top, on the left-hand side, there is a leprosarium. It is run by sturdy Catholic sisters, some Indian and some Spanish. I arrived late at night and was quite tired and would have preferred to have thrown a bucket of water over myself and lain down. But Sister Mary insisted that I walk round the leprosarium with her and I have found it a mistake to disagree with Catholic sisters.

'So round we went and to my astonishment there were little collections of people sitting round hurricane lamps on the ground, and I said to the sister, "What are they doing?" She said that the young patients were teaching the old people to read and write. And so they were – with the children saying, "No granny, you don't do it that way but like this". The only things that Oxfam had provided were the slates, the chalk and the little hurricane lamps.

'When we got to the gates of the leprosarium I saw

Who was the third person in the frame, in a Marks and Spencer sweater, size 40, do not boil? How did he fit?

they were closed, but in the gloom you could see on the far side a little gang of people and the sister said to me, "Guy, open the gates". I did so and a family carried in a man. The sister led the way and they put the man on a table in the clinic. If they had put him on the ground he would have fallen down because his legs stopped at his knees. The sister knelt down and looked at the patient and she said to me, "There are worms in his wounds" and I looked and there were. Then a strange thing happened and it was rather like a camera going click, click. I could see who the sister was, she was somebody who could bring effective help to the patient. And I could see who the patient was, he needed help and badly. But who was the third person in the frame, in a Marks and Spencer sweater, size 40, do not boil? How did he fit?

'The deduction from this of course is that if you are to be concerned in trying to help the poor, the handicapped and the deprived you must be totally involved. You must try to project in what you write and say in your advertisements and public addresses the courage of the people, their determination to advance the lives of their families, their responsibility one to another and you must never at any time undervalue them.'

Flying a kite

'El Salvador has probably the worst record for human rights in the world. It is a tiny country the size of Wales, but people are murdered at night and if you wish to see your friends again you visit the city rubbish dump and there you will find their bodies. That's where they are battered to death. As a result a large number of families are in church refuges where they live under the care and defence of the church,

Do not forget that techniques and skills themselves are limited. What you must do is to stand up and encourage and develop a vision of a new society.

because if they left these places they would end up, as so many others do, outside the city.

'I visited one with about 200 families and hundreds of tiny children. It was a classic demonstration of the ability of women because the place was immaculate. I would have got it in a muddle in five minutes flat. There was only one small piece of land open to the sky which was surrounded by a very high wire fence. The children congregated in masses on this tiny piece of playground – the only bit of open air to be found. And they were making paper kites with newspaper, little bits of stick and some string. But of course if you fly a kite you need wind and you need some space and the children found it extremely difficult to get their kites off the ground. The result was that the big wire fence was simply covered with battered kites.

'Eventually I left to go, walked out into the road, looked up and down – it is always wise in El Salvador to see who is about – and walked down the road to turn right at a corner at the bottom. Before I did I turned round and looked up and two little kites had cleared the fence and were lifting up jerking bit by bit into the dark blue sky. Some people would say that this is just some string, a bit of newspaper, some little sticks and two little boys, but in fact it is more than that. It is a triumph of the human spirit over the grim environment in which so many dwell.

'You came here to learn about fundraising and will have learned much about new techniques and skills in your time here. I hope you have enjoyed it, but do not forget that techniques and skills themselves are limited. What you must do is to stand up and encourage and develop a vision of a new society in which all of us may dwell in peace and harmony.'

More than a job

In quoting Guy's words I can't invoke the sincerity and passion of his delivery or recreate the emotional charge in his voice that ensures there's not a dry eye in the house. Guy's stories are magic. They give fundraisers a lift and remind us that our profession is more special than most other trades or businesses. For me, that makes Guy's closing address perhaps the most important part of each year's International Fund Raising Workshop.

Fundraising is more than a job. In the right hands, it is a powerful force for change and while that change is under way it should be an inspirational beacon of hope. Fundraisers have good reason to be proud of their profession.

If I have missed anything important while preparing this book, I'm sorry and trust you will let me know so I can put it right in the future. For further information on a wide range of fundraising and marketing subjects please refer to the bibliography on page 323 of this book.

ACTION POINTS

A similar list of action points appears at the end of each chapter of this book. I hope you will use them as convenient *aide-mémoires* to enable you more easily to put relationship fundraising into practice.

▲ Prepare to change your approach to fundraising to become a 'relationship fundraiser'.

▲ Learn from commercial practice. But adapt the methods used rather than adopt them.

▲ Be aware of the variety of ways in which donors help

your organisation. Make sure others are aware of it too.

▲ Never attempt to disguise a mistake.

▲ See your donors as partners in a common aim. Enable them to feel a sense of co-ownership.

▲ Make sure that donors' money is well spent and that their trust is not misplaced.

▲ Don't forget that people who give their time can be as valuable as those who give money.

DONOR PROFILE

Mary Tewson

Mary Tewson lives in a well-to-do modern housing development on the outskirts of a large town in the North of England. She is 54 years old, unmarried and lives with Agnes, who is eight years older and her only surviving sister. They share Mary's detached three-bedroomed house which Mary bought on a mortgage nearly 20 years ago and has now almost paid off. The house is just two miles from where Mary works as receptionist for a veterinary surgeon. She is popular with her colleagues and highly regarded by her employer. Mary earns a reasonable salary and has few outgoings. The house is comfortable and well furnished.

Mary is of medium height, in very good health and is particularly proud that her long black hair has so far avoided any signs of grey. Always smartly dressed, she drives a Ford Fiesta car with a 1600 cc engine which she likes because it gives her that extra bit of acceleration.

Both Mary and her sister are regular churchgoers. Most of their social life revolves around a variety of church-related clubs and committees. These activities keep both sisters very busy and of course they see a lot of each other. But, from time to time, Mary likes to go out on her own, to the pictures or shopping in town. Last year she also went on holiday alone, to Tenerife, breaking the habit of a lifetime of holidays spent in Britain with her sister.

Mary is actively involved with her local hospice and in fundraising for the local group of friends of the nearby general hospital. Although she's not interested in politics she is much concerned about world affairs, particularly injustice. She shows her love of children and her concern for their problems by supporting several children's charities both at home and abroad. She sponsors two children, one in India and one in Africa, and gains great comfort from providing this practical and tangible help. She eagerly awaits news from either of the sponsored children, or their projects.

Mary receives a lot of mail from charities, some of which she supports and some of which she doesn't. She welcomes opportunities to be useful, particularly if it helps children. She recently accepted nomination for the committee of the local branch of a national child care charity, and was delighted to be elected. In due course she hopes to be able to use her secretarial skills as branch secretary.

Mary hasn't made a will, but plans to in the near future. She no longer thinks that one day she might get married. Her priority now is to be as useful as she can be to as many people as possible.

2 Fundraising now

'I am still looking for the modern-day equivalent of those Quakers who ran successful businesses, made money because they offered honest products and treated their people decently, worked hard, spent honestly, saved honestly, gave honest value for money, put back more than they took out and told no lies. This business creed, sadly, seems long forgotten.'

Anita Roddick
Body and Soul

Coming out at parties

I don't know of anyone who, from an early age, was telling their parents that what they really wanted to be in life was a fundraiser. Most of us have only drifted into it by accident and some may feel they just 'ended up' in fundraising. Part of the reason for this is that fundraising in Britain has not hitherto been seen as a legitimate career area and most of us had never even heard of it until we found ourselves doing it.

Fundraising is a relatively new career. Most people still don't know what it means or what it involves. Surprisingly it has a fairly low public image relative to its importance, although a few years ago fundraising's image was, if anything, even worse. I know this because it was brought home to me dramatically at parties and other social gatherings when I started in fundraising. I used to respond confidently to the customary question,

It takes courage to come out as a fundraiser, to acknowledge publicly your chosen career in front of friends, acquaintances and those you might be wishing to impress.

'And what do you do ...?' by explaining that, 'I am a fundraiser. I raise money for charity.' In my naïvety I expected to be met by enthusiastic acclaim, admiration and expressions of interest. But instead people reacted as if I'd just announced myself to be a badger gasser or apprentice on a North Sea sludge dumper. I was left in no doubt that asking people for money was not considered a suitable occupation for a grown man. Thereafter – for a short while at least – I took to saying I was in 'overseas development' or 'with a Third World agency' or something equally vague so people felt too embarrassed to ask any further. It's rather like the insurance salesman who terms himself 'investment counsellor' because it sounds better when he tells his mum what he does for a living.

Always negative, these reactions to my being a fundraiser were sometimes openly antagonistic or overtly critical and at times, I suspect, from people who did not give much to charity and appeared to feel rather bad about the fact. I am sure most fundraisers have experienced this chilling reception. It takes courage to come out as a fundraiser, to acknowledge publicly your chosen career in front of friends, acquaintances and those you might be wishing to impress.

Limited public image

Yet this negative view of fundraising is a strange reversal of reality. It's not just a question of job satisfaction. Few career areas present as many opportunities for real responsibility, which often can come at a comparatively early age. At the age of 26 I was appointed UK director of an international charity with more than 100 staff in Britain. I had responsibility for a multi-million pound business with a team of regional fundraisers, a chain of shops, a catalogue marketing operation, a substantial advertising budget, a press and public relations programme, a publications unit, headquarters administration and a new computer system. I wasn't particularly qualified for all this responsibility, so like many other fundraisers I learned the hard way. Nevertheless I managed to cope reasonably successfully with everything except the computer. I doubt I could have found comparable career development opportunities anywhere else. Even now, many years later, I find fundraising still offers some of the best opportunities for real responsibility and challenge as well as, of course, unparalleled job satisfaction. But the downside is the public rarely, if ever, appreciate this. Whilst you have to learn to live with it, you can also fight to change it. Many of the reasons for the public's poor perception lie at our own door, for we have promoted what we do rather badly.

And it's not only the general public that has a low opinion of fundraising. Many organisations that depend on fundraising still undervalue the process and the individuals that carry it out. One of the saddest and most limiting aspects of our profession is the refusal of some trustees and senior charity management to acknowledge the economic realities of their position and accord to fundraisers proper resources, consideration and encouragement. Too many fundraisers still see their trustees as an obstacle rather than an asset.

There have been some changes in fundraising's status in recent years, both good and bad. My off-putting impressions of public lack of esteem for fundraisers were formed before the great fundraising boom of the 1980s when, in the UK at least, careers in fundraising started to blossom along with the growth of charity direct marketing, the use of professional external agencies and the proliferation of the fundraising

I find fundraisers are often strangely shy of admitting what they really do for a living. They prefer to say they're in marketing, or advertising, or public relations or whatever.

consultant. But still I find fundraisers themselves are often strangely shy of admitting what they really do for a living. They prefer to say they're in marketing, or advertising, or public relations or whatever. The truth is the fundraiser is *all* these things and more. If we don't believe in ourselves, why should anyone else believe in us?

Generally low public image is getting worse in some ways. We see ourselves as nobly applying professional techniques and understanding to improving the lot of our fellows. They still see us as benevolent busybodies, gracious ladies (and sometimes gents) whose quaint and condescending hobby is more designed to push us up the social ladder than kick off the shackles of injustice. It may just be that, from being entirely ignorant of our existence a few years ago, some of the public now see us as 'those people who send me that awful junk mail'.

Pride in our profession

The voluntary sector is no longer marginal, it is central to our society. Voluntary giving has always been important, but government policies in recent years have increasingly de-emphasised the role of the State in social provision, resulting in an inevitable increase in society's reliance on a strong and diverse voluntary sector. The voluntary sector is increasingly being called upon to complement and substitute for government action in areas where the State has withdrawn and commercial enterprise has proved to be inappropriate, inadequate or inefficient. This trend is unlikely to reverse and can be seen in several countries. Voluntary action is likely to become even more important in the future.

But the extent and diversity of the voluntary sector in developed countries throughout the world is not widely appreciated. In Britain charitable giving is estimated to be between £3.5 and £5 billion per annum. That's

somewhere around one per cent of Britain's gross
national product and bigger than several of its other
major industries such as agriculture and the combined
value of the UK domestic consumption of coal, gas, oil
and electricity.

Clearly this is a big business by anyone's standards.
It is also a growing business. Although growth may have
slowed during the latter part of the last decade, most
industry sectors would envy the real expansion of the
voluntary sector over the past ten years. In the USA,
after accounting for inflation, growth from 1981 to
1990 was 78 per cent.* It has been equally impressive
in the UK.

Individuals in Britain give around 80 per cent of the
total and around 80 per cent of adults give something
during the course of the year – a fairly creditable market
penetration. (That figure is broadly consistent in other
countries such as the USA, Canada and Australia.)
However, the vast majority of people give tiny, virtually
negligible amounts.

In America the voluntary sector is reported to be the
largest employer of labour and its value represents 2.24
per cent of the country's gross national product. By
contrast some 19 per cent of the French population over
the age of 18 volunteer, giving an average of 18 hours per
month, the equivalent of 650,000 full-time employees at
work. But by comparison with the British and
Americans the French do not yet donate generously to
their non-profit sector. Other European countries lag
even further behind, but the statistics available are poor
so comparison is difficult.

There are over 172,000 registered charities in Britain
and their number is increasing at the rate of 4,000 every
year. Only a fraction of these are fundraising in the
public arena, but of course this small part includes all the

* Sources: *Charity Trends* 1991 and *Giving USA* 1990.

It's not hard to see why these are such interesting times for fundraisers.

largest charities and, while not recorded, the number of causes raising money from the public is almost certainly growing faster now than ever before.

The average gift in the UK is low (and may even have fallen) but this simply shows the considerable potential there is for growth in improving the public's perceptions about giving, encouraging planned giving, encouraging more people to leave a legacy to charity in their will and in targeting specific groups and individuals known to respond to fundraising appeals. (Much is made in the media about fluctuations in this average figure. In practice, a universal average is irrelevant to fundraisers as most of our effort is rightly geared towards a smaller market segment that comprises our real customers – the donors.)

In this already large industry sector there is significant opportunity for further financial growth. There is also considerably increased competition for funds. It's not hard to see why these are such interesting times for fundraisers.

So fundraisers have scale, growth and opportunity in their profession. What else should motivate the new recruit? It's unlikely to be high pay, good benefits and job security because as yet these aren't often found in fundraising.

But there are more positives than negatives. In the first chapter I outlined the importance of fundraising to our society. The work fundraisers do is interesting and challenging. It frequently takes them to exciting places and enables them to meet interesting people. Many fundraisers travel the world, gaining vital firsthand experience of often highly dramatic situations. They also seem constantly to be meeting celebrities, important political figures, the media and even royalty. Fundraisers get access to the people of the moment.

Fundraising is the perfect occupation for the wishful thinker, as success in fundraising means he or she can turn those wishes directly into reality.

Fundraisers can also gain great satisfaction in knowing that what they are doing is really worthwhile. Not only can they bring about change, they can influence people's thinking and extend their interest and involvement in a range of worthwhile activities.

Fundraising is the perfect occupation for the wishful thinker, as success in fundraising means he or she can turn those wishes directly into reality.

Fundraising organisations have other benefits. They encourage compassion and provide millions of people with a practical means of direct involvement in solving the problems and serving the needs of others. They provide opportunities for volunteers (see what pleasure and companionship some men and women get from their local charity shop – which also recycles clothes and other goods), they campaign for social and even political change. Unlike commercial organisations charities don't produce dividends. The fruits of their labours are something more special – changed lives.

Fundraising also is, or soon will be, a true equal opportunities profession. There are at least as many effective women fundraisers as men and although men may still dominate in senior positions that won't last. So when referring to fundraisers in this book I will say 'he or she' whenever practicable. Sometimes that gets a bit cumbersome, so then I've reverted to 'he' or 'she' at random. Ethnic background and physical abilities or disabilities are also largely irrelevant to effectiveness as a fundraiser, so there really is no valid reason why the fundraising profession should not be a model of equal opportunities.

Not-for-profit doesn't mean not profitable
Charitable works often come in for criticism and voluntary organisations are frequently accused of

How many commercial organisations do you know that can claim anything like 80 per cent profit on turnover?

inefficiency and bad management. While all organisations have some shortcomings and some charities have more than their share, my experience of working with commercial clients indicates that by and large the public is quite harsh in its views of charity management. Perhaps it is a good thing that it is as it keeps the sector on its toes, but I think charities could certainly do much to improve their collective image.

After all, most charities are obliged to apply at least 80 per cent of their total income directly towards their charitable objectives. This factor, known as the expense ratio (80 per cent charitable, 20 per cent expenses), is in fact a remarkable achievement in commercial terms, for that 80 per cent represents what most companies would call net profit (ie after all direct costs, administrative costs, overheads and cost of sales, etc have been deducted). How many commercial organisations do you know that can claim anything like 80 per cent profit on turnover? That represents, usually, quite staggering efficiency on behalf of charities and the public should be very proud of this.

Of course, this is an unfair comparison. Voluntary organisations don't have raw material costs or manufacturing costs and can include their costs of service provision in their overall distribution figures. So direct comparison with commercial enterprises is difficult. Nevertheless the gap between the average company's profit ambition (around ten per cent keeps most companies happy) and the charity's need to distribute 80 per cent of its funds is huge, more than enough to cover all costs of sales.

And raising funds for a cause is a much more complicated and difficult process than selling.

Fundraisers are not professional beggars – beggars are almost invariably asking for themselves and give

How could I have any faith that my donation wouldn't be completely wasted if the proper administrative machinery wasn't in place?

little or nothing in return. We ask on behalf of others and we have to be prepared to give a lot. Nor is asking for money on behalf of a third party anything to be even remotely ashamed about – quite the reverse. We promote a unique product. It is something people *want* to buy.

Essential overheads

I am fond of responding to the traditional accusation that charities spend too much on administration by explaining that I wouldn't be prepared to give any of my money to a charity that *didn't* spend a sizeable part of its income on administration. Because, if it didn't, how could I have any faith that my donation wouldn't be completely wasted if the proper administrative machinery wasn't in place? I have never yet found a donor who couldn't follow that logic.

The general public, unfortunately, is often considerably less well informed than donors and few subjects are more calculated to raise the public's ire than visions of a charity overspending on administration. Sadly this paranoia often rubs off on donors who should know better. In some ways the concern has become an *idée fixe* in Britain's collective consciousness.

Fundraisers, therefore, need to recognise this concern, to treat it seriously and to tackle it comprehensively. Like most serious issues, it won't go away if we ignore it.

Different organisations need widely differing administrative machineries and the reasons for this are not difficult to explain. A grant-making charity inevitably requires less administration than one that manages its own programmes. An overseas aid charity may have to spend far more on transport and distribution than it does on service delivery, purely because of a project's location. Most donors can be persuaded to accept that this does not mean a project near a port is any more worthy of support than one that is deep inland. For a charity such as The Samaritans their major cost is in administration – telephone bills, premises, etc – because that organisation is so effective at recruiting volunteers to provide their round-the-clock life-saving service.

The *Report of the Charity Commissioners for England and Wales 1989* is worth quoting on this subject.

'The cost of administering charities is a matter which arouses strong feelings and varied opinions. It is sometimes assumed that people who work for charity should do it for nothing, or, at most, for a pittance. Donors often express a wish that their money should go exclusively to the objects and beneficiaries, and not towards the cost of administration. Charities have on occasion colluded with such attitudes, advertising that no part of any contribution from the public will be spent on administration, and some claiming ever lower administrative costs in a competitive downward spiral. Such attitudes, however, imply that administration is a bad thing, and that the ideal administrative cost is nil. If carried into actual practice, such an attitude can only lead to badly administered charities and to inefficiency and abuse.

'Effective and efficient administration cannot be bought on the cheap. ... The critical task is, therefore, not simply to reduce administrative costs as an end in itself ... it is to identify what level of administration is necessary in each case and to ensure that the strength of a lean and efficient administration is wholly devoted to the objects of the charity in question.'

I'd go along with that. If that's what Britain's major government agency for the voluntary sector is saying on the subject, fundraisers have little excuse for failing individually to publicise their necessary costs of administration and doing so with pride.

If there is any kind of need on any scale, however urgent, emotive or unlikely, it concerns fundraisers.

Any need, on any scale ...

Fundraising is remarkably diverse. Appeals range from campaigning to save the whale to caring for the terminally ill, from medical and scientific research to anti-vivisection and the exploitation of animals, from wheelchair access for disabled people to sports facilities for disadvantaged youth, from preservation of our heritage to the protection of abused children.

If there is any kind of need on any scale, however urgent, emotive or unlikely, it concerns fundraisers.

Without doubt the products of our sector, both in inspiration and in actual good works, are infinitely more useful and valuable to the human condition than those of virtually any other business area.

I've seen enough of fundraising organisations to realise that whatever their shortcomings they are an indispensable force for good in our world. They provide a unique avenue through which the ordinary individual can take action to help put the world's troubles to right.

Public preferences in giving are remarkably consistent. An analysis of the top 200 charities in the UK shows the most popular destinations of donations are medical and health-related charities (33 per cent), general welfare (26 per cent), international aid (21 per cent), animal protection (eight per cent), environment/heritage (six per cent), and religious causes (four per cent). Youth, arts and education trail behind with tiny percentages but the last two may gain ground in the future as they start fundraising in earnest.

When it comes to leaving legacies public preferences are generally equally consistent. Money is left to the same areas in the same order, with the unsurprising exception that animal protection and international aid change places.

The overwhelming tragedy which limits the potential of the voluntary sector more, perhaps, is the alarmingly high turnover of good-quality, well-motivated staff ...

Value for money

Despite the important work they do, many members of the public seem to feel that charity executives (and that includes a lot of fundraisers) should not be well paid nor should they be seen to be well paid. This may be a consequence of the low esteem in which charity workers and fundraisers are held, and may also derive from the poor job we fundraisers have done of explaining ourselves, selling ourselves and generally of encouraging the climate of respect we seem to think we deserve.

More seriously for the voluntary sector, however, is the thought that holding back on salaries may be a spectacular false economy. (False economy is something to which charities are remarkably prone.) This is not just a question of peanuts and monkeys. The overwhelming tragedy which limits the potential of the voluntary sector more, perhaps, than any other single thing today is the alarmingly high turnover of good-quality, well-motivated staff who join this sector for a few short years and then leave it, often to secure a better salary and living conditions the only way they can, by joining a commercial organisation.

Fundraisers' salaries have improved in recent years but by common consent they still lag behind other commercial equivalents by as much as one-third or even a half. So more is spent in recruitment and training of staff, only to see them move on just as they become most effective.

Is that the best way to help the poor and needy? It doesn't seem likely to me.

The director of appeals for one of Britain's largest charities recently visited the headquarters of one of America's most successful fundraising campaigns. He was greatly impressed by the high morale, the quality and the dedication of the staff he met. The organisation radiated an atmosphere of commitment and success.

'Do you pay your people market rate, or below?' he asked. 'Oh no,' was the reply. 'Neither. Our policy is to pay ten per cent *above* market rate because we need to employ the best. We work them hard, we make tough demands, but we get value for money.'

Not surprisingly, that organisation raises more than $4 billion each year.

Charities particularly are large and complex businesses with many levels of customers, many operational restrictions, some peculiar advantages and a moral as well as a legal imperative to be properly run. They need to attract the best, because second best will simply not do for this kind of work. Somehow we have failed the public if we have allowed them to think that cheese-paring will suffice when it comes to finding our top management material.

Charities shouldn't compromise just because of some vague notion that they can't afford the best. It's more likely that they can't afford *not* to have the best. But if they can get the best, whatever it may be, for free or at a reduced rate, then the charity should pursue that gift with vigour, without any fear or inhibition.

Charities shouldn't be afraid of asking, but equally they shouldn't be afraid of paying.

Double agents

Perhaps the public's attitude to and view of fundraisers would be improved if we had a clearer vision of ourselves and what we do. According to a recent article by David Boaz in *Fund Raising Management*, America's monthly journal for fundraisers, there are three basic roles we might adopt as fundraisers, depending on the way we see ourselves. These are the chess player, Robin Hood and the double agent.

Two days working in the post room would give the new trainee the chance to see at first hand the generosity, the interests, the concerns and the criticisms of the people that power the cause – the donors.

The chess player sees himself, or herself, as part of a great game of chess, shifting money from one part of the board to the other, every move efficiently and meticulously calculated, each step one move closer to the goal – completion of the target – checkmate.

The Robin Hood character, on the other hand, has a much more noble and righteous view of his calling. His mission is to take money from the 'haves' and redistribute it to the 'have nots'. He is keenly aware of the injustice which has made this task necessary. If he sees that the charity he serves has enough money to be considered a have itself, rather than a have not, this usually causes him something of a dilemma.

The third role model is the double agent. She serves two different groups equally faithfully, the donor and the cause. Her role as fundraiser makes her the perfect agent of both with no compromise involved. She is the enabler in between who brings satisfaction to both sides when her job is well done.

I prefer the latter analogy. It's quite important to have a vision of what we are doing – and I always wanted to be a double agent.

The initiation

If I were in charge of training new fundraising recruits I'd make sure that each and every one of them spent at least their first two days working in the post room, opening and answering the incoming mail. It's one of the best ways I know of finding out what – and who – an organisation is for.

It is also certain to be two days of fascinating experience for the new trainee, during which the hopeful apprentice will see at first hand the generosity, the interests, the concerns and the criticisms of the people that power the cause – the donors. He or she will also

learn a lot about the other contacts of the business –
suppliers, other agencies, government, volunteers and
so on. Such an introduction should be mandatory in all
fundraising organisations.

Just like the driving test, it should be revisited every
few years for a refresher course.

One of Guy Stringer's favourite management
techniques is similar to the 'two days in the post room'.
It is equally easy to put into practice and also very
effective. Guy calls it 'management by walking
about'. Each day Guy would stroll around the
departments of Oxfam, talking to people, seeing
what was going on, being seen, accessible. No
fundraiser should hide behind a desk. It's a simple
point, but well worth remembering.

ACTION POINTS

▲ Take pride in your profession.

▲ Explain fundraising's purpose and peculiarities
whenever you can and be prepared to defend it if you
have to.

▲ Help promote fundraising as a worthwhile profession
and a quality career area.

▲ Campaign vigorously for competitive salaries and
better conditions for fundraisers.

▲ Don't feel inhibited about asking for donations for
your cause or about paying for what you need.

▲ Think of your fundraising role as that of a double
agent, providing a service to two different markets – the
donor and the cause.

▲ Spend at least two days in the post room. Go back there, every now and then, just to keep in touch.

▲ Practise 'management by walking about'.

DONOR PROFILE

Fred and Eleanor Sykes

Fred Sykes is a builder with a substantial reputation in his home town. Despite some rocky years at the beginning his business prospered and when Fred retired last year he found that he and his wife were very comfortably off indeed. The only problem for Fred was that he didn't like having so much time on his hands. Retirement meant little change for Eleanor, who spends most of her time looking after Fred.

Their five children are grown up now and living away from home. They've all got jobs, including the girls, much to Fred's surprise – good jobs too. None of them have ever asked mum and dad for financial help, although Fred would have liked nothing better than to help his own kids along.

Fred is a well-known figure in most of the town's institutions – the Chamber of Commerce, Rotary, the Round Table. Never one to let the grass grow under his feet, his first act on retirement was to take on as many functions and activities as he could, not just to keep busy but to give life a sense of purpose. Nevertheless, time still hangs.

With his customary gusto Fred has thrown himself into his latest appointment, Chairman of the Appeal Committee for the local polytechnic. One of his boys went there, so he has direct links. The polytechnic also felt he had the right business connections and wouldn't be shy when it came to asking for money. Fred likes his new role as fundraiser and is fully aware that he is expected to come up with a pretty substantial gift to show others the way. That's not a problem for Fred.

Fred supports several charities through deeds of

covenant, particularly housing charities and those with some local connection, or whose work he can see for himself in his own area. His largest covenant is to research into spinal injury. It goes back to three years before he retired when one of his site foremen broke his back in an accident at work. Fred reads everything they send him, but doesn't pay much attention to most of the other stuff, even though he's happy to keep on supporting the charities who send it.

Fred made his will 16 years ago, and last updated it two years ago. He hasn't thought of including anything to a charity.

3

Key principles

'The object of a business is not to make money. The object is to serve its customers. The result is to make money.'

John Fraser-Robinson
Total Quality Marketing

In my early years as a fundraiser I had the good fortune to be guided and advised by Harold Sumption, who was and still is a trustee of the charity I worked for. If all trustees were as practically useful and encouraging as Harold was to me fundraisers' lives would be much easier and probably there would be little need for this book. Twelve years ago Harold Sumption co-founded the International Fund Raising Workshop. Many years before that, his wise counsel was benefiting numerous good causes including some of the largest and most effective charities in Britain. Harold is instinctively a relationship fundraiser and from him I learned most of the fundamentals of fundraising. There are no absolute rules in fundraising and slavish adherence to formulae will win no donors, but there are some basic principles and I have found these to be consistent and helpful in virtually every fundraising endeavour. They are worth remembering.

1 Fundraising is not about raising money. It's about meeting needs and bringing about change.

A donor's greatest desire is to be recognised.

2 People give to people, not to organisations or even causes. Fundraising is a people business. Personal requests work best. Fund development is *people* development.

3 Friend-making comes before fundraising.

4 Open their hearts. Then open their minds. Then open their cheque books.

5 Communicate need, to bring the problem to the donor.

6 Set clear targets. Communicate your goals to your donors. Communicate action and success to encourage full involvement.

7 Know how much to ask each prospect for, and when.

8 The most important two words are thank you. Acknowledge every donation with a friendly, personal letter. Give larger donors special treatment.

9 Encourage donors to identify with your organisation, to feel a sense of shared ownership.

10 Always be honest, open and truthful with donors. Share your problems as well as your successes.

This list is universal but it is certainly not comprehensive and may exclude some important principles that relate particularly to your organisation. Whatever your principles I advise you to capture them: write them down, communicate them to colleagues, trustees, donors and suppliers. And when you prepare a fundraising or marketing plan (see chapter 7) check how it measures up to your principles of fundraising.

Why do people give?

Ask an American fundraiser this question and he'll say without hesitation that a donor's greatest desire is to be recognised. The approval and respect of one's friends and colleagues would certainly figure high on many donors' unwritten list of motivations for giving. Some

It pays fundraisers to study their donors closely and find out what buttons they can press to encourage giving.

other reasons are included below and there are probably quite a few more.

Tax planning to escape, say, inheritance tax
Ego, self-esteem (that's the kind of person I am!)
The quest for immortality
Emotional response
Self-preservation (eg cancer/heart research)
Vested interest (eg school, sports facility)
In memoriam
Giving something back
Identifying with the cause
Religious heritage
Social ambition
Guilt
Altruism
Compassion
Authority
Value for money
Because they were asked
Because it feels good. People like to give.

Much has been written about the psychology of giving and it certainly pays fundraisers to study their donors closely and find out what buttons they can press to encourage giving. In my experience people have widely varying reasons for supporting charities. There is rarely a single motivation for making a donation and often donors are impelled by a combination of the feelings listed above. Donors respond emotionally to the plight of starving people in Africa. Their religious beliefs tell them they should help, they feel some guilt because by comparison they have so much, they feel their gift is good value for money and will be well used, they feel good that they can make a gift and sometimes will tell

This would be a sorry world indeed if people were not to be encouraged to give when they can.

others that they have done so. They may even feel that giving grants them an authority to be involved, some kind of ownership of the problem or need. They may feel all these things simultaneously and yet still not give until they are asked. People are like that.

I suspect that the underlying reasons for giving have changed little over the years and won't change much in the future. I'm just glad that people will keep on giving. Despite criticisms of paternalism and dependence, which we must certainly guard against, I believe this would be a sorry world indeed if people were not to be encouraged to give when they can, and as much as they can, to help others in great need.

What makes a successful fundraiser?

In the opening pages of his book *Born to Raise* Jerold Panas details a seemingly endless list of qualities indispensable to a good fundraiser. These include boundless energy, zest for hard work, single-mindedness, intuition, patience, dogged determination, the ability to be unrelenting, unwavering, optimistic, good at listening, creative, aggressive, consistent, lucky, courageous, willing to take a risk ...

These all apply and I am sure you could add to the list but we run the risk of seeming a little sanctimonious. I suspect other professions too could create similar lists and I don't want to encourage a host of 'what makes a good airline pilot' or 'what makes a good bricklayer' copies. Perhaps there are equivalent handbooks to Jerold Panas', such as *Born to be an Actuary* or *Born to Collect Taxes*.

Fundraisers also need to be sales people. If the idea of selling is unappealing then fundraising is not for you. Certainly intuition and the ability to listen would come towards the top of my list of essential qualities for a

Who is the right person to ask ... when is the right time to ask, the right time to wait?

relationship fundraiser. Intuition is vital: who is the right person to ask, who should head a particular campaign or event, when is the right time to ask, the right time to wait? I would also include persuasiveness, being a good talker, a good writer, well organised ... This is a demanding job. The list could go on and on. But the key word missing from the list, the word that describes the most important ingredient of any fundraiser, is ...

This is a cue for the one and only fundraising joke I know. I might as well tell it now and get it over with.

A young apprentice fundraiser is being shown the ropes by an older and wiser hand. Eventually, his head spinning with new information, the young tyro asks the sage the $64,000 question, 'What is the most important quality of a good fundraiser?' Without hesitation the sage replies, 'The most important quality of a good fundraiser is commitment. Mere involvement is not enough. You must be committed.'

This response puzzles the youth, who can't see that there is any difference between commitment and involvement. 'The difference between commitment and involvement', explains the sage, 'is the difference between bacon and eggs. In bacon and eggs the hen is involved, but the pig is committed.'

I think this is very true. A capacity for commitment is our most important qualification. While we may need to have all those other admirable attributes, we must above all be really committed to the work that we do. If not, donors will see through it instantly and nothing will more swiftly and more surely deter them from giving any further support. But when they see the fundraiser's commitment come shining through in everything he or she says, or does, that will do more to reinforce their faith and commitment to the cause than anything else.

This potential for commitment is just one of the

differences between fundraising and other marketing activities that makes fundraising so special.

It is a difference fundraisers ignore at their peril.

ACTION POINTS

▲ Remember there are no rules in fundraising. Very few things work for absolutely everybody. Use your judgement to decide what is best for you, then test before you proceed.

▲ Make a list of your principles of fundraising. Share that list with others if you can and keep it handy, for you never know when you'll need it.

▲ Study your donors carefully. Find out what they give, who they give to and most importantly why they give to your organisation.

▲ Consider the qualities that make a successful fundraiser and see if you can match up to them.

▲ Be proud of your commitment to your work. Let it show.

DONOR PROFILE

Rose Lister

Every morning Rose Lister turns up at the door of the charity shop just as the manageress, Liz Medley, is turning the key. Rose is never late. She does 9 to 12, the morning shift, every Monday to Friday. She is never off sick, has never tried to change her time and is so regular you could set your clock by her. Liz puts it all down to the fact that Rose enjoys her job so much.

Along with Rose, Liz usually finds a few other things on her doorstep. Several black plastic bags of old clothes, sometimes some carrier bags, occasionally some loose bundles and, of course, always a bottle of milk for the tea. From time to time there is also a customer or two waiting in the morning cold to have first crack at the bargains.

Liz hardly has time to close the door behind her before Rose sets to work sorting out the new material. Anything that looks in nearly new condition is displayed and the rest goes to the dry-cleaner or the ragman, depending on what it is worth. Any books or bric-a-brac are separated and carefully put to one side. They are like gold dust. Then Rose goes round all the rails and dump bins, sorting, rehanging, tidying, making the place look presentable and appealing.

The display of the charity's work is Rose's particular achievement. Most of the other volunteers are not all that interested but Rose has a flair for display. You can see it when she does the shop windows and her montage of posters has turned a dull pile of leaflets into an exhibition.

Rose is a model volunteer and Liz is proud of her. She is also a little puzzled. Most of the others come in to fill their time but Rose seems to enjoy an active life outside the shop. There's a mystery in Rose's life too.

When there was an emergency appeal in the shop recently Liz couldn't help but notice that rather than putting in a few coins in the collecting box or saying she gave time not money, as many of the others had, Rose had quietly filled out a donation form. Liz hadn't been nosey, of course, but she couldn't fail to see that Rose was writing in the number of her credit card on the form and her donation had been for no less than £200.

And then Rose had just quietly sealed her envelope and gone on with her work.

4 The vital ingredient for success

'The future will be a future of more and more intensified relationships.'

Professor Theodore Levitt
The Marketing Imagination

In explaining why I decided to write this book (see chapter 1) I outlined very briefly the concept of relationship fundraising – a donor-based approach to the business of making money.

It is a simple concept and it's not new. Although relationship marketing is a currently fashionable term, it is something fundraisers have been practising almost instinctively for years. Many fundraisers are already undertaking relationship fundraising and are well aware of what they are doing and why. But as fundraisers adopt ever more sophisticated marketing techniques and donors, the inevitable victims of unregulated growth, become more and more resistant to these techniques, relationship fundraising becomes increasingly important and increasingly likely to prove more profitable and sustaining in the long term.

What is 'relationship fundraising'?
'Relationship fundraising' is fundraising where people matter most, a sort of Fritz Schumacher approach to fundraising. (Schumacher invented the concept 'small is

Donors generally are distressed to see blatant commercialism from the charities they support.

beautiful' and through his book of that name started the appropriate technology movement which concentrates on using only low-cost, available materials rather than expensive imported technology.) Small *is* beautiful. Relationship fundraising advocates a return to the close intimacy of the one-to-one relationship between donor and cause but, thanks to the miracle of modern technology, one made possible on a national scale for thousands, even millions, of people at the same time. How and why it should be done are the subjects of this book.

Above all, relationship fundraising is not just about raising funds. If you feel a definition would be useful, here is mine. I am sorry I couldn't condense it into one succinct sentence.

Relationship fundraising is an approach to the marketing of a cause which centres not around raising money but on developing to its full potential the unique and special relationship that exists between a charity and its supporter. Whatever strategies and techniques are employed to boost funds, the overriding consideration in relationship fundraising is to care for and develop that special bond and not to do anything that might damage or jeopardise it. In relationship fundraising every activity of the organisation is therefore geared towards making donors feel important, valued and considered. In this way relationship fundraising will ensure more funds per donor in the long term.

I'm not, incidentally, advocating conversion to relationship fundraising because I'm sentimental about fundraising. I'm advocating this because I speak to a lot of charity supporters and this is the kind of thing they're telling me more and more. Donors generally are distressed to see blatant commercialism from the charities they support. They often resent the repeated

They should have been moving away from a transaction orientation in business and moving towards a relationship orientation.

process of being asked for money with precious little offered in return. They dislike being written to by a marketing machine and feel conned by the transparent techniques of direct mail and telephone appeals.

I hasten to say that what I am opposed to are the transparent techniques, not direct mail or even telephone fundraising *per se*. They are potentially efficient means to a very important end.

Donors repeatedly reaffirm their willingness to hear from their chosen charities but they express great concern about *how* that contact will be carried out.

The current generation of professional fundraisers has been vigorously extending and upgrading its transactions with donors – their 'customers'. They should have been moving away from a transaction orientation in business and moving towards a relationship orientation.

People coming into the fundraising profession now are more likely to be trained in an appropriate professional discipline, such as marketing or finance, but may perhaps be less well-versed in some of the thinking behind the fundraiser's art. This new blood might prove to be of great value to our profession, but if it is unable to appreciate and adopt the theory and practice of relationship fundraising then it is more likely to do lasting damage to fundraising in Britain. There are some signs that this has already happened in America where, rather like the used-car salesman, the well-rehearsed and trained professional fundraiser is not always held in great esteem.

For fundraisers increased professionalism doesn't automatically equate with increased status. Unless it is carefully managed, the effect of increased profession-alism can be quite the reverse.

So we changed our approach. Instead of directly asking schools to raise money, we became very indirect indeed.

The benefits of a new approach

The first charity I worked with was ActionAid, an international development organisation which assists children and families in the Third World. I saw a wonderful example of relationship fundraising in my first few months with ActionAid when we came to evaluate our fundraising efforts in schools.

ActionAid is now a major international charity but at that time it was much smaller, a relatively unknown and new organisation. Certainly, ActionAid was a very minor player among the many national charities that had targeted schools – particularly primary schools – as a lucrative source of funds. We found considerable resistance from teachers to yet another fundraising effort. They were busy people, they couldn't support every cause so, not surprisingly, little ActionAid lost out most of the time to the bigger boys.

So we changed our approach. Instead of directly asking schools to raise money, we became very indirect indeed. The ActionAid Education Service was started and our offer to schools was not that we would organise a sponsored walk or swim for them to raise funds, but that we would provide schools with a detailed illustrated lesson on Third World development which they could slot conveniently into their timetable. We had a model African hut children could build themselves in the classroom, and lots of tangible, tactile examples of how different life is for children of a similar age in Africa. There was no fundraising sales pitch at all.

The schoolchildren loved it. So did the teachers. It gave them time off – they could leave the lesson to the lady from ActionAid. We even provided hand-out notes. Soon the word spread and ActionAid didn't have as much difficulty getting into schools after that.

But then came the extraordinary motivation to give.

It's a good illustration of a charity allowing its donors' enthusiasm for the cause to be the driving force that will increase the fundraiser's 'market share'.

Children who had learned so much about the lives of others of their age overseas began to ask how they could help ease some of the difficulties these other children faced. Teachers began to request details of ActionAid projects for which they and their pupils would be keen to raise funds.

In a short while ActionAid was raising more money from schools than ever before.

This is just one example of relationship fundraising in practice, but it's a good illustration of a charity thinking about its donors, putting itself in their shoes and allowing its donors' enthusiasm for the cause to be the driving force that will increase the fundraiser's 'market share'. It's also a good example of 'the double agent' at work.

A total philosophy

Although there are many such examples to illustrate the point, relationship fundraising is not a series of isolated incidents, it is a total philosophy, an approach to dealing with every aspect of donor contact, channelling that contact towards building a specific lifelong relationship and to ensuring that the relationship is as fruitful as possible for both parties.

It involves notions which to many may seem unnecessary or even uneconomic, such as quickly and effectively answering every letter and acknowledging by return of post every donation, however small, sending a personal letter that any donor might wish to receive.

The commercial logic in this is simply that small donors leave large legacies. Not all of them, of course. But the relationship fundraiser assumes they all will or at least treats them as if they will.

The relationship fundraiser also notes the warnings in negative, critical letters and responds appropriately

A lot of useful relationships got off to a very good start thanks to an efficient and effective complaints procedure.

and positively. People, even complainers, write because they care. American fundraiser Richard Felton calls it 'criticism with love'. If they didn't care they wouldn't bother. Worse by far is that they ignore you.

Lawrence Stroud, fundraiser at Botton Village in Yorkshire, the largest of the Camphill Village Trust communities for mentally handicapped adults, was surprised to see how many donations he received from people who had initially written to him to complain, most often because they had received unsolicited mailings from Botton. Lawrence's policy has always been to write a warm and friendly letter honestly explaining how the village had acquired their name and describing in some detail Botton's direct mail programme and how it is benefiting the village. He also includes details of the Mailing Preference Service and helpful advice on how to avoid receiving unwanted mail in future.

It doesn't surprise me that this approach has brought in donations. I am also not surprised that it has prompted many congratulations and comments such as 'I wish other charities reacted as you did'.

So a lot of useful relationships for Botton Village got off to a very good start – thanks to an efficient and effective complaints procedure.

What relationship fundraising can do for you

In this noisy world, with so many competing promotional voices clamouring for our customers' attention, we all know that our communications have just seconds in which to make an impression. When our carefully prepared and costly appeal package is finally delivered through the door of Mr and Mrs Donor, we know we stand only a three-to-one chance that it will even get opened before it is consigned to the bin. Our attempts to inject compulsion to open and to make

Consider what a difference there is when Mr and Mrs Donor receive a letter from a friend.

reading irresistible are, by and large, rather futile and pathetic. If our promotion is read, it is as often an indulgence as an inevitability. Our donors, always drawn from the more intelligent and rational sectors of society, are now among the most sophisticated and aware people on earth – most of them.

They know when they're being sold to and they may tolerate it but they don't like it. They know when they're being written to by a marketing machine and they don't like that either.

They may respond to our most recent mailing just as they did the time before because of their commitment to the cause, but that doesn't mean they like the way they've been asked. And while we are congratulating ourselves on achieving a 20 per cent response to our latest warm mailing, what about the 80 per cent who didn't respond? What do they think of our aggressive fundraising approach and what, ultimately, will they do about it?

But consider what a difference there is when Mr and Mrs Donor receive a letter from a friend. We all know the apathy with which most people greet junk mail, but don't forget that millions of people still rush to their front door to see what the postman has brought. When they see it is from someone they like they eagerly open that letter first to see what news and information their friend has sent.

Imagine how nice it would be if donors were to telephone you to enquire, rather worriedly, as to why they hadn't received the last issue of your newsletter and to say how much they looked forward to hearing from you. I know of one charity whose donors are so involved and interested that it does get such calls and letters (although less so now that their publication schedules are a little more regular and reliable).

Fundraisers are most often writing to people who have already shown that they believe in the cause. And they are writing about subjects that are almost invariably interesting, dramatic, newsworthy, touching, exciting and positive.

So there is no excuse whatever for fundraisers to produce junk mail or junk anything.

There is every reason for fundraisers to strive to produce interesting, exciting and relevant information which they can send to friends who share their interest and commitment.

But that's just a start. Relationship fundraising can help you to find out all you need to know about your donors, it can help you to locate and recruit others like them, it can encourage your donors to introduce their friends, it can help you to write appropriately and personally to your donors as individuals, it can help you identify the right offer to make them. Relationship fundraising can show you how to avoid making mistakes in dealing with donors, how to avoid wasting money and make your promotion pay, how to increase their annual giving and extend their 'life' as donors, how to manage your staff and present your organisation, how to approach your marketing strategy, how to make your donor your friend, how to increase the value of your donors and how to ensure a gigantic leap in your income from legacies.

It can also be very satisfying and rewarding.

Letters to friends

The relationship fundraiser gears his (or her) offers to what his donors want to buy, not what he wants to sell. He recognises that people are different. He knows that they not only differ from each other in the way they give, but that each individual will not always give the same to

We may yet be able to choose our own personal daily newspaper with the foreign coverage of The Observer, *the sport of* The Guardian, The Times' *crossword and page 3 of* The Sun, *if we feel so inclined.*

every appeal. As we all know they frequently don't give to some appeals, which seems to me to provide an interesting answer to the apparently endless question of 'how many letters should we send?' If you listen to your donors, some would receive just one appeal each year, some as many as 10 or 12 and most of the others would receive some number in between.

It depends on the donor.

Of course, if you give donors the choice they may choose to receive your appeals less times than you would wish them to. This is where the relationship fundraiser has to get clever (see chapter 7).

Fundraisers tend to think automatically of their communications with donors as 'appeals'. We talk of 'mailings' and 'packs'. I'm as guilty as the next person, but really we should think of them as letters and we shouldn't always expect or ask for a response.

Because each donor is different the relationship fundraiser is also aware that it makes little sense to send the same mailing package with the same offer, letter, leaflet, etc, to every donor. While the practical difficulties are obvious, technological change is providing fundraisers with the means to do something about this. Magazines are now being published where you can choose the editorial mix that most interests you. Who knows? We may yet be able to choose our own personal daily newspaper with the foreign coverage of *The Observer*, the sport of *The Guardian, The Times'* crossword and page 3 of *The Sun*, if we feel so inclined. It would make for happier readers and many more newspaper sales.

As my experience has grown I have become increasingly convinced that developing a relationship with donors is the key to success in fundraising. Our business is donor development and that is only possible through the formation of a tangible relationship. As donors, by and large, are honest and intelligent people it is a process that can only be done with honesty and intelligence. You may be able to pull the wool over the eyes of some of your donors for a while, but you can't do it in the long term and successful relationships are based on long-term concepts.

Neglecting the relationship can be expensive too. I once worked with a national charity that, as policy, didn't send any acknowledgement to donors giving less than £5.00 and sent a pre-printed receipt to those giving between £5.00 and £10.00. Their purpose was to discourage small donors, who probably went to another charity and left their legacy to them.

Hard times

As I write this, Britain, like much of the rest of the world, is in the depths of a recession. Charities are not immune from its harrowing effects. Like every other business, charities don't need sympathy in difficult times, they need ingenuity and imagination to market their way out of difficulties. But they also need the underlying strength of a sound business base, and that strength in times of recession can only come from a wide spread of well-established and well-maintained relationships. When times are hard, relationship fundraising is even more important than usual.

Victims of success

However, it makes sense to proceed with care. It might prove unwise for some organisations to attempt to rush the theory of relationship fundraising into practice overnight. There is a cost, even if it is an initial cost that is later repaid several times over, that is inevitably associated with the introduction of relationship fundraising.

If any fundraiser can put hand on heart and say 'I do all this', then he or she is not doing too badly.

Relationship fundraising may be particularly prone to a rather common dilemma in fundraising, where the organisation literally becomes a victim of its own success. Better materials, better communications, more care and attention all result in more satisfied customers which leads to greater take-up of services and increased costs in all service functions. So it is important to plan and to introduce these costs in a manageable way. And it is equally important to relate these costs to benefits.

The nine keys to building a relationship
There are a number of cornerstones in the process of building and sustaining lasting and mutually beneficial relationships with hundreds, even thousands, of individual donors. Inevitably, when written down, these seem trite and obvious but they are worth listing here. If any fundraiser can put hand on heart and say 'I do all this', then he or she is not doing too badly.

Be honest
If any business area should be honest, it is fundraising (or, perhaps, the police ...). The public expects fundraisers to be honest. Those that don't view fundraisers as inherently honest and trustworthy certainly don't give, so it pays to be seen to be honest.

It also pays to *be* honest. Jeremy Shaw, now managing director of Smith Bundy and Partners, London, when he was running Barnardo's Publications, the trading arm of Britain's biggest child care charity, offered his customers a product: a machine that plays chess with you.

It sold well, but after a while Jeremy began to get a large number of returns – 25 per cent as opposed to the usual five per cent.

Puzzled, Jeremy conducted some basic telephone

research. He found that the machines worked all right, they just weren't sufficiently advanced.

So he wrote back to all the customers who had complained, offering them a full refund. Then he went on to ask if they might want to buy a machine that was much more advanced, but cost three times as much.

Twenty-five per cent bought the new machine. A relationship was established because Barnardo's behaved honourably.

And they made more money. It pays to be honest.

Be sincere and let your commitment show
Donors are donors because they care enough to take action and support your cause. Let them see that you care too and that that is why you're there as well. When this happens, immediately you and they are on the same side, with a common concern and aim. Your commitment will then encourage them to go even further for the cause.

Be prompt
Reply quickly and efficiently to any request. Answer letters the next day, or sooner if possible. If the issue is important telephone the donor and explain what action you are going to take. If it will take time to provide a full answer, write or telephone the donor quickly to say that an answer is being prepared and let them know when to expect it. Prompt response shows you take your donor's concerns seriously.

Be regular
Regular planned communication keeps donors in touch, informed and involved. If you are irregular in your communications be aware that other fundraisers are not so lax. They also have access to your donors, so they'll be

in touch when you are not.

Be interesting and memorable
By their very nature charities have access to dramatic, interesting and compelling material. Use it to the full, present it well. Tell a story. Make all your material stand out for its interesting content, style and presentation. And its unforgettable visuals.

Be involving
Don't allow donors to take a passive role. Ask for their opinions, contributions and even complaints. Encourage feedback in any way you can. Invite them to events, offer visits to projects. Make the dialogue as two-way as you possibly can.

Be cheerful and helpful
Advertise your helpfulness. Never let donors feel that asking is a trouble. That's what you are there for – to help them. Teach customer care to all your colleagues. I have never forgotten a simple piece of advice from the days when I sold advertising space over the telephone – smile and dial. When you smile, it sounds much better at the other end. It really works. Try it. (Tell your colleagues first, otherwise they'll think you've gone mad.)

Be faithful
Always stick to your promises. Let donors see that you are honourable and trustworthy. Stand by your organisation's mission and don't compromise what it stands for.

Be cost effective
Donors expect and appreciate good stewardship of their

This familiar old triangle crops up again and again wherever fundraisers congregate.

gifts but are generally well aware of the potential for false economies which they dislike as much as conspicuous waste. Be open and informative, explain your reasons for financial decisions and show them that their money is in good hands.

As usual, this list is not exhaustive. But if you can inject these key elements into your relationship with donors they will not only be encouraged enough to continue their support, they will derive increased satisfaction from their giving and will even go out and tell their friends, encouraging them to do the same. And that, I believe, is what fundraising is all about.

The donor pyramid

This familiar old triangle, the donor pyramid, crops up again and again wherever fundraisers congregate and it is useful as a simple way of illustrating the traditional idea of the donor life cycle, the not quite universal fact that a donor's involvement starts with a general enquiry and then moves or is led through various stages of ever-increasing involvement to the ultimate gift – a legacy. It is inevitably limited, as all simplifications are, but it is also potentially misleading.

The pyramid represents the approximate numerical values of a charity's supporters at their different stages and levels of involvement (see page 61). So immediately outside the pyramid is what might be considered the as yet untouched potential, or the entirely indifferent: the general public. The lowest rung within the pyramid, if pyramids have rungs, is the general enquirer, the person who has been in contact but not yet given. Above these is the first-time giver, next is the committed donor, then the covenanter or regular giver, followed by the big gift donor and, ultimately, those rare few who leave a

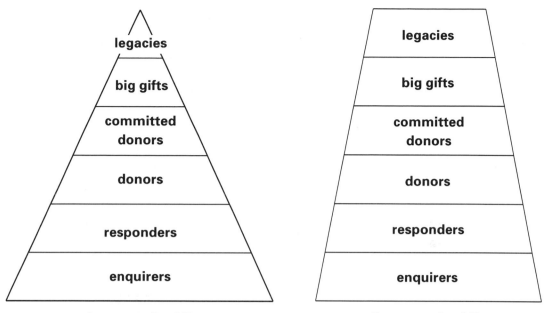

legacies

big gifts

committed donors

donors

responders

enquirers

the general public

legacies

big gifts

committed donors

donors

responders

enquirers

the general public

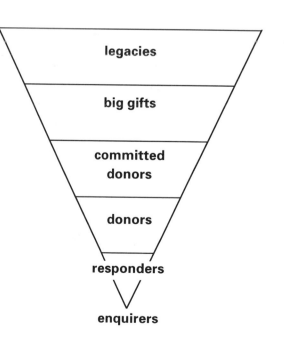

legacies

big gifts

committed donors

donors

responders

enquirers

The traditional donor pyramid (top left), the more optimistic donor trapezium which relationship fundraisers will follow (top right) and the donor wedge (bottom right) which, unlike the other two, classifies donors in terms of ascending monetary value rather than total number of individuals.

Think of the implications for your fundraising income if you were to work a donor trapezuim rather than a donor pyramid.

legacy. These are broad band divisions, of course, and the assumption is that as fundraisers do their job and upgrade supporters through each stage then the numbers involved will become sharply fewer until from the broad base we started with we are ultimately talking to very few people indeed.

This, I think, is at best a negative view. Why should fundraisers accept that so many supporters will be lost along the way? Would it not be better if this pyramid were considered as a ladder, a ladder of involvement? You can move people more easily up a ladder than up a pyramid and a ladder *has* got rungs.

Of course, it would be foolish to delude ourselves that we won't lose people along the way as we attempt to gently upgrade our supporters, and often we will lose them for quite good reasons.

Nevertheless I feel that the donor pyramid is not quite complete as a model and we should add to it two more shapes (again, see page 61).

The donor trapezium

This has the same bands and levels as the donor pyramid but is steeper at the sides and flat at the top. Looked at another way it might be seen as a roadway, disappearing in the distance towards the horizon. However, it assumes that far fewer people will drop out and – the ultimate reward for the relationship fundraiser – a lot more people will make it to the top band and leave a legacy.

These are mere scribbles, of course, just a convenient way of illustrating an abstract theory. But think of the implications for your fundraising income if you were to work a donor trapezium rather than a donor pyramid. The financial difference in the long term is immense so the donor trapezium is a simplified way of illustrating what relationship fundraising is all about.

The donor wedge

This intriguing shape, simply the donor pyramid turned upside down, results from looking at supporters not in terms of numbers but in terms of their combined financial value. The bands are the same and in the same vertical order. So we see that the rewards of donor development are that each individual gives vastly more as he or she progresses to each different level of support. There may be numerically many fewer legators but they still tend to give the largest amount of money. If the donor trapezium is approached in the same way the top line would be very long indeed and the inverted triangle, or wedge, would have rather a flat point. (Put another way, it is a small but significant point.)

Setting up and maintaining a relationship database

In practice, the one essential key to effective relationship fundraising is not an abstract principle, it is a tangible piece of technology and it is vital to the success of any strategy for relationship fundraising. It's what I refer to as a relationship database. It is the core of relationship fundraising and without it true individual marketing is impossible. With a relationship database fundraisers can return to the intimacy and individuality of the corner shop. A database is simply a list of individuals. It can be very small and contained in a card index file. More likely it will be computerised and quite sophisticated, if not horrendously complicated.

But computerised customer lists have come a long, long way in recent years and the technology now exists to make our retention, selection and application of customer information very sophisticated indeed. The miracle of the modern database is that it enables the fundraiser simultaneously to talk individually to thousands, even tens of thousands of donors, sending

The fundamental core of relationship fundraising is the creative use of your database.

unique messages to every one, all at the same time.

For the non-computer specialist, the difficulty is in finding an affordable system that is easy to operate and does exactly what you want. There is a bewildering choice.

To keep proper records of your donors you need to do six things.

• To choose an adequate system with multiple fields of information.

• To input data carefully.

• To undertake continual, thorough cleaning.

• To update your records continuously with all donor transactions.

• To add regularly any new information gleaned from correspondence, mailing returns, research, the telephone, or any other source.

• To use your data conscientiously and responsibly. In the UK any user of data has to register with the Data Protection Registrar and to abide by their rules and standards.

The fundamental core of relationship fundraising is the creative use of your database. It is the keystone. With an effective relationship database and a commitment to the theory of relationship fundraising, everything else will fall into place.

But a word of warning: if you ask your computer consultant for a relationship database he'll look at you blankly. I made that term up. You'll need to explain to him exactly what you want that database to do.

The fact that it is a list or is computerised is almost irrelevant. What matters is what it enables you to do – keep an individual track of *all* your communications with *all* your donors.

ACTION POINTS

▲ Practise relationship fundraising as a total philosophy, not as a series of isolated actions.

▲ Take care when putting the theory into practice not to try to do too much too soon. Remember the initial cost of relationship fundraising.

▲ Devise a policy for responding to complaints. Include an explanation of what you are doing and why. Offer practical help where possible.

▲ Acknowledge every gift, however small.

▲ Carefully assess *every* communication with your donors. Make sure it is interesting, relevant and timely. Erase any possibility of 'junk mail' from your organisation.

▲ Give your donors the choice – let them tell you how they want to be communicated with.

▲ Smile and dial.

▲ Follow the nine key steps to relationship building: be honest, sincere, prompt, regular, interesting, involving, helpful, faithful and cost-effective – and show you are!

▲ Set up a relationship database. Handle data with care because your ability to communicate accurately depends on it.

DONOR PROFILE

Richard West

Richard West runs a high-class restaurant in a small Surrey town. He lives well in a large house in the country with extensive grounds, dresses very sharply and drives a big expensive car. By anybody's standards, Richard West appears to be a success. In part the wherewithal for his expensive lifestyle comes from the profits of his restaurant, and that's what he likes people to believe. But the truth is that the business is not going as well as it originally did and for most of the past ten years Richard has, out of necessity, had to fall back on his capital. Luckily for him he has rather large amounts of that inherited from his mother, and the interest on this alone is more than enough to provide for all his and his family's needs.

Richard West's wife, Lisa, also likes the high life and doesn't mind spending to keep up appearances. Their children are not yet grown up so haven't developed their own expensive tastes; however, their schooling more than makes up for that. One way and another, large amounts of money leave the West household on an almost daily basis, but it was ever thus and Richard keeps fairly close track of each individual's expenditure. He doesn't take his wealth for granted but he has grown up with it and accepts it.

The restaurant keeps Richard busy. With that, the family and his passion for sailing he has little time for much else. He doesn't join clubs or serve on committees. He does have a social conscience, however. If you asked him he could list five or six charities that he currently supports, but if you asked those charities only one could find him anywhere on their database. He is a member of a leading animal welfare charity and pays his annual membership fee of £8 by standing order.

Last year, a close friend approached him on behalf of a building appeal for a new hospice, organised by one of the local churches. Richard has no connections with any church, but the appeal sounded urgent and worthwhile. Richard's friend was asking for a large amount of money so Richard gave him £10,000. He could easily have given more.

5 Understanding your donor

'While the individual man is an absolute puzzle, in aggregate he becomes a mathematical certainty.'

Sherlock Holmes
The Sign of Four by Sir Arthur Conan Doyle

Relationship fundraising starts with finding out what your donors want and need and then supplying it to them as completely as possible, in the most cost-effective way. So detailed research into who your donors are and what they think and feel is essential.

Basic research

Research is one of fundraising's most under-used tools. Those charities who have done it have usually struggled to afford it and have often under-invested. Yet some basic research can cost little or nothing to carry out. When fundraisers find out what research can do for them and how it can help increase their income, then they quickly reassess its importance. Many charities now are setting aside sufficient resources to carry out research properly and continuously.

It's obvious good sense, of course. With good research information you can confirm your hunches, track shifts in your important markets, find out which offers and styles of presentation have most appeal, what people think of your publications, whether your priorities are out of step with your donors' and a whole range of other vital things. The more you know about your supporters, the more accurately you can structure your relationship fundraising.

Here are some of the things you need to know.

- Why have people become your supporters?
- What do they like about what you do and what do they dislike?
- Are your instincts and gut feelings borne out?
- What should you be doing to improve your relationships and thereby encourage donors to support you more?
- What is their basic lifestyle and demographic information (ie individual characteristics)?
- Is there a geographical difference, age difference, etc?
- Who else do they support and why?
- How do they compare what you do with those other charities?
- Do longer-established supporters view you in the same way as new recruits?
- What is your supporters' attitude to legacies?
- Why do some enquirers never become donors?
- What (in detail) do your current supporters and potential supporters think of your magazine, or your press ads, or your mailings?
- What does the general public think of you, or your press ads, or your mailings?

And so on.

You could, of course, do some of the most basic research in-house among your existing records. Here's another question you need to answer: what percentage of your warm list actually *gives* each year? The answer to this and similar questions can only be found from your own information.

Very few charities know the answer. It can vary from

Research is a continuous process. It should be planned on an annual basis so you can track changes in attitudes and perceptions over the years.

five to 75 per cent. This also highlights another possible area of confusion. Never assume that database means the same thing as donor base. They can be quite different.

How to do research

Research is a continuous process. It should be planned and budgeted for on an annual basis so you can not only find out about your donors, but can track changes in attitudes and perceptions over the years. The characteristics of your supporters may not shift, but if your relationship fundraising materials (see chapter 9) are doing their job you should be able to see changes in how they view your organisation and its work.

For the purposes of this book, most of what follows is concerned with market research amongst individual private donors. Fundraisers are also becoming increasingly sophisticated at researching other groups such as company directors, shareholders and various types of larger donor. An increasingly important aspect of this work is the tracing of networks. Specialist firms can now be employed who will tell you all you need to know about a given donor – what clubs or institutions he or she belongs to, who else she knows, who her co-directors are and even who she went to school with.

There are six common methods of research amongst individual donors:

1 Postal questionnaires: a printed questionnaire is sent to a random, numerically valid segment of the list you want to research.

2 Telephone research: a random selection of your target group is talked through a questionnaire over the phone.

3 Focus groups/group discussions: usually conducted on neutral territory or in the donor's home by a trained researcher.

4 'Omnibus' surveys: your question is added in with a whole range of other unconnected issues to a standard sample of society.

5 Meeting supporters: you simply go out and talk to people face to face, for free.

These research methods are listed on page 72 with my views of their advantages and disadvantages. The last method is the least expensive and most obvious – yet many fundraisers don't take advantage of its splendid simplicity and so lose out. They forget that continually meeting supporters, individually and in groups, is an indispensable fundraising aid. (It should be compulsory for chief executives and trustees.)

Postal questionnaires

Of the others, my favourite is the oft-maligned postal questionnaire. It may not be 100 per cent reliable in the mathematical sense, but if you accept its shortcomings it will always tell you a lot and has the advantages of being relatively inexpensive and easy to organise. Open-ended questions are of most value but don't include too many as response will be reduced if the questionnaire is too long or arduous to complete. If you can sit down one evening with a pile of around 100 completed question-naires and just flip through I guarantee that you will have a fascinating evening, at the end of which you'll know what interests and concerns your supporters. You'll have created a mental picture of them and it will be of great value to you.

It is worth writing down this mental picture. If you have segmented your list or if the age range of returned questionnaires is noticeable you may be able to create more than one picture of different parts of your list.

The covering letter that introduces and explains the

Advantages	*Disadvantages*
1 Postal questionnaire	
Low cost	Needs professional analysis
You can do it yourself (very simple questionnaires only)	Questions might be leading if not professionally prepared
Specific questions	Only most active supporters respond
Quantitative	
Not obtrusive	Low response levels compared to some other methods
2 Telephone research	
Accurate cross-section	Needs professionals
Immediate response	Costly finding phone numbers
Very few refusals	Danger of deviation
Qualitative and quantitative	Intrusive
A chance to listen	
3 Personal interview	
Qualitative and quantitative	Requires careful preparation
Very detailed	High cost
Reliability can be immediately assessed	Needs professional interviewers
	Attracts activists
No leading questions	
4 Focus groups (group interviews)	
Honesty	High cost
You can join in and listen	Needs professional interviewers
Qualitative	Attracts activists
Reliability can be immediately assessed	Strong may intimidate the weak
5 'Omnibus' surveys	
Inexpensive	Interviewer may not have any experience of charity matters
Representative of population	
Quick	Lacks in-depth advantage
General public only	
6 Regularly meeting supporters	
Cheap	None
Rewarding	

Don't keep research results to yourself. Share them with donors and invite comment.

questionnaire is vital as is properly thanking participants and if possible reassuring them that, in due course,
they will learn the results of the survey. Don't keep
research results to yourself. Share them with donors and
invite comment. It will almost always do you good.

Charities can expect much higher returns from postal
questionnaires than companies experience when
researching customers by post. Nevertheless you want
to get as high a percentage of completed questionnaires
as possible so it is often worth sending a reminder three
or four weeks later. In my experience this can increase
response by up to 50 per cent.

Once you have your picture of your typical donor,
don't file it away with last year's questionnaires.
Circulate it within your organisation and get everyone
to agree to it. Refer to it when defining the objectives of a
new publication. Use it when you are briefing writers
and designers when you prepare any new promotion.
Use it for list and media selection. Segment your list so
you can write to the different groupings (see page 149).
But don't forget you are communicating with
individuals and while this picture will help you focus
your message it is still a composite and may not exactly
correspond to anyone on your list.

Confidentiality

Research surveys usually promise absolute
confidentiality and of course this encourages a larger
response. However, you have to be careful that the
promise of confidentiality does not unnecessarily
restrict your subsequent use of valuable data. It is worth
explaining in the covering letter as many of the potential
uses of this data as possible and making clear that, for
example, the information in certain sections of the
questionnaire will be used to help you update your

records. If you intend to add any of the information gathered via research to your donor's individual file on your database then you must say so clearly on the questionnaire and the accompanying letter.

Focus groups

Focus groups, also known as group discussions, are worth special consideration because they give you qualitative analysis – a chance to dig below the figures to find out in detail what people really think. Focus groups have to be drawn from a representative sample or a specific segment of your list and the research sessions must be conducted by an independent and professional researcher. They can be quite expensive, but they are also great fun and can be very instructive.

Be sure to participate in at least one of the groups. Go as part of the research team so that there is no possibility of inhibiting donors from talking honestly in front of someone from the charity and be careful not to influence responses, however strongly you feel about what you are hearing.

The possible benefits from this exercise are enormous and I do urge you to try it. It gives you the chance to probe your donors and to find out what turns them on and what switches them off (what the Americans refer to as 'hot buttons' and 'road blocks').

With both group and telephone interviews it is recommended, if possible, that you send an advance letter from the charity, alerting potential responders to the research and the reasons for it. This is particularly important for elderly donors who may be less familiar with research and may not like answering the phone or may be nervous about opening the door.

It may also make sense to check your findings from a small number of focus groups with wider quantitative

For fundraisers any kind of research has one important drawback – the process of giving research information is entirely different from the process involved in giving to a cause.

research, such as a questionnaire.

Telephone research

I think research is one of the best and most inoffensive uses of the telephone, but some people do find it intrusive. Everybody hates telemarketing, of course (except those who have tried it – see chapter 7).

The fact is, more people by far respond to the telephone. It is the most economical form of direct personal contact, with all the obvious benefits that brings. Fundraisers should use the telephone far more than they do (it's also invaluable for lobbying – see pages 234 to 235).

As with telefundraising, a simple script has to be prepared to introduce the call and explain the questionnaire and its purpose. This is a crucial opportunity to strengthen donor relationships but of course is just as easily an opportunity to offend. The questions must be prepared professionally so as not to lead or encourage an unrepresentative response, and the interviewer should be professionally trained, entirely competent and relaxed. Telephone research is costly and must be carried out efficiently within time restraints, but a good relationship fundraiser will take this opportunity to listen, to let donors talk on about the subjects that interest them and will never exert pressure to move on or close the conversation.

The hidden flaw

For fundraisers any kind of research has one important drawback – the process of giving research information is entirely different from the process involved in giving to a cause. Answers to research questions are guided by logical thought, reasoned responses to a series of reasonable questions. This is what people think they will feel, or think they will do, in given situations. But as we all know, the true motivation of a charitable gift is very often not logical at all. Responses are often emotional, spontaneous and sometimes even irrational. No amount of clinical research will pick that up. This is one reason why I place great emphasis on a fundraiser's gut feelings – instincts often overruled by marketers in favour of more concrete, but sometimes suspect, research data.

This hidden flaw is unfortunate, but it doesn't invalidate research for fundraisers – far from it. It simply has to be borne in mind, and research findings have to be viewed against this background. Major misunderstandings have occurred, when people who should have known better have misled the public and charities themselves by quoting research figures as absolute fact, while ignoring the hidden flaw. Research is a useful guide, it is not a rigid path.

Beware of nice people

In addition to the hidden flaw, you also have to bear in mind that donors tend to tell their favourite charity what they think that charity wants to hear. They are often reluctant to be critical (although some can be vitriolic!). If you know your donors, you'll be aware of how likely or not that is and can weight your results accordingly.

This is not a unique problem for fundraisers. Market researchers found a similar situation when conducting product research in the high streets of Japan. The Japanese, of course, are such well-meaning, polite people, they can't bring themselves to say anything nasty or unpleasant about any product – odious or not. So beware of nice people. Researchers want objectivity.

The hazards of faulty research

Some things are particularly difficult to find out even through the most stringent and demanding research

This expensive test was then duly given the thumbs down by a random sample of British averageness.

methods. Most notorious of these is the virtual impossibility of assessing whether a particular television, press, or poster advertisement (here I am referring particularly to indirect rather than direct response advertising) has any immediately recordable impact on product sales.

It is also virtually impossible to pre-test advertisements accurately by research methods. A famous example of this is Maureen Lipman's splendid 'Beattie' advertisements for British Telecom. When these were pre-tested as draft scripts to focus groups they were pronounced an obvious flop. However, BT had faith in the concept (a rare client) and agreed to pay to have an actual commercial made. This expensive test was then duly given the thumbs down by a random sample of British averageness. But British Telecom had spent so much that they felt they had to go ahead, whatever the public might think. As a result, one of television's most popular characters was launched on the world, an event that did British Telecom no harm at all.

These ads, incidentally, were intended to do more than just project the image of British Telecom. Their other purpose was to improve the culture of the telephone, to let people see it as a useful, friendly, easy-to-use, everyday tool, not as the black thing in the hall that only rings when there's bad news. This culture of the telephone is an important consideration for telefundraisers (see page 228).

Another campaign that failed twice in pre-tests was Heineken Lager's wonderful series of ads which claimed that Heineken 'refreshes the parts that other beers cannot reach'. Watch out for this when you test your advertisement visuals on focus groups. Sometimes they have little better than a random chance of getting it right.

Of course I'm being a little unfair to the market

research fraternity by selecting two spectacular failures without mentioning any successes. Pre-testing often does get it right and is almost always useful for establishing consumers' interests and areas of concern as well as what turns them on and off. But faulty research can be expensive and damaging to your relationship with donors, so all results should be analysed and viewed with care.

The final protection against faulty research or the natural flaws in any research is, as I said previously, not to neglect the dictates of your own 'gut feelings'. While this in no way invalidates the need for research, most experienced and competent fundraisers will find their instincts are pretty near the mark – but it helps to have this confirmed by research!

Implementing your findings

A major key to success in the 1990s will be knowing how to use your data. But one of the most common faults with commissioned research is the 'filing cabinet' syndrome. Research, expensively commissioned, is summarily scanned and then filed away without further action because what it uncovered has implications and putting those into practice will be, at best, inconvenient.

This of course is a wasted opportunity. Research will not repay your investment or reveal its potential unless you are prepared to act on its findings. It has to be agreed at the highest level necessary that results will be acted upon, before you undertake any research project.

Categorising your donors

We all know that not everybody gives, or is likely to give, to charity. Our universe is not universal. To find new donors therefore we need to identify those sub-sections of our society that have a proven track record of

People constantly refuse to conform to the labels we put on them, with almost total disregard for the fact that our lives would be much easier if they did.

giving to our cause or similar causes or, because of characteristics shared with existing donors, seem likely to be prospects for our kind of appeal.

Wouldn't it be nice therefore if we could divide society up into convenient little groups that correspond to the different behaviour patterns we want or expect? Clearly this is dangerous ground, because we are trying to classify the unclassifiable. People, thankfully, are individuals and constantly refuse to conform to the labels we put on them, with almost total disregard for the fact that our lives would be much easier if they did.

But imperfect and limited in use as they may be, most systems of classification are still likely to be more helpful than sticking to the idea that our donors are all little old ladies living in Tunbridge Wells.

Two areas seem worthy of further attention from fundraisers.

1 Can we usefully categorise the population to help us identify those people most likely to become donors?
2 Can we predict any changes in society that might influence who will be our donors in the future?

To look at these we need to understand two common pieces of research jargon: demographics and psychographics.

Demographics are sets of characteristics about people that relate to their behaviour as consumers. This includes age, gender, race, marital status, education. We are all aware that people who have specific demographic characteristics are more likely to support us than those who have not.

Psychographics are, according to American sociologist Arnold Mitchell, 'the collective essence of an individual's attitudes, beliefs, opinions, prejudices, hopes, fears, needs, desires and aspirations that, taken together, govern how he or she behaves and that, as a

... some of the 'lifestyle' lists and attempts at donor profiling are producing impressive results for fundraising charities in the UK.

whole, expresses itself in a "lifestyle"'.

It can also be clearly seen that psychographic features, too, will have a distinct influence on whether or not someone might become our donor.

Numerous other pieces of classification jargon have entered our language, such as geodemographics, behaviourgraphics, Target Group Index, profiling, targeting, market segmentation ... I won't go into these here, although the last two at least are discussed in chapter 7.

Is it possible to categorise people psychographically? And is it possible to overlay demographic factors on to psychographic categories and locate our ideal prospective donors?

The answer to both questions is yes. Or rather yes, but ... Yes, but don't blame me if you are rather confused by the outcome. As I've said, people have a habit of irrational behaviour that confounds most classifications. But, that accepted, some attempts at classification can be of value and certainly some of the 'lifestyle' lists and attempts at donor profiling are producing impressive results for fundraising charities in the UK just now.

A few years ago Arnold Mitchell invented a system for categorising the population called VALS (values and lifestyles) which is perhaps the best-known marketing model covering these. VALS is described as a comprehensive framework for characterising the way of life of Americans. Despite this, it, or something similar, may have some value for fundraisers elsewhere, as you will see. It also has some major limitations and has been criticised for overlap between the different groups. But it's a start.

VALS divides people into four major categories comprising nine lifestyle types. Very briefly, these are:

1 Need-driven people: they have limited resources and are driven more by need than choice.

They subdivide into *survivors,* who exist in extreme poverty; and *sustainers,* who struggle at the edge of poverty.

Need-driven people account for about 10 per cent of America's people.

2 Outer-directed people: they respond strongly to real or fancied signals from others. They are guided by what they think others will think.

They subdivide into *belongers,* the stabilisers of society, solid, comfortable, middle class; *emulators,* people trying to move up; and *achievers,* business and professional leaders.

Outer-directed people account for about 69 per cent of America's people.

3 Inner-directed people: they conduct their lives in accordance with inner values.

They subdivide into three groups – *I-am-me,* a highly individualistic transition stage; *experiential,* more mature, seeking involvement; and *societally conscious,* the cosmically aware.

Inner-directed people account for about 19 per cent of America's people.

4 Integrated people: they are inspired, generous, visionary. They have put it all together. They are rare, accounting for just two per cent of America's people.

Research into these groupings has shown some marked characteristics in relation to charitable giving and choice of causes. (If, as I did, you doubt that there are any such words as experiential and societal, they are listed in the *Oxford English Dictionary.* I was surprised too.)

Of course, most donors are outer-directed belongers, the preservers and defenders of the status quo, described

It is inescapable that values and personal beliefs are crucial to the decision to give to charity.

in the VALS typology as conservative, conventional, nostalgic, sentimental, puritanical and conforming. They like to belong and not to stand out. Their world is well posted and well lit and the road is straight and narrow. Family, church and tradition loom large. They know what is right and they stick to the rules. This description, I think, would fit many fundraisers' donor profile.

Experiential inner-directeds are good volunteers and 71 per cent of outer-directed achievers donate to health associations, 50 per cent support religious organisations and 24 per cent educational institutions.

If, say, you are involved as fundraising adviser to a hospital and a university, these differences could be significant.

VALS claims to put a face on different donor segments. Whether or not you believe in a system such as VALS, it is inescapable that values and personal beliefs are crucial to the decision to give to charity. Until somebody comes along with a better model this may be the best way we have of finding who might be tomorrow's donors.

Further information on VALS can be obtained by reading Judith Nichols' *Changing Demographics: Fundraising in the 1990s* or by contacting the VALS Program, SRI International, 333 Ravenswood Avenue, Menlo Park, CA 94025 USA, telephone (415) 859 3882.

The golden generation
People are not only living longer, they are also retiring earlier and they're reaping the benefits of increased prosperity and better financial planning for things like pensions and that 'rainy day' insurance. They have more spare time and they're more affluent.

Older people fall into four basic groups.

It will help if fundraisers can combine to create a positive image of older people and to banish myths such as those that equate old age with inactivity, poor health and decline.

1 The older, 50–64: the golden generation. The children have grown up and left home, the mortgage is paid off. They can revel in the knowledge that they have the highest disposable income of any age group and they've got time to enjoy it. They're also our prime targets.
2 The elderly, 65–74: these are unsettling years. The number of female-headed households begins to climb.
3 The aged, 75–84: by now the majority is female. At 80+ it's two-thirds. Life now is more insular.
4 The very old, 85+: not surprisingly, this group has higher than average assets.

As they get older, research tells us that people tend to stick together in clear geographical clusters. England's best-known 'retirement area' is along the south coast from Hastings to Worthing, but there are many other clearly identifiable enclaves of elderly people.

These are vitally important groups for fundraisers. Recognising their needs, interests, concerns and then providing marketing communications to address them will ensure success for any fundraiser. But, of course, this is an area fraught with ethical dangers and the need for strict adherence to a clear code of practice is obvious.

Jeff Ostroff, author of *Successful Marketing to the 50+ Consumer*, identifies seven areas of need for the ageing population: the home; health care; leisure time; personal and business counselling; education services; financial products and services; and products that combat ageing. Fundraisers, says Mr Ostroff, should position themselves as providing solutions to these needs.

It will help if fundraisers can combine to create a positive image of older people and to banish myths and stereotypes such as those that equate old age with inactivity, poor health and decline.

There are some special tips for writing to older

Such an assumption may well be horribly wrong because our society is changing quite radically for a whole variety of reasons.

people, such as saying '50 years old or over' rather than 'older'; writing long, explanatory copy giving reasons in detail (older people have the time, like to read and like to make up their own minds) and, of course, it pays to set the type in 10 point at least, with adequate spacing between the lines, so older people can read what you have to say in comfort. (How one charity turned this information to advantage is briefly described on page 298.)

Donors of the future

Who will be the donors of the future? What will they be like and how will they feel? How will we find them? How will they differ from today's donors? These are crucial questions for fundraisers. Competition is increasing. We all want the committed donor. We all want 'relationship' donors.

One might be forgiven for assuming that, if the best way to find a new donor is to find someone exactly like our current donor, then the donors of the future will be exactly like our current donors.

Such an assumption may well be horribly wrong because our society is changing quite radically for a whole variety of reasons. Each passing year sees an increase both in the numbers and the affluence of older people. We are all living longer and planning better and this, with the baby boom of the postwar years, will ensure a growing and increasingly affluent elderly population for many years to come. Also the explosion in the numbers of working women since the end of the Second World War, described as the single most significant social trend of the twentieth century, means that a different kind of woman is now coming up to retirement (prime donor) age with, perhaps, a significantly different set of interests and motivations.

Baby boomers are the first generation raised on television. Will this make a difference for fund-raisers? If so, what?

And, finally, the hippy generation of the 1960s, with its revolutionary standards of morals and outlook, is now middle-aged. These are the baby boomers whose numbers should swell the ranks of prospective donors, but will their different values and attitudes mean they are more, or less, likely to support our cause?

The traditional donor pyramid may well be changing (see chapter 4 page 60). According to Judith Nichols it already has in America. Instead of the good old 80:20 rule the ratio now is more likely to be 95:5. For example, Britain's Royal National Lifeboat Institution, which at some time or other touches everyone in the land, gets more than 80 per cent of its annual income from less than 2,000 people. This rule, known as the Pareto principle, asserts the almost universal truth that whatever area of business you are in – retailing, licensed trade, bookmaking, fundraising or whatever – around 80 per cent of your sales will come from around 20 per cent of your customers. Examine your business and if this is true it is a fair clue as to where you should be concentrating your resources.

Also the 'age of prospecting', the last 10 years during which so many charities expanded their supporter lists in quantum leaps, has created a bulging middle section in the pyramid with all those newly recruited donors waiting to be moved up. The bottom of the pyramid, unfortunately, has apparently remained the same except, perhaps, that many of the prime targets for recruitment have been creamed off.

Baby boomers are the first generation raised on television. Will this make a difference for fundraisers? If so, what?

Unsettling though they may be, most of these social changes at least seem likely to be positive for fundraisers. In the USA during the 1990s the baby boomers will move into their prime earning years causing the number of affluent households to sky-rocket. The number of house owners will increase by 40 per cent and those with income of $75,000 and above will multiply by an incredible 300 per cent.

According to American demographers, fundraisers in America are segregating their baby boomers by VALS type to see where their donors are going to come from. These not-so-young-now people have quite different attitudes from the preceding generation and these may have substantial implications for the future of fundraising. (After the baby boomers, apparently, come the baby busters and the baby boomlet – but that's another matter.) According to Cheryl Russell, author of *100 Predictions for the Baby Boom*, baby boomers differ from their parents in that they

- are more likely to be university educated
- are two-income couples
- believe men and women should be equally responsible for cleaning the house
- own VCRs and microwaves; may have home computers and telephone answering machines
- frequently go to the cinema, plays, concerts and museums
- think divorce is acceptable and abortion should be legal
- are more suspicious of authority
- stress fun and enjoyment rather than duty and obligation
- focus on opportunity rather than security
- are likely to be candid rather than tactful
- are self-concerned rather than loyal to organisations
- stress individuality and differences rather than groups and sameness
- prefer experience to possessions.

Of course, we all change as we get older – but we don't all become the same.

I've left a few out of this list that I didn't think were so applicable outside the United States, but most of the rest I think are fairly accurate. Can it be that a generation that is so different from its predecessor will behave in the same way when it comes to making donations?

I think it is unlikely.

Of course, we all change as we get older – but we don't all become the same.

So if basic values are different, how should fundraisers market to the new middle-aged?

It's an urgent question for many charities, who are seeing their current list atrophy as donors grow old and die. While this may bode well for immediate legacy income, it's not very encouraging for the future if these donors are not being satisfactorily replaced.

Fundraisers also need to find an appropriate language for appeal materials to make sure that they do indeed appeal to this new audience. Older donors don't like slickness or padding. They appreciate straight talking and are quite prepared to accept honest emotion in appeals.

Detailed accounting for what charities have done and are doing with donors' funds will also be important, as will flexibility in devising ways of helping and in planning special schemes, such as planned gifts and even legacies. Schemes that clearly recognise a donor's contribution will also pay off. Tomorrow's donors, raised on increasingly sophisticated media, will also expect quality communication (no more bleak, grey, badly designed publications) and will expect to be communicated with via the most modern media, such as fax and video.

Of course, it may be some time before the baby boomers become tomorrow's donors in appreciable numbers, but it'll pay to bring them in now, if you can find appropriate ways. Concern as to how this new breed will behave can be balanced against the undeniable fact that as people's disposable income grows they become more generous. This will happen to baby boomers too.

Consumer attitudes are changing

There's no doubt that fundraisers are living in times of rapid change and consumer attitudes are changing too. Consider how your donors view direct mail now compared to their understanding of it just ten – or even five – years ago (an important consideration when you contemplate the future of fundraising direct mail).

The only way to keep up with people's feelings and how they affect you is through a carefully planned and consistent programme of properly conducted research. If you can't afford to do it on your own, join in with other similar charities and share the cost.

Concentrate first on the basics – a questionnaire and maybe some focus groups among your own supporters. But again the most simple, yet most essential and best, research is just to go out and meet your supporters and talk to them – regularly.

You can take psychographics a long way. For example, you may wish to direct your fundraising particularly towards women. But what kind of women?

A woman with a career is very different to one who views work just as a job and different again to someone who has never worked in any job outside the home. Age, education and social background also subdivide your target group. Women are individuals.

It is worth reading Judith Nichols' book, even though it is discussing people in America. Much of what she says has universal application.

The degree to which most donors have faith in their favourite causes and trust them to do the right thing is something fundraisers should never underestimate or take for granted.

What donors will allow

One of the surprises that research (and meeting people) has shown me is just how tolerant, understanding and encouraging donors can be. The general public seems to be constantly moaning about charities, trying to undermine everything they do through destructive criticism that is usually misinformed or imagined. I suspect this quite often only thinly conceals a cynical attempt to disguise guilt feelings brought on by not giving enough.

Donors don't share this lack of confidence. They have greater respect for and faith in the organisations they support, which is perhaps not surprising. In supporting your cause they have made a commitment and don't want to be proved wrong. The degree to which most donors have faith in their favourite causes and trust them to do the right thing is something fundraisers should never underestimate or take for granted. This trust is one of the motivating rewards that comes to the fundraiser and helps to compensate for the lack of more tangible benefits of the job.

Donors like to be asked their opinions and like to feel those opinions are listened to, but most will turn the question around and tell you that they'll be happy to go along with whatever the fundraising organisation wants to do. So don't always expect your research among donors to reveal staggering truths and insights into where you should be going. Most of your responses will, in fact, be telling you precisely what the donor thinks you want to hear, because the donor likes you, believes in you, wants to help you and certainly doesn't want to create offence. (There are, of course, some who revel in the chance to be as critical as they can be!)

Donors are wonderful people. In my experience they are generally prepared to endorse brave decisions, to

... every one of them has put their hands in their pockets and freely given of their own money to meet a need, help an ideal or achieve a dream.

accept that charities like all organisations have to take calculated risks. They will understand that, at times, mistakes will be made. If they are fully informed of a situation and the decision that needs to be made, I have found they will not seek to make it themselves but will back the organisation 100 per cent, whatever the consequences, providing they can believe the decision was honestly based on what the organisation believed was right.

Donors are not fools (although naturally such a varied group inevitably attracts all types, particularly the unusual). They know that charities have to meet costs and can readily understand that they have to spend money properly in order to be effective and efficient. I find they are as likely to despise false economies as much as they dislike conspicuous extravagance. When the arguments are explained to them, without exception, they seem to understand the need for achieving value for money. That includes the value of investing in a sound administration – see page 29.

Donors are very tolerant of fundraisers because they have faith. The trust, faith and pride that donors feel in the organisations they support are great assets for fundraisers, assets that will prove their value again and again and are worth nurturing against every threat. Fundraisers should realise that, just as they are committed to their cause, so too are the donors. In a remarkable demonstration of their belief, every one of them has put their hands in their pockets and freely given of their own money to meet a need, help an ideal or achieve a dream. In doing so, each donor invests a part of himself or herself. His commitment has been demonstrated. It is a very tangible thing.

It's a very precious resource for the fundraiser.

Fundraising is perhaps, after undertaking, the

ultimate 'people' business. To fundraise effectively you need the people's understanding. How can you expect them to understand you if you don't understand them? The way to understand your donors, and to avoid making mistakes, is through research.

The next chapter is about avoiding – and making – mistakes.

ACTION POINTS

▲ Research makes fundraising relevant, so ensure you understand your donors as completely as possible.

▲ Meet your donors as often as you can. Ask their opinions on the things you need to know.

▲ Plan a questionnaire and/or some focus groups. If you have to, share the cost. Then spend an evening with a pile of completed questionnaires.

▲ Create a written picture of your typical donor. Circulate it. Get your organisation to adopt it as part of your fundraising plan.

▲ Clearly explain to donors how you will use the data they will provide and why it will be useful to you.

▲ If you intend to add any research information to your database, clearly spell this out on your survey materials.

▲ Thank donors for taking part in your research.

▲ Don't assume database means the same thing as donor base. They can be quite different.

▲ Keep reminding yourself of the dangers of faulty research, and see its results as a useful guide rather than holy writ.

▲ Make sure your findings are fully used and implemented, not filed away.

▲ Publish a summary of your findings in your supporter newsletter. Invite comments. But take care to present your findings in a way that donors will understand and accept.

▲ Concentrate the bulk of your attentions and your resources on the small group of individuals who provide most of your income.

▲ Plan for changes in society. Try to identify and track down the donor of the future.

▲ Make your research part of an ongoing annual programme.

DONOR PROFILE

Mrs Chester

Mrs Chester didn't like to have to come to London but she did love her annual meetings. They were definitely a high spot of the year.

She had been coming for 18 years. 'In those days they were held in a church hall just off the Euston Road. I doubt if there were more than 50 of us, including the staff,' she explains.

She had told this story to someone or other every year because Mrs Chester was very good at making new friends, particularly at annual meetings.

'Now, well, there are thousands of us, aren't there?' she would exclaim looking around. She obviously felt considerable pride in what the organisation had become and the small part she had played in it.

'You see, I *am* the charity in my home town, you know,' she would explain in a very modest way. 'I am the secretary and the treasurer combined for our branch and I make sure to organise one major event each year and several small things too. I get lots of help but it takes quite a lot of organisation. It's been a big commitment but I wouldn't have missed it for the world.'

There's no complaint in what she says, just enthusiasm, so it comes as quite a surprise to her new-found companion to discover that this charity isn't the only cause Mrs Chester supports.

'Oh no,' Mrs Chester realises her friend's assumption. 'This is only Mondays, Tuesdays and Wednesdays. Thursdays, Fridays and Saturdays I'm local organiser for – ' and she mentions another national charity, operating in a similar field of concern. In the latter half of each week she does just as much for them and has been doing so for just as long.

Then the conversation hots up. Mrs Chester loves both organisations and wouldn't hear a bad word said against either, but her 18 years with both have given her plenty of opportunity to compare and contrast. Nothing either of them could do would put Mrs Chester off, for really she doesn't support these organisations, she supports the cause – the needy children both organisations exist to help.

But one of her two charities has upset her quite a lot – the one that keeps writing alarming letters and that always seems in need of more money than she is able to give. She's told them before that she'd rather give her time than her money, yet they still keep writing. Mrs Chester wishes 'they' would listen but doesn't believe they will. Really, she doesn't feel she knows who 'they' are.

She also wishes they were a bit more like her other charity. But it doesn't bother her too much – not yet.

6 Errors and pitfalls

'I think the gentleman who created King Kong would have been more gainfully employed in making a set of concrete steps at the Ashton Road end of Bracechurch Street to help old people get to the bus without having to make half-mile detours.'

Letter to the Editor
Birmingham Evening Mail

How to recognise and avoid mistakes

Human beings are fallible and fundraisers are just human beings in disguise. As in any field it is instructive to look at and learn from the mistakes of others – the mariner to sail with is he who has been shipwrecked, for he knows where the reefs are.

I sometimes feel it's a pity that at most of the seminars and workshops on fundraising that I attend the speakers seem to concentrate primarily on giving case histories of their successes. They rarely ever refer in any detail to their failures. Perhaps this is just human nature, but I am sure we could all learn at least as much from studying when, how and why things went wrong as we can from looking at those few campaigns where, apparently, everything went right.

In this chapter I want to consider some of the danger areas for fundraisers and to look at what's happening to donor relationships as a result.

... in careless hands there are few more certain and deadly foes than technology.

These are times of rapid change for fundraisers (I've said it before and I'll probably say it again). One characteristic of change is that it makes things more risky and that means more of the players will make mistakes. The emergence of all the amazing technology we now possess, along with bringing its undeniable range of benefits, has perversely led us into some peculiar areas of risk.

Fundraisers should go out of their way to avoid errors and pitfalls – donors cost such a lot to find and to develop that it seems a real shame to lose them later through avoidable mistakes.

In the heart of the machine

Some years ago George Smith presented a paper to the International Fund Raising Workshop in the Netherlands called 'People to People' and I am going to quote liberally from it. His subject then was what he saw as the enemy of fundraising relationships – technology.

While most fundraisers would say that, correctly applied, technology is one of our very best friends and greatest assets, even our salvation (see chapter 7), I would agree wholeheartedly with George that in careless hands there are few more certain and deadly foes.

'First you are an individual donor,' bemoans George. 'Then you become an entry on a supporters' file. Then you are part of a database ...'

You can almost hear the machine swallowing him.

It's not so much that the public resent their details being included in some gigantic anonymous lump of high technology – the fact is people rarely think about it. What they do notice, however, is when the machine gets it wrong. Usually that's because some flesh-and-blood being injected the frailty in the first place and the damn machine is too detached and clinical to stop repeating

You can't say it'll never happen to you because every fundraiser knows it can, it does and it will.

the error every time you decide to write to your donors.

Let's go back to that hoary old question of 'how many times can you write to your supporters?' Imagine the damage that might be done to your precious relationships when every time you do write you get your friend's name wrong!

You can't say it'll never happen to you because every fundraiser knows it can, it does and it will.

The cold hand of technology

Take the example of a well-known environmental agency (names have been withheld to protect the guilty) which, within the space of just a few weeks, managed to allow technology's cold hand to come between itself and two potentially very valuable donors. The first instance was when a colleague of mine received four virtually identical mailing packs, different only in that three of them had at least one important component wrong in her name or address. Two of them had addressed her as Mr, a fairly basic gender insult. Such waste, particularly of paper, must have seemed doubly ironic to my colleague as the subject of all four appeals was nothing other than the campaign to save the tropical rainforests. (Even the sophisticated recipient who knows that tropical rainforests aren't used to make paper would nevertheless abhor this obvious waste from an environmental organisation.)

Then, to add indifference to insult, the same organisation wrote to another colleague of mine. This time the letter was a brilliant example of how not to say thank you (for a recent generous donation). Above his name my colleague was dismayed to see a long line of ten computer numbers. This allows sufficient scope to allocate a different number to very nearly 200 times the entire population of the United Kingdom. But, not

This seems to be an example of the culture of mass marketing invading the culture of fundraising.

satisfied with this impersonalisation, the charity added a further line of 17 more digits at the foot of the letter. For the recipient, this was the ultimate experience of being written to by a machine. But then, to compound the insult, instead of the director's own signature, the letter had been signed *per pro* by some indecipherable person with the handwriting of a 12 year old.

Lost opportunities both, of course, but much worse. Offence could easily have been caused.

Computers give rise to many amusing salutations which could also offend. Humorous examples include the legendary Mr Obe, who sounds West African but OBE was just one of his decorations, and Mr Prince, who in real life was (and still is) Prince Rainier of Monaco.

A charity I once worked with received a very irate complaint from a certain Miss Fishpool, because the salutation of their most recent letter had omitted the final 'l' from her surname.

Some people have good reason to be sensitive about what we might do to their name.

Funny, of course, but there is a serious problem for relationship fundraisers here. Such incidents can create lasting damage. The environmental organisation in my first example should have been creating the kind of atmosphere that will encourage a donor's support, not polluting their prospects' letter-boxes with the mailings of machines.

This seems to be an example of the culture of mass marketing invading the culture of fundraising. Yet if the principles of relationship fundraising are practised it can be the other way around.

The culture of fundraising *can* invade the culture of mass marketing. Then much greater care would be taken to ensure duplicates are not sent out. List providers – the owners and the brokers – would be told in the strongest

... if you rely too heavily on composite descriptions you might make some horrendous mistakes.

terms by a unity of substantial customers that unclean lists would no longer be tolerated under any circumstances. And removing those unsightly computer numbers, even replacing them with a discreet bar code or similar indirect identification device, would be simplicity itself. As would ensuring that the real person, or a facsimile thereof, actually signed the letter so that when it arrived it looked as it was meant to be – an individual letter of thanks, recognising the gift of a friend on a personal one-to-one basis (see pages 215 to 218).

The little old lady from SW1

The lengthy advice I gave you in chapter 5, to research the demographics and psychographics of your supporters so that you can prepare a donor profile, of course, also conceals a lurking danger in its wisdom – the tendency to suppose we are dealing with norms and caricatures and not real, individual human beings.

Your profile is a composite and must be treated as such. People are not composites. They are all different and need to be treated as individuals.

Every one of our supporters is difficult to classify in their own way and if you rely too heavily on composite descriptions you might make some horrendous mistakes. Some will merely be annoying; others may cost you your relationship.

Take George Smith's little old lady of SW1.

'She is a 65-year-old lady who lives in a pre-First World War house in inner London. Her four grown-up children have all left home and her husband is unemployed. She herself has never worked for a living. Her credit status is zero. In fact she lives in a part of London where mail order companies refuse to offer credit facilities.

'By now you will be feeling duly sorry for this sad

That's how the donor is able to see what kind of people we are, whether we are honest and trustworthy.

remnant of urban society, this impoverished old dear shuffling sadly to the launderette and to the post office every week to pick up her pension.

'Let your eyes be undimmed with tears. What you have just read is a demographically accurate description of Her Majesty Queen Elizabeth II.'

The story makes the all-important point, the one which makes fundraising such an unendingly interesting area. We may be using the most sophisticated of modern systems but we are communicating with people. To do this successfully we require warmth, humanity, understanding and great care that we don't ever think of them as lists, or appear to think of them as lists, but we always think of them as people.

Bad language

If we are bland in our descriptions and our views of the people with whom we communicate, it is inevitable that we will be equally bland in the language we use when we write to them. If we rely on formulae for the letters we use (the peeling [not appealing] computer label, the four-page letter, leaflet, standard reply form, message on the envelope and so on) will not our words be equally formula-driven and sterile as a result? Will we be sending formats instead of letters? Of course we will.

The way we talk to people is critical to our relationship with donors. For the most part we communicate via the printed word. That's how we express ourselves and depict our need. And it's how the donor is able to see what kind of people we are, whether we are honest and trustworthy.

Frequently the gurus of direct mail will tell us that copy doesn't matter, or that at most its importance is limited when considered alongside audience, offer and format. This view may have some merit when

... they often think little of relegating the crucial task of writing their warm mailings to enthusiastic staff with little or no qualifications or experience for the job.

considering the tiny percentage who respond to your cold mailings, but it is absolutely untrue and frankly dangerous when applied to your regular communications with donors.

Yet whilst fundraisers frequently employ professional copywriters to craft their cold direct mail packages, they often think little of relegating the crucial task of writing their warm mailings, their newsletter or information sheets to enthusiastic staff with little or no qualifications or experience for the job. It is a curious reversal of logic.

If you still think copy is unimportant, compare and contrast the following two pieces of text from an annual report – George Smith again, this time writing about arthritis research.

'I am raising funds for arthritis research. And I could say this ...

'... Recent advances in clinical research bring the long-awaited cure for osteo-arthritis ever nearer. No fewer than ten million people suffer from the disease and we desperately need your help to fund a long-term programme of remedial work to reduce the terrible price paid by society for this most crippling of diseases. It is estimated that six million working days a year are lost through arthritis and that 95 per cent of the population will be affected at some stage by the disease.

'This is typical annual report text, but if I said that out loud to a potential donor I would risk boredom, confusion, inattention and a lot of other fruitless reactions. But let's suppose I adopted the first person mode that comes instinctively with natural speech and said this ...

'... My mother is crippled with arthritis. She can't get out of her chair now and she can't handle a knife and fork. There's probably someone in your family whose

'The difference is always worth exploring. Read your message out loud. Does it survive the test?'

life has been made miserable by the disease. For there is not much we can do about it right now. The only answer is research and that costs money. Every pound you can give me goes to help. Can you please send us a donation? The cure will be too late for my mother, but it might not be too late for you or your children. Every time you get out of a chair and pick up a knife and fork, say a little thank you for your own luck and do something to help.

'All right, it's corny, deliberately so in this case because it helps make the point. But does anyone doubt that the second piece of copy is more effective than the first? It sounds like someone talking, not someone going through the motions. The difference is always worth exploring. Read your message out loud. Does it survive the test?'

The point is, words matter and they should be handled with care. Remember that you are trying to communicate a promotional message which you will then send uninvited in a free distribution publication. That makes it one of the hardest messages of all to get people to read. So they have to *want* to read what you say and the job of your writing is to make that happen so easily and skilfully that the reader will be happily and effortlessly drawn into your story.

The kind of writing that produces the best response in direct mail is concise, to the point, unpretentious and unambiguous, for any style you attempt will most probably get in the way of the message. Avoid formality and any hint of self-satisfaction. Write to your donors in their language, not yours, and write with warmth and sincerity, featuring real people and describing the things that you do that influence their lives.

It usually pays to be brief, or at least not to waffle. I have some sympathy with Sir Winston Churchill, who sent the following memo to his First Lord of the Admiralty, 'Pray state this day, on one side of a sheet of paper, how the Royal Navy is being adapted to meet the conditions of modern warfare.'

Concentrates the mind, doesn't it?

Good writing is quite a challenge and is rare in fundraising publications. But if it isn't good writing it won't be good reading and if it isn't good reading it won't be read. These days people have better things to do with their time.

That's the challenge that makes good writing well worth working for.

The mail mountain

One major potential problem facing fundraisers and donors is that there is so much fundraising direct mail. Who would have thought just a few years ago that UK charities would be using direct mail on such a scale and in such a variety of ways? I think this growth has also occurred in most European countries and, as usual, it is following even greater growth in the United States.

It is obvious to most people with even a superficial knowledge of fundraising that one of the biggest changes for charities in recent years has been the explosion of direct mail fundraising.

Direct mail is now arguably the most important and most widely used weapon in the fundraiser's armoury.

In the early 1980s, when growth in direct mail fundraising began to accelerate, many people resisted it because they suspected donors would not like it.

The common cry was, 'We can't mail our supporters more than once or maybe twice a year. What works in the United States won't work here.'

Not many fundraising organisations still feel like that. There aren't nearly so many organisations now

We used to say in hushed tones, 'You know some donors in the USA get 30 or more appeal mailings each month – incredible isn't it? We couldn't ever imagine it happening here.'

who mail donors just once or twice a year.

For experience has clearly shown that more regular mailing (usually) works very well. It does pay to mail your donors more often. Donors seem to feel, 'We support ABC charity, but we give our money to XYZ charity because they write and ask for it.' The same people support many charities but they are likely to give most to the charity that keeps in touch.

Direct mail fundraising, we all know, can work fabulously well. So in a surprisingly short space of time charity appeal mailings have grown ... and grown ... and grown.

But, of course, the number of available mailing lists hasn't grown at anything like the same pace – certainly not the good ones.

The last two decades also didn't see any substantial changes in either the number of, or the characteristics of the typical charity donor – the little old lady from Tunbridge Wells or from Fontainebleau or from Mönchengladbach for that matter.

We used to say in hushed tones, 'You know some donors in the USA get 30 or more appeal mailings each month – incredible isn't it? We couldn't ever imagine it happening here.'

Now in the UK, many people do receive charity fundraising mailings on a very regular basis, if not every day then every week and often several times a week.

What does this escalation mean to donors?

Quite simply it means they're seeing far more of it, they're recognising it for what it is – a marketing communication – they're realising that they don't want to be communicated with in this way and they're responding to it less and less.

There is a limit to how many times we can sensibly write to our donors but there are many different views as

... like the little boy and the emperor with no clothes on, I can only own up that I see what I see.

to what that limit might be. I believe we should only write when it is economically viable to do so and when we have something relevant and important to say.

If fundraisers don't take care to avoid over-mailing donors will start to take their business elsewhere, or simply cease to be donors altogether, perhaps even striking one or two particularly offensive charities out of their wills.

Perhaps the whole process is simply going through a phase of natural selection and will, in time, become automatically self-regulating. As more and more fundraisers subject a limited universe of prospects to more and more direct mail so responses begin to fall to the point that direct mail fundraising becomes uneconomic for the less 'publicly appealing' causes. These then have to switch their recruitment to other sources, thus leaving cold donor recruitment via direct mail to the few most popular – and largest – charities.

Junk fundraising

There seems to be a silent conspiracy among people in direct marketing to expunge the term 'junk mail' from our vocabulary. They appear to believe that by never mentioning the hideous phrase the issue will blow over, the public will forget their irritation, perhaps even come to love direct mail and the threatened disaster for direct marketing – regulatory intervention from on high – will be averted.

I think this is wishful thinking of the sort that ostriches do. If in saying so I am considered disloyal to the industry that provides my bread and butter then I am sorry but, like the little boy and the emperor with no clothes on, I can only own up that I see what I see.

You see, the evidence that junk mail exists – and might even be on the increase – comes through my

When direct mail is done well it can be a joy to send and a joy to receive. But that happens too rarely.

letterbox every day of the week. By 'junk mail' I mean inappropriate, irrelevant, badly prepared and badly targeted mailings. In other words, unwanted and irritating rubbish.

This doesn't mean I am antipathetic to direct mail. Far from it. I think it is one of the most challenging and demanding of advertising media. When direct mail is done well it can be a joy to send and a joy to receive. But that happens too rarely. Unfortunately most direct mail is mediocre and is met with indifference. Of the rest, quite a lot is junk, including quite a lot of junk fundraising, and that is causing damage to all fundraising organisations, particularly charities. It is even threatening the continuation of direct mail fundraising as we know it.

One consumer described junk mail as 'like a drunken stranger who comes up to you in the street and rambles on at you. You just want him to get out of the way as soon as possible.' That's not the way fundraisers want their communications to be viewed, is it?

That's not the way we'd expect donors to view us if we met them in the street. Why then are we making such a bad job of our written communications?

Lukewarm

Junk mail is just as much of a threat to warm mailing as it is to cold.

Personal visits to donors are rarely viable in very large quantities. Large-scale telephoning of donors is often practical and very effective, but its value will be reduced if used too often. So direct mail is the only practical means of communicating regularly with large numbers of donors on a long-term basis. If donors become resistant to direct mail generally (remember that your supporters also receive mailings from other charities, from banks, insurance companies, building societies, travel firms, wine retailers, time-share operators, Uncle Tom Cobbley and all) then the outlook for fundraising communications, however relationship-oriented they may be, is pretty bleak. That's why I hate junk mail.

I feel it has to be acknowledged, brought out into the open and eradicated as quickly and as openly as possible so that the public can clearly see that fundraising, at least, has its promotional house in order.

'Junk' of course isn't unique to direct mail. You can have junk phone calls (we've all been on the receiving end of these) and equally you can have phone calls that make donors feel proud and happy and personally involved. Imagine you're a keen supporter of Third World causes. You learn on television of a disaster in the Horn of Africa and one of the charities whose work in that area you have supported in the past telephones you at home that very night to say, 'I know of your interest in this area and its people and I thought you would like to know what we (XYZ charity) are doing to respond quickly to this situation'. Most donors would be impressed and moved by such a personal report and would welcome the chance to help, if invited to do so.

Yet 'junk' telephone calls cause most people to classify all promotional telephone calls in the same way. The public's natural reaction is to shoot first and ask questions later. As with direct mail, they'll resort to shooting all the messengers, whether or not they are bringing bad news, simply because too many similar looking messengers have brought too much bad news in the past.

I don't blame them. But it doesn't have to be like that.

The damage junk fundraising can do to our

Many people in our society are vulnerable to approaches from unscrupulous or badly trained and unsupervised fundraisers.

profession is easily imagined. Many people in our society are vulnerable to approaches from unscrupulous or badly trained and unsupervised fundraisers.

Imagine the confused and lonely old lady whose hearing is less than perfect, whose responses are slow and uncertain who receives a telephone call from a charity she is inclined to support. The charity's emissary, recruited that afternoon from a nearby polytechnic, is following a carefully structured script designed to lead remorselessly one question after another towards an extracted promise to give, to give a large and specific donation and then even to agree to give it under deed of covenant 'the form for which, Mrs Prospect, will be in tomorrow's post ...'

It doesn't bear thinking about. But it has certainly happened and will happen again regularly unless telephone fundraisers can be regulated by a respected and universally accepted code of behaviour that can then be vigorously enforced.

The difference between the two telephone calls I've just cited could not be more extreme. One is imaginative, relevant relationship fundraising. The other is junk.

The Institute of Charity Fundraising Managers is currently preparing a draft code of practice for self-regulation of direct mail in the United Kingdom. Another, similar code of practice is now proposed for telephone fundraising.

For these codes to be effective we need to devise some way of dealing appropriately with any organisation that transgresses them. There are few things more futile than a toothless law.

All this may be entirely academic, because at the time of writing there are two major threats hovering over the fundraising community in Europe that might restrict or even curtail direct mail and telephone fundraising as we

Let's not pretend it doesn't exist. That does nobody, neither consumer nor marketer, any good at all.

know it. These threats are in the shape of some of the most extreme provisions of Britain's 1991 Charities Bill which, in its original form, suggested quite impracticable restrictions on anyone who prepares direct mail or telemarketing campaigns for a charity, and the notorious European Community directives proposed to bring all regulations relating to the storage, exchange and transmission of personal data in line for the start of the single European market in 1993.

Various effective initiatives have been taken to resist these proposed pieces of unworkable legislation and – for the time being at least – it seems that the major dangers to fundraisers are likely to be averted, although this is by no means a foregone conclusion.

But the threat of unwelcome mail and intrusive telephone calls remains. In this we are our own worst enemy and must take action to clean up our act. If we are not seen to be taking firm and comprehensive action to control these threats then we can be sure some other power, national or international, will intervene to do so and the interests of fundraisers will then inevitably take second place.

The tragedy is that if restrictions are placed on our ability to use data, junk mail and telephoning is more likely to increase than reduce. For accurate, up-to-date data enables us to *exclude* inappropriate individuals and to write or phone relevantly and in an informed way to the rest. With no access to such data, marketers will return to the bad old days of uncontrolled mass mailings – real junk.

Junk is not limited to the mail and the phone. We have all seen it on the television, on posters, press advertisements. It's everywhere.

Let's not pretend it doesn't exist. That does nobody, neither consumer nor marketer, any good at all. It's like

Drastic, perhaps, but if enough of the public were to do this then the unwanted mail would have to stop.

drugs or smoking. The best way to tackle the problem is to bring it out into the open.

The final solution
Although the public may not generally realise it, there is a ready-made and easy solution to the problem of too much junk mail from fundraisers. It is one we provide ourselves – the freepost reply envelope.

All recipients need do is take the unwanted mailing and return it to the sender via the freepost envelope so conveniently provided. Drastic, perhaps, but if enough of the public were to do this then the unwanted mail would have to stop, as charities would be picking up an intolerable freepost bill.

Low organisational self-image
Some charities make a number of mistakes brought on by their self-imposed tendency to wear sackcloth and ashes, derived from their low view of themselves as a charity. They commonly say, 'As a charity we can't be seen to waste money', which is quite correct. But often what they really mean is, 'As a charity we can't be seen to spend money' and that, as I have said before, leads to many false economies. It results in charities spending £5 and completely wasting their money when they could have spent £10 and achieved real value. Donors, of course, would much prefer the charity to get value for money and if expenditure is clearly explained and justified will happily endorse the decision.

Charities generally have almost totally failed to educate their supporters towards a mature understanding of the reality of their position, with the result that some of their supporters have been given quite unrealistic expectations of the organisation's financial capabilities. So they make unrealistic demands

This kind of dishonesty by omission simply creates a rod for the charity's back.

such as 'little or no administrative costs' and 'expense ratio of five per cent' and so on.

I don't blame the public for this kind of wishful thinking. The fact is that, in the past, charities have made a poor job of explaining the commercial facts of life to their donors and to the public at large. It is this situation that leads to charities presenting accounts that are designed to conceal rather than to reveal, by angling charts and diagrams to show figures in a misleading perspective and by leaving out those statistics that don't help to perpetuate the deception. This kind of dishonesty by omission simply creates a rod for the charity's back.

As always, how people perceive what you say depends as much on how you say it as on what you are saying. That's what promotion is all about. But you have to be open and honest.

So rather than tell a concerned donor that a part of his donation will go towards fundraising costs, is it not better to explain that by spending 25 per cent of his gift on fundraising you can actually turn every pound of that part of his gift into an extra £4 for the cause?

Of course it is. Donors think that's great.

The need for positive projection of the facts was shown clearly long ago when a certain king required his portrait to be painted. He commissioned three painters each to try their different styles and the winner was to be handsomely rewarded with gold. Unfortunately, by a second accident of birth this young king was severely crippled. One of his legs was shorter than the other, his back was bent and he was blind in one eye.

The first painter was absolutely honest and painted his king exactly as he was. The king was shocked and threw the artist in jail.

The second painter portrayed his king as a dazzling

You must tell the truth, but it helps if you present it in an acceptable way.

Greek god. The king felt he was taking the mickey and had him deported.

The third artist painted a hunting scene – the king's favourite sport – in which his majesty was depicted with one foot on a tree stump (the shorter leg, naturally), his back was bent as he took aim and his blind eye was closed to fire his rifle.

The king was delighted, even though the painter had pictured him entirely faithfully, and the happy artist was duly awarded his bag of gold.

The moral of this story is that you must tell the truth, but it helps if you present it in an acceptable way.

A neglected public face

Presenting things in a more acceptable way is a lesson many fundraising organisations could fruitfully take to heart when considering another area of common concern for relationship fundraisers – the public face of the organisation.

By this I don't mean the image projected to the media, I mean the face your public see when they visit or telephone your organisation perhaps with an enquiry, a request, or just on the off chance.

This is an area many fundraisers overlook, but they do so at their peril. To show what I mean, consider the following results of anonymous tests carried out by my company on 50 of the UK's largest fundraising organisations.

A colleague of mine recently telephoned the top 50 charities in the UK, asking for general information on behalf of a potential donor. Most were polite and helpful. Only one was downright rude, but several were hesitant, or suspicious, or asked awkward questions and made the caller feel uncomfortable. Ten out of the 50 sent very poor, ill thought-out information. The material sent

Your telephonist/ receptionist is a relationship fundraiser too.

by many of the others was not very good. Only 19 included some kind of clear response device. Worse still, having said they would, 11 out of the 50 failed to send anything at all.

Perhaps that is some indication of the quality of donor service among Britain's top fundraising charities.

Depressing though it is, it is a somewhat better picture than when we did a similar exercise five years earlier. Then only two out of 47 organisations approached made any further contact with the person who had requested their information.

Funny, isn't it? But it may not be quite so amusing when you consider how your organisation would fare. I strongly recommend you to try this yourself. Next time you are out of the office subject your own organisation to a 'donor friendliness' road test. It can be very illuminating. If your voice is likely to be recognised get a friend to do it for you but do try to listen in.

You may be very pleased and proud of your organisation. But if not, think what effect that unhelpful voice is having when it answers your donors.

Ask yourself how well trained your staff are in basic telephone techniques, in answering the public, in making donors feel good and in providing an accurate and speedy response to their requests. Are they familiar with the annual report, so that when asked can give a positive and helpful answer? If stocks are low, do they know how to get more, or whom to ask?

I work with many charities. I know quite a few who are very hot in this regard. I know others who have never given it a second thought.

Your telephonist/receptionist is a relationship fundraiser too. He or she needs to know as much as you do about what donors want and how he or she should respond. Perhaps you could encourage this by buying them a copy of this book ...

The voice that answers your telephone is often the public's first and sometimes their only contact with your organisation. It has a very special role to play in your relationship fundraising and can do a great deal of harm if it doesn't sound right or say the right things.

What kind of a reception is that?

Another area at high risk of fundraisers' neglect is the reception area. Now your donor can not only hear the receptionist, he can see her (or him) as well. What else can your donor see? A good display of promotional material? A neat display of press cuttings? Some interesting brochures to take away? A few copies of the annual report, some neatly framed posters? Somewhere comfortable to sit?

The chances are your donor might see none of these things. Instead he'll have to stand waiting for what seems an interminable time in a narrow corridor strewn with sundry leaflets, stacked with parcels, boxes and the photocopier, next to peeling posters and paintwork with nowhere to put his cup of coffee.

He does, of course, get a cup of coffee, which is something. This is just neglect, not abuse.

It has its charm and it's very appropriate for the church bazaar or the local youth club.

But not for a nationally known fundraising charity seeking to present a positive image and inspiring impression to the world of potential donors, all of whom might one day come to visit.

One national charity I know has recognised that the people who come to visit are important and has constructed its reception area to create a good first impression. The focal point is a video and audio display unit containing short messages which are changed at

They're all potential or current supporters. You might be surprised.

intervals. Along one wall, neatly displayed, are all of the charity's recent press releases and a display of press cuttings. A colourful target chart illustrating the progress of the latest appeal is also on show as are a series of bright posters that surround the small library. And there is plentiful and comfortable seating. I like going there.

People tend to put a lot of emphasis on first impressions. Rightly or wrongly we judge people by the way they dress. What kind of an impression will your reception make on your donors? Will it speak volumes about a successful, competent organisation? Will it project an air of achievement and progress?

Or will it present a depressing atmosphere of decay and decline?

Fundraisers from many organisations will feel that the reception area is not part of their responsibilities, it is none of their business. But that is a mistake.

A good reception area has an important part to play in your relationship fundraising. Ask your receptionist to keep a record of all visitors for one week – the people from the ad agency, 'her from East Anglia', the computer engineer, the man who repairs the photocopier ...

They're all potential or current supporters. You might be surprised.

Or maybe you think it doesn't matter because you don't get many visitors. Perhaps that's because you have a lousy reception area.

Check enough seats are available, train the receptionist, buy some flowers, get advice on mounting and maintaining a good display of leaflets and brochures. Have your posters framed. Keep your reception area clear and clean. And go and sit in it yourself from time to time.

That's terrific. But that means the largest part of your donor list didn't respond. You achieved a 75 per cent non-response. Why?

The importance of non-response

The potential errors and pitfalls described above have all been visible and easily identified. It's not too difficult to create a mental picture of what happens in these areas when things go wrong.

I now want to consider an area of at least equal importance but because it is invisible it is therefore much harder to define and quantify. This is perhaps best described as the danger of forgetting those who *don't* respond.

By this I mean the larger part of our donor list, those who manage not to reply to most of our mailings, however appealing we may make them.

Fundraisers tend to ignore these people. We are always fanatically interested in our response levels. 'Oh great, we've just got a 25 per cent response to our Christmas warm mailing!'

That's terrific. But that means the largest part of your donor list *didn't* respond. You achieved a 75 per cent *non-response*. Why – what did you do wrong? What do your donors think of you? Did they mean to respond but not get round to it? Have they decided only to reply once a year? Will they ever respond again? Did they not like your mailing?

In fact, while most fundraisers could tell you whether they get, on average, a 15 per cent or a 30 per cent response to their mailings, many won't be able to tell you how many people on their list won't respond at all, how many only respond once a year, how many respond several times each year, how many respond every time.

We have come to be so interested in the bottom line we tend to overlook those who don't reply. This is a serious error.

Of course we can find some things out about these

The difference between what one charity and another refers to as a warm list can be quite staggering.

people through focus groups or, perhaps, a telephone survey, but how many fundraisers do? Wouldn't it be fascinating to know what non-responders thought of what we sent? We assume, more or less, what the donors who responded feel, but how about the rest? Are they really donors? Why didn't they respond? What changes, suggestions or improvements could they make?

This subject is further complicated by the different definitions some fundraisers have of when a donor is a donor (after the second gift, say I), whether and when charities decide to clean their lists and at what point they decide to remove a donor who hasn't responded (after two years, I say) and put them on a tepid (reactivation) list. Of course, before any reactivation programme is put into operation – see pages 170 to 172 – the relationship fundraiser needs to do everything practical to find out *why* a donor hasn't responded.

The question of 'when is a donor really a donor' is a very important point. Before any individual can be usefully categorised as a donor there has to be some concrete evidence of their potential long-term support for the cause. A donor isn't someone who responds once as a knee-jerk reaction to a particularly emotive appeal. There must be at least a second gift as evidence of sustained commitment.

The difference between what one charity and another refers to as a warm list can be quite staggering. One charity my company prepared a questionnaire for received a five per cent response, when others with apparently similar donors and appeal received 65–75 per cent. What the first charity referred to as their donor list of 400,000 names in fact probably came down to 20,000 real donors and 380,000 dead people they had just traditionally squandered their postage budget on.

The fact is that although a typical fundraising

promotion may not generate a direct response from the whole donor file it almost certainly will have a considerable effect on a very large part of it. Research can prove this. Fundraisers need to know what that effect is, for the advertising impression made on non-responders can be a crucial component of what you get for your expenditure on advertising. This doesn't just relate to direct mail but applies also to press advertising, inserts and any other response advertising.

We should stop talking about direct response as if that were the only thing that matters. We are interested in 'response'. Whether it is direct or indirect is merely a matter of how long we have to wait to get our money.

If we take the views and interests of 'non-responders' into account, surely that will influence the kind of response marketing materials – direct mail, press ads and so forth – that we produce?

The power and the perils of emotion

Emotion, one of our greatest assets as fundraisers, is also one of our greatest dangers. There is no doubt that emotion pulls response. It opens cheque books as well as hearts, but unbridled use or abuse of emotion can cause offence to the many while perhaps unjustly raising the expectations of the few.

The dilemma surrounding the use and abuse of emotion has been controversial as long as I've been in fundraising and probably since fundraising began.

In fact it is insoluble. There is no practical answer to this far from simple issue. But it is a subject that bears some further examination for it is fundamental to most charities' communications with their supporters.

Clearly, while bland communications don't work and are a great waste of money, some limits have to be imposed by those who frame our laws to prevent

What is obscene is the casual displacement of these images by other, more immediate news ...

excessive use of emotion by fundraisers.

Emotion is essential to any appeal. Tests repeatedly prove that almost any audience will give more if the emotional lever is pulled. We all know the power and the potential that is in a child's eyes. Most charities, by their very nature, have access to powerful emotive images and messages. The more emotive its appeal, the more popular and successful the charity .

Would the British public have responded so generously to the famine in Ethiopia in 1984 if they had not had delivered directly into their living rooms via the most powerful medium of all, television, those stark images of long lines of passive, starving children so movingly filmed by Mohammed Amin, accompanied by the chilling emotive words of Michael Buerk?

Of course they wouldn't. In that situation, emotion is spontaneous and unstoppable. No one could see the scene without being emotionally involved. It is right and proper that such suffering should be exposed, in its full and awful vividness, so that the scandal of starvation in a world of plenty can be brought home, and people be given the chance to act.

It is not the images or the use of the emotion that are obscene. What is obscene is the casual displacement of these images by other, more immediate news, such as the report of the test match or the latest share prices. What is obscene, I believe, is switching off or turning over in the hope that by so doing the problem, as well as the emotive images, will go away.

I don't see a dilemma in using to the full such clear and obvious images of suffering by humans or animals. If your cause can draw on such legitimate emotion it will successfully raise funds. If it can't, it will have to try less basic and reliable means. It cannot tackle the problem without the funds.

... it may lead to inaccurate images, stereotypes and ultimately to abuse of the very people the fundraiser exists to help.

Not everyone who works in overseas development shares this view. People who are starving still have dignity and rights. But Third World charities also seek help for people who are not starving but who are poor. Where a question of acceptability arises is when images of poor people are presented as if they were starving, where images of black people are presented as if they were poor, and where poverty is presented automatically as unhappiness.

Programmes of long-term development perhaps face these dilemmas more than appeals for disaster relief where the need is both immediate, obvious and paramount. The people in need of development help still have the same rights, feelings and dignity, but the dilemma arises when the fundraiser has to present their situation in the best way. The best way for raising funds will inevitably be the most emotive, but that may not be in the best interest of the people so pictured, for it may lead to inaccurate images, stereotypes and ultimately to abuse of these people who are the very people the fundraiser exists to help.

British children are protected by law from potential exploitation by fundraisers. Parental permission is necessary before any photographs of children are reproduced and signed approval should always be sought. No such regulations protect the image of the Third World child. Any chance of protection is left in the gentle hands of the fundraiser, which brings me to the story of Mbazimutima.

When I was a fundraiser at ActionAid we recruited supporters via newspaper advertisements in the quality press. Because it was a relatively expensive exercise we were always testing – different copy, different sizes, different media – and our tests were rigorously scientific. We used photographs of African or Indian

We must never forget that we are dealing with real people who, if they were given the chance, would care about what we do with their image.

children waiting to be sponsored. As soon as one child was sponsored, we changed the photograph. No permission for this had ever been sought or given, but we had no complaints, mainly I suppose because the parents of these children weren't likely to read the papers in which we advertised.

One evening I was asked to approve a rush proof of an A/B split copy test we were running. The only change in this particular test was in the child used. The relative pulling power of different children was being tested. Now there's nothing wrong with that. We all know that we need to use attractive, appealing images in our ads. In this respect charities are no different to washing powders. But one of my colleagues noticed that the picture which was captioned Mbazimutima, aged eight, Burundi, wasn't him. Someone at the agency or the newspaper had used the wrong picture. I was very new at the time and was under some pressure from the newspaper and the agency to approve the ad quickly. No one would know the difference. If Mbazimutima's replacement was to walk down Oxford Street, no one would know he was the wrong guy.

We discussed it and agreed that whatever the consequences we would change the picture so the right name would appear under the right photograph.

So Mbazimutima's name appeared under his photograph, as he would have a right to expect. I am sure that was the correct thing to do. As fundraisers we must never forget that we are dealing with real people who, if they were given the chance, would care about what we do with their image.

I once sent a photographer to India to document development work in Kerala. He came back with many stunning images but one of a ragged-haired, wide-eyed naked boy was particularly dramatic and appealing. I used his picture in a small poster campaign and wrote a headline which was set across his lower torso, thereby covering his dignity. I never had his permission but it was a very popular poster and made him famous across the country. I don't suppose he ever knew.

Later our advertising agency selected the same picture for another national poster campaign, but here the headline wasn't so obliging and we had the problem of deciding whether or not to run a poster which showed in full a naked boy. I was very much against it, but was persuaded that rather than replacing the photograph, which wouldn't be easy, it could be retouched to remove effectively the offending part by blurring the image at the appropriate spot. In the end the retoucher transformed our stunning little boy into a no less beautiful and appealing little girl. But we had no right to do this and I have regretted it ever since.

Fundraisers for overseas causes have an awesome responsibility and not all of us discharge it faultlessly. When UK charities such as the National Society for the Prevention of Cruelty to Children (NSPCC) and the National Children's Home use images of children they have to employ models. These can then be art directed and made up as required and the public readily understands the need to protect the identity of the real cases. These charities' promotions are no less effective because of it.

So if it is necessary in the UK, some similar rights and protection should also be given to people from other lands and cultures. This is a grey area for fundraisers.

I don't know how it would work, but yet another code of practice needs to be devised to allow fundraisers to portray legitimate emotional images without demeaning, exploiting or misleading either the public or the people whose images are being used but who can't

A solution must be found which enables fundraisers to present effective advertising that is positive, honest and accurate.

give permission and can't protect themselves.

UK charities also sometimes face similar dilemmas. I once took a photographer to a well-known London teaching hospital to photograph open heart surgery for a major heart research organisation. The hospital was quite happy to allow us to take any photographs we wanted. The operation we were filming was on a middle-aged woman who was already unconscious on a slab. I remember thinking she looked like a lump of meat, she was so completely out of it. As we all, medical staff and photographers, went about our business, she was almost totally ignored. We took detailed shots of the operation which, it seemed to me, were the ultimate invasion of privacy. Later we discovered that the woman's permission had not been obtained so we correctly decided not to use any of the shots which showed her even though she herself would be in no way identifiable. Later she recovered from her operation and did allow the charity to use her picture.

The dilemma posed by the images fundraisers use to portray people with disabilities is even deeper and more complex. Ann Macfarlane, writing in Arthritis Care's house magazine, *Arthritis News*, said, 'The majority of disabled people believe that not only is much charity advertising personally insulting, it also portrays untruths.'

This observation may well be true and if it is then the tragedy is that, just as with distorted views of overseas aid, damage is being done by fundraisers to the very people they are seeking to help. Somehow a solution must be found which enables fundraisers to present effective advertising that is positive, honest and accurate. If then it still offends, perhaps the problem is more with the perception of the offended than with any actual offence.

The majority of charity publications fail because they are dull.

Emotion can be used positively. It can make people think and so educate and inform where bland advertising would miss out. Disabled people can be consulted about the images fundraisers use, and should be. In varying degrees, in most of the charities I work with, they are, although they may not always get their own way. The solution is consultation, fair represent-ation and even-handed discussion. As former Prime Minister Harold Macmillan was fond of saying, 'Slow calm deliberation untangles every knot.'

Perhaps one way forward, as Ann Macfarlane goes on to suggest, would be the preparation of a set of guidelines and principles for good practice in charity advertising. The trouble with guidelines, of course, is that inevitably they are also restrictions, they rarely cover all situations and they sometimes create as many problems as they resolve.

But it would be a start.

Boring, boring, boring ...

There are lots of other potential errors and pitfalls that threaten danger to your relationship fundraising. Sloppy letters and boring cramped news-sheets reinforce the traditional image of charities as well-intentioned rather old-fashioned amateurs. The majority of charity publications fail because they are dull. As such they present a picture of their organisation as boring and ineffective, which is a sad waste because so often nothing could be further from the truth.

A few years ago I was invited to be one of the judges of the UK's Charity Annual Reports Awards. It was a sobering experience. More than 400 organisations submitted their publications and at least 90 per cent of them were fit only for the wastepaper basket. Several clients of my company have won that award in the past but it is little consolation being the best of such a bad bunch. However, the awards have done a great deal of good and have made a major contribution towards elevating the status of charity publications.

Things have improved in recent years and many more fundraising organisations now realise the folly of failing to invest time, care and money in producing good, effective publications. But good intentions themselves are not enough. Another major danger is failing to listen to your donors.

This can frequently be seen in charities continuing to provide services that donors don't want to fund, but it's also frequently visible in a charity's own publications.

From time to time I run workshops for fundraisers on publication design and production, particularly with regard to fundraising annual reports. One of my favourite devices for unfailingly attracting the audience's attention is to show some examples of really appalling charity annual reports. It is rather wicked, I know, but I make no apology because once your annual report is published and distributed it is in the public arena and therefore is fair game for anyone to praise or condemn as they choose. The reason this device never fails to attract attention is that each member of the audience sits nervously through each ridiculed report thinking 'I wonder if mine will be next?'

It rarely happens, but one day, as I was showing a particularly dreadful, dull and boring report, a hesitant hand went up in the audience and a timid voice confessed that she was, in fact, the originator of this dismal production. I, of course, began to backtrack like a mad thing but was stopped in my tracks rather bravely by this woman who now boldly stated that it was OK, she had no emotional stake in that production and had since read my book on annual reports. She felt she now

She had certainly made dramatic changes, but they were all of the wrong sort.

clearly realised what was wrong with her first effort and had since introduced major changes. 'Would you mind', she asked, 'if I gave you a copy of my new report for your comments?'

After the seminar she did indeed give me her new report. It was certainly different. It was absolutely hideous – so over-designed it was virtually unreadable and so 'far out' in style that most recipients wouldn't want to try. Besides, its zany, unconventional shape meant it wouldn't fit easily in my wastepaper basket.

I hurried off to make slides of it for my next annual report presentation. Such disasters are, thankfully, becoming quite hard to find.

The point is that she had certainly made dramatic changes, but they were all of the wrong sort. She had failed in the most important area of all, she hadn't listened to her readers.

Although most charities have now improved their annual reports, many still neglect other important publications. For example, very few charities produce a good welcome pack (see page 271), yet the information sent as an introduction to a new supporter can be a crucial part of forming a long-term relationship. If your relationships get off to a good start, they are almost certain to flourish. If not they may never recover.

Other errors

There are a number of other errors and pitfalls which can easily get in the way of your relationship fundraising, but these are either small matters, thus deserving only a brief mention here, or matters of personal opinion with which, perhaps, many of my readers will disagree and so are maybe best kept largely to myself.

An example of the latter is fundraising by collecting box. I know many organisations get worthwhile income

Watch the eyes of passers-by to see how the public loathe street collections.

this way, but I don't like it. It seems to me to be the antithesis of relationship fundraising. This is just a personal opinion, as I've said, but I know many people agree with me.

With street collections people only give when they have to. They rarely even know the name of the cause and we, the fundraisers, have no way of explaining our purpose or going back later to solicit a further gift. Watch the eyes of passers-by to see how the public loathe street collections. They smack of the begging bowl and do little good for fundraiser or donor in helping to enhance the position of either. They are a major contributor to the public's low esteem for charities.

A research exercise in New York some years ago showed that the public are quite prepared to give to a fictitious cause called 'The League of Two-headed Babies'. The fact is that many people don't care who or what the collection is for, so long as the collector goes away quickly. Hardly positive fundraising. I did recently depart from my personal rule of avoiding street collectors because I was so impressed by the fortitude of a solitary woman collecting for one of the overseas aid charities. She struggled in the rain against a sea of indifference while doggedly shouting her campaign slogan. That struck me as worth a pound of my money. Only later did I remember that collectors are not allowed to shout slogans or to do much other than just hold the tin and be there.

But that is an exception. Street collections won't win many converts, I suspect they are more likely simply to breed resentment. The late Cecil Jackson Cole (known as CJC), the remarkable man who founded Help the Aged, helped found Oxfam and gave me my first job in fundraising, once said that a penny in the tin is a vote for

To win the hearts and minds of people you need a lot more time than it takes to pop a coin in the slot and a much better place to do it in than a busy street.

the cause. I don't believe this is so. To win the hearts and minds of people you need a lot more time than it takes to pop a coin in the slot and a much better place to do it in than a busy street.

CJC was right, however, in his basic assumption that encouraging people to give also encourages them to think about the cause they have given to – but street collections seem to me to be one of the least ideal ways of doing it. As far as I know, Oxfam was the first fundraising organisation in Britain to commit resources to educating its donors, thereby echoing CJC's foresight.

On the positive side, street collectors do raise substantial sums of money and they are one of the few methods by which charities actually reach the man in the street. But I still don't like them. For much the same reason I am not keen on house-to-house collections, although at least then your collectors can leaflet, answer questions and collect names, addresses and telephone numbers of interested parties (see page 193).

I am also against much of the commercial selling of advertising space that charities do in journals and programmes. The reason for this is that they usually deliver very limited value for money so should be promoted as donations, not commercial advertisements. It is not always the case, I know, but too often professional advertising sales reps bludgeon small businesses into taking unwanted ads in tacky, badly designed publications that have no worthwhile circulation and because of their low quality are rarely, if ever, read. This breeds resentment among the advertisers and is certainly not a positive cooperation between industry and charity. Some charities have in-house advertising sales staff who are more scrupulous than the normal freelance ad sales outfit, but even these require more supervision than most charities can give.

I also dislike any hard selling by charities, however good the cause, and most potential sponsors and large donors would agree with me. Our business area is not appropriate to hard selling. Few businesses are. You don't get very far by pestering. All you do is queer the pitch for those who follow.

The benefits and risks of marketing

Marketing imposes an essential series of disciplines on fundraisers. It enables the implementation of a planned series of tried and tested strategies and techniques, all of which are designed to help fundraisers achieve their ultimate aim – to raise more money.

Marketing helps the fundraiser to organise research, to identify prospects, to target supporters and potential supporters at different levels, to identify and test different products and propositions to put to them, to consider and evaluate price structures, public awareness and perceptions. It encourages and enables fundraisers to segment their donor list into a host of relevant sub-divisions and then to approach each of these groups in a relevant and economic way. It causes fundraisers to evaluate each and every area of promotional endeavour and constantly to seek to improve cost-efficiency.

Many fundraising organisations can illustrate dramatically the improvements that successful introduction of marketing techniques has made to their bottom-line figures.

But marketing can also enable you to screw up your relationship with donors completely.

A dangerous love affair

Charities' love for marketing is still in relatively new bloom and, although one or two little indiscretions have sullied the initial idyllic expectations, there is no real

Beware the marriage guidance counsellor who also rents tuxedos.

sign that the affair is anything like over. In fact there is every hope that, given a few steadying outside influences and a little knuckling down to realities from both sides of the relationship, a long and happy marriage may result.

I hope so, for there's no doubt whatsoever that effective marketing can do a great deal for charities. And there is reason to expect that fundraisers can do a great deal for marketing too.

But there are clear dangers and considerable risks. Before charities plunge into too deep an embrace, these must be carefully considered. These days, it pays to take precautions.

Also there are a number of siren voices, particularly those of direct marketing agencies, currently urging charities to undertake more aggressive marketing activities. Beware the marriage guidance counsellor who also rents tuxedos.

Beware also of the tendency among agencies to see direct mail in the abstract, in terms of marketing theory, rather than as donors see it, arriving uninvited through the letterbox and landing with a thud in a jumbled heap on the hall floor.

It is unlikely, perhaps, that your direct marketing agent will have been a fundraiser, but it helps a lot if he or she has at least been a donor.

Marketing damage – and how to avoid it

One definition of marketing for fundraisers might be that it is the process that enables fundraisers to target the needs and wants of donors and potential donors and to satisfy them through the design, pricing, communications and delivery of competitively viable fundraising products and services.

It enables fundraisers to plan, prepare and view all

If donors feel they are being sold to, or addressed by a marketing machine they will pretty quickly cease to be donors.

their strategies on a regular basis and to allocate resources according to the needs thus identified.

I think if you read that again you'll see the danger that I am referring to.

It is the language of marketing, but it isn't the language of fundraising. If you use that kind of language with donors you'll pretty soon come unstuck. And many people from marketing backgrounds do use that kind of language when talking about and to donors.

I think that's a shame and it should be discouraged. We don't want to 'educate' donors so that they understand the terminology and issues that involve fundraisers today. The unique relationship between fundraisers and donors will only be protected and strengthened if fundraisers accept that we should talk to our donors in their language, not ours. By language I don't mean just words, but pictures and the combination of words and pictures together which, if presented carefully, can be five times more powerful than either words or pictures on their own. Language also means gestures and the way we present ourselves generally.

If donors feel they are being sold to, or addressed by a marketing machine they will pretty quickly cease to be donors. Therefore, we should not be treating our customers in the same way as our commercial counterparts treat theirs.

That fundraising is different must be recognised in our communications with donors. This means we need a different language, the language of fundraising, not the language of marketing.

Fundraising has taken many spectacular leaps forward in recent years, but these were almost always technology-based or marketing-based. We borrowed the systems and processes of commercial product marketing. We perfected the techniques of direct mail

Only a small percentage will reply so go full guns for them, the rest don't matter.

and began to write to our donors far more vigorously and far more often. We set up databases to enable us to contact our donors with mathematical precision. Our fundraising programmes came to rely on the cold hand of technology. We introduced bland generalisations about people, we called them our targets, our prospects. We classified them and we gave them profiles. We even started to address them as 'Dear Friend'. How bland can you get? 'Dear Friend', I ask you!

In the 1980s the culture of mass marketing began to invade the culture of fundraising.

We can see this invasion in the rigid formulae that inhabit the letters we send to our donors – the window envelopes, computer labels, the obligatory underlining, phony postscripts, and so forth.

We see it in all the imperfections, blips and blemishes that inevitably creep into our databases.

We see this invasion of mass marketing when we no longer think of our donors as people but as lists and numbers.

Following the crowd

A famous advertising copywriter once claimed that the beginning of success is to be different, the beginning of failure is to be the same. If this is true, fundraisers are failing their donors.

Take, for example, the way charities have embraced the techniques of selling by direct mail, and the formula we have adopted to carry our sales message to our customers.

Commercial direct mail appeals to the lowest common denominator. Only a small percentage will reply so go full guns for them, the rest don't matter. If it works well once, keep milking it until it stops working and then move on.

We have taken over the commercial direct mail formula, with only a few minor adaptations and fitted it for fundraising's needs. It's a formula we're all familiar with – the DL or C5 envelope, the carefully laid out four-page letter with lots of underlining, the obligatory PS and a photograph of the writer (when did you last include your photograph in a letter you wrote to a friend, or underline, or even write a PS?), the ubiquitous appeal leaflet and reply form, the handwritten reply envelope and so on.

We've all seen hundreds of them and they're all beginning to look very alike.

Now of course this formula is tried and tested. It can be trusted. It still works well so has more than earned its place in our affections.

But isn't it a fact that most donors can see through it? Therein lies the danger.

The bottom line indicates that only sales matter. Relationship fundraising says this isn't so.

If we can show our donors that there is more depth, substance and sincerity in our communications than they've come to expect from other sources, then I am sure we will benefit in the long term.

If we are not to compound the errors of the past and fall into some of the traps we've fallen into before, then we fundraisers are going to have to be different, and distinctly different, from all the rest.

In that way the culture of fundraising may indeed begin to invade the culture of marketing, rather than the other way round.

ACTION POINTS

▲ **Try to learn from mistakes – preferably other people's.**

▲ Beware of the modern machine. Use it wisely and cautiously.

▲ Banish computer numbers from your correspondence. Try bar codes instead – people don't appear to notice bar codes but they can be very put off by computer numbers.

▲ Treat donors as individuals. View your composite descriptions as useful indications and generalisations only.

▲ Avoid the bland and the dull. Inject life into your copy so your enthusiasm and commitment come shining through. Similarly, steer clear of formulae, or producing anything that might look just like everyone else's production.

▲ Don't hide from the problems of junk mail. Confront them. Don't do junk marketing and don't let anybody else get away with doing it either.

▲ Be honest and open with donors. Don't conceal problems. Tell the truth in a positive way.

▲ 'Road test' your charity. Ring in posing as a donor and check the response you get.

▲ Check your reception and monitor everyone who answers the phone or meets the public. If their performance is not exemplary and their training faultless, introduce simple guidelines and explain why things must change.

▲ Check who visits your reception. Go and sit in it yourself from time to time. Phone in and out through your switchboard.

▲ Find out how good your publications are. Listen to your readers. If they're not doing a first-class job of selling your cause, make changes. Dull publications are rarely read. Make yours reflect your cause.

▲ Think carefully about how you use images in your advertising. Balance emotional impact with honesty and integrity.

▲ Don't forget your non-responders. Find out how they feel.

DONOR PROFILE

John Collins

John was angry. He put the phone down, not quite with a crash but very firmly.

'Honestly,' he said out loud, although he knew he was talking to himself. 'Why can't these people check their facts. Talk about inefficiency ...'

Having got that largely out of his system, but still inwardly mumbling about too much spent on administration and what are they doing calling at this time, anyway, John went to the fridge and poured himself a drink. Balancing his microwaved pizza on top of his foaming beer he shut the fridge door with his boot, a technique that over the years had worn away the enamel on the door, and swayed into his living room. He flopped down on to the sofa, flicked on the telly and forgot about it.

Meanwhile, the telephone fundraising organisation that had rung John to solicit the long overdue renewal of his subscription to a well-known environmental organisation was preparing to query this lapsed renewal – among others – with the client. The caller noted that John had informed him that he was still a member and had renewed his membership quite recently. Mistakes do happen and the telefundraising organisation wasn't going to take any chances of creating offence.

But John wasn't a current member. He hadn't renewed his subscription for more than two years.

If you had stopped John on his way to work the next morning and asked him he would have told you with absolute conviction that he was a fully paid-up member not just of that environmental organisation, but of several others, all in similar areas.

John cares, make no mistake. He really cares. The only thing is it's more than a year since he renewed *any* of his subscriptions. He thinks he's a member, they think he's lapsed.

John never reads appeal mailings but he knows he still gets quite a lot, so he must be a member. And he gets quite a few newsletters too.

As John would say, 'How am I supposed to know?'

7

Marketing to raise money

'Change used to be something that happened every ten years or so. Now it seems it's always with us, always different and not always what we'd like.'

Charles Handy
Inside Organisations

According to Stan Rapp and Tom Collins, in their excellent book *MaxiMarketing*, the late 1980s saw the beginning of the most important business development this century. They described this event quite simply as the death of mass marketing and the birth of individual marketing.

If this is true, it represents the greatest single opportunity for fundraisers ever. But there's more to it than that. All kinds of businesses throughout the world are finding that their relationships with customers are changing. We are seeing a shift from 'get that sale now at any cost' to the construction and management of customer databases that can create a complete record of relationships with customers throughout their lives.

Most marketers have yet to realise the opportunities this represents. Fundraisers must respond to the chance they now have to make Rapp and Collins' prediction come true. They have the once-in-a-lifetime opportunity to show the kind of lead that will make relationship fundraising a model for the rest of the marketing fraternity.

Marketing – and relationship fundraising for that matter – is only of value to fundraisers if it helps them to raise more money more efficiently.

It is somewhat ironic that fundraising in Britain has in the past decade just begun to embrace conventional marketing techniques and wisdom and to employ trained marketing people, at the precise time that marketing itself is undergoing a fundamental metamorphosis. Some charities are caught in a dilemma. They have begun to appreciate the power of commercial sales and marketing techniques and have enthusiastically embraced aggressive sales tactics, particularly in copying direct marketing techniques. Now they are being told that maybe they are being a bit short-sighted.

A central theme of this book is that the traditional approaches of product marketing were in many respects inappropriate and counter-productive for fundraisers and that, while the old marketing was clearly bringing many short-term gains, it was also stirring up a host of problems for the future. In fairness, the importance of customer relationships has always been recognised in professional marketing, but practitioners often underestimate its importance or overlook this in their drive for increased profit.

The new marketing need have no such in-built destructive tendencies. The new marketing, based as it is on the cultivation of individual direct relationships, is ideally suited to fundraising, and fundraising is the perfect area in which to show how well the new marketing works.

Marketing – and relationship fundraising for that matter – is only of value to fundraisers if it helps them to raise more money more efficiently. There is no value in getting carried away with the idea of a mutually supportive relationship with your donors unless the ultimate effect of that relationship is to increase the flow of funds for your cause.

Marketing for a fundraising organisation is inevitably and irrevocably different to marketing a product such as washing powder or motor cars.

What is marketing?

Marketing involves finding out what consumers want or need and then supplying it at a profit. Research, strategy, product design, advertising, public relations, communication and even after-sales service are all part of marketing. Marketing involves constant monitoring of consumer reactions to product, price and delivery and enables you to establish whether or not your product is viable. Any strategy for marketing should be conceived against a background that takes full account of internal resources such as your own management and staff, the existing external market of current customers and prospects, any competitors, and local, national and perhaps international media. It also includes macro considerations such as the economy, demographic shifts, politics and so on. Analysing these various elements is the first step in preparing a marketing plan.

Everybody in your organisation should be part of your marketing plan. From the chief executive officer to the person who answers the switchboard, everyone has an important role to play in marketing your organisation and should be clearly aware that they do.

The marketing plan for fundraising may well be part of a larger strategic plan for the whole organisation which covers such areas as service provision, associated organisations, campaigning, staff policy and other activities not normally part of fundraising. If so, fundraising planning has to adapt to fit in with that overall strategic plan. Readers should note, however, that reference to the marketing plan from here relates only to marketing for the fundraising operation.

Marketing for a fundraising organisation is inevitably and irrevocably different to marketing a product such as washing powder or motor cars. This may be less significant for fundraisers in a hospital or

Every one an original.

That suggests some very

satisfied customers.

university, where a clearly defined product or service exists, than it is for a charity or cause promoting a less tangible need or service to a disadvantaged third party.

Fundraisers will only succeed in marketing if they start by recognising these differences, capitalise on the strength this gives them and plan their marketing to take the differences fully into account. This was always the case. But the new age of individual marketing means fundraisers have to be even more aware of the underlying factors that contribute to their unique relationship with their customers.

The age of choice

The old mass marketing is indeed dead. Gone are the days of the Model T Ford, when you could have any colour or shape you wanted as long as it was black and looked like all the others. Choice now is almost limitless and customers themselves are being involved more and more in deciding how they want to make their choices. So luxury car manufacturers already offer buyers more than just the opportunity to choose internal and external colour schemes – they can also select the upholstery materials used, some internal components, and an endless array of optional extras. Just around the corner is General Motors Saturn plant where owners will virtually be able to design their car themselves to be manufactured to order by computer-driven robots.

Every one an original. That suggests some very satisfied customers.

Choice is not just the province of car manufacturers. Revlon makes 157 shades of lipstick, 41 of them pink. Whiskas cat food offers 30 different flavours. *Catalyst*, the customer loyalty package which took the gold trophy in the 1990 British Direct Marketing Awards (see page 8), offers customers the opportunity to choose

The personal service of the village shopkeeper is now in the hands of the national fundraiser.

which areas of editorial interest them in their free quarterly magazine – travel, motoring, cookery, business, etc. So, instead of receiving the bland, generalised content typical of most airline or hotel magazines, *Catalyst* readers choose their own reading matter, thereby guaranteeing their interest (in theory).

This kind of individual choice was impossible before the development of the computer database (which enables the publisher to solicit the customers' views and store them for easy access) and the technology by which that database can be applied to select, print and bind each individual copy of the magazine according to the choices stored in the database. These are the components that make individual marketing possible to tens of thousands of people simultaneously. It is of these that fundraisers must now take full advantage.

Database is not new. Businesses have kept lists of their customers since selling began and many, notably corner shopkeepers, have not only known their customers by name but have known all their families names and all about their private affairs. What is different now is the computer and the potential it gives us to remember names, addresses, dates, donations, frequencies, amounts, facts and figures by the millions. Computers can also find out about your donors, by matching, cross-checking, analysing ... and the cost of all this is going down all the time.

Marketing has moved full circle. Potentially the personal service of the village shopkeeper is now in the hands of the national fundraiser.

Some marketing considerations
Sometimes good intentions can frustrate a charity's marketing activities and few good intentions are as frustrating as those of dedicated charity employees

Potential donors were denied the opportunity of helping a cause they obviously were interested in. They weren't even given the chance to say 'no'.

trying to protect their donors.

I had an early example of this at ActionAid. Two of my colleagues, when asked why they were failing to keep records of the names and addresses of people who had sent in money, explained their fear that I would use their addresses to write and pester these good people for more money, and that would upset them.

Crazy and misguided though it seems, there is a germ of truth in this argument and I suspect it is still a view shared by many charity trustees. I would certainly have written to those good people, but I hope I wouldn't have upset them. As it is, potential donors were denied the opportunity of helping a cause they obviously were interested in. They weren't even given the chance to say 'no'.

The other classic which happened at about the same time – and I swear this is true – was when the head of the post room asked that if I must run a Christmas appeal could I organise it at some other time of the year as the post room was always very busy anyway in the few weeks leading up to Christmas?

As a first step towards preparing your marketing plan it is necessary to carry out a marketing audit to evaluate and record the current state of your organisation's marketing. I suspect that even nowadays many organisations would find, as I did all those years ago at ActionAid, that formal marketing is non-existent, or worse. (I didn't know any of this at the time. With hindsight it was a case of the blind leading the blind – but we were successful in spite of that.) It's all changed now, of course, and ActionAid's marketing department is one of the most sophisticated to be found anywhere. But even if no marketing apparatus exists in your organisation the exercise is nevertheless worth doing and can be very illuminating. From the lessons thus learned the next step is to construct your plan. This essential preparation done, then all you have to do is implement it!

Here are some considerations for fundraisers, questions you might ask yourselves when contemplating your marketing audit:

• What is different or unique about us and what we do? Are we first, or best, or biggest? Can we find a niche that is uniquely ours?

• Who are our major markets? Research by the American Heart Association showed that it wanted to address 41 different markets, so you'll probably be talking to more than one.

• What is our position in relation to other causes, similar appeals, or services?

• What are our objectives?

• What is our product and what are its benefits (eg a television station might produce programmes but it gives customers entertainment and information)?

• Different people react differently to different propositions. How do people react to ours?

• How can we change the proposition to improve the response (without necessarily changing the product)?

• What is our pricing policy (if it exists at all)? Are we controlling how much donors give or are we leaving it to them? Is our price high enough for our needs, or too high for our donors' pockets?

• How are we packaged, ie what is our reception area like? What do our visible communications look like?

• Do we have a brand image or identity? How do our donors, our prospects and our service users perceive us? (See chapter 5.)

• How do we perform on after-sale service – speed and quality of response, thank you policy, etc?

• Can we make any special offers, promotions, or incentives, eg invitations to open days, visits to centres, etc?

We are in the donor development business not in child care, or Third World development, or higher education, or whatever.

• How good is our promotion – advertising, use of media, publications, displays, personal presentations?
• How effective is our distribution – volunteers, local groups, shops, regional staff? How do our distributors use our materials?

And so on.

An even more basic question, to top the list, might be 'what business are we in?' Mary Parker Follett, America's first management consultant, had a client who thought they were in the curtain business. She persuaded them they were in the light control business, and transformed their entire approach.

In *The Telephone Book* Robert Leiderman also quotes an instance of an organisation that failed to understand what business it was in. The extract he relates comes from an essay by leading marketing academic Professor Theodore Levitt and concerns the decline of the American railroads.

'The railroads did not stop growing because the need for passenger and freight transportation declined. In fact, that grew. The railroads are in trouble not because the need was filled by others (cars, trucks, airplanes, even telephones) but because the need was not filled by the railroads themselves. They let others take customers away from them because they assumed they were in the railroad business, rather than in the transportation business. They were product-oriented, instead of customer-oriented.'

As fundraisers, we are in the donor development business not, as you might think, in child care, or Third World development, or higher education, or whatever.

How to turn change into innovation
Most people resist change and many fundraising organisations go out of their way to avoid it. But the

opportunity to change can be just what your marketing needs and your marketing plan can help you achieve it.

• See change as an opportunity, not a threat.

• When your organisation is at its most successful is a good time to refocus and to change. Don't become complacent for that leads to decline.

• Find the right person to lead change. Any new initiative needs someone who loves it.

• Challenge people who say, 'We've always done it this way'.

• Identify specific objectives. Measure them before and after. Get everyone involved to agree on these objectives.

• Change your people's behaviour not their attitudes. The change in attitudes will follow.

• Recognise your different publics. Develop and exploit any niches that are special to you.

• Test your changes at every stage. Remember that non-customers will always outnumber customers, so research what they want too.

The marketing mix – creating an effective marketing strategy

An organisation's marketing strategy will flow from the earlier stages of marketing audit and preparing the goals and objects. The strategy is important because it translates all the information and insights that emerged from the initial process into a workable long-term plan.

An effective strategy will be customer-centred, distinctive, innovative, sustainable and flexible. It should be easy to communicate the basics of the plan to others and should be capable of motivating everyone involved into enthusiastic commitment. It will identify the markets being tackled and the products that are right for each segment of the market and will use, as

Savour the task of preparing your plan. It should be fun, challenging and approached by all with open minds.

appropriate, the whole range of fundraising methods available: direct marketing, of course, but also personal solicitation, events, big gift campaigns, joint promotions with companies, local groups, etc.

The marketing plan

The process of planning is as important, if not more important, than the plan itself. So savour the task of preparing your plan. It should be fun, challenging and approached by all with open minds. Donors should be involved in your planning too – they'll love it, you'll learn and the bond between you and them will strengthen. But don't over plan – beware of paralysis by analysis.

How actually to prepare the plan is beyond the scope or purpose of this book. However, there are one or two reasonably accessible books which are recognised guides to marketing planning. These include McDonald and Leppard's *The Marketing Audit: Translating Marketing Theory into Practice*, *Marketing Plans* by Malcolm McDonald and *The 12-Day Marketing Plan* by James Makens. One of the easiest to use is *The Marketing Plan. A Pictorial Guide for Managers* by Malcolm McDonald and Peter Morris which, as its name suggests, is not only useful but is about as much fun as marketing planning can be.

If not always fun, marketing for fundraisers should nevertheless be accountable, appropriate, acceptable, affordable, action-oriented and it should give added value – all the As.

All marketing starts with the prospect. But before you can reach people who might be receptive to your message you've got to know where to find them.

Targeting

Targeting is described as the art and science of

identifying, describing, locating and contacting one or more groups of prime prospects for whatever you are selling. (Here is the first hidden danger of marketing. It's full of unnecessary complexity. Everyone knows what targeting means. It neatly says in one word what a marketer will describe less well in twenty.)

Fundraisers build their donor bases by effectively targeting those individuals and groups most likely to give to support their cause. Target-marketing can involve combinations of geographic, demographic and psychographic consumer characteristics to narrow down potential prospects. To target accurately we not only need to segment consumers according to the full range of their attributes (geographic – regional, economic, cultural, geographical; demographic – age, sex, race, education, religious background, family size, residence; and psychographic – social values, beliefs, attitudes, interests, opinions, lifestyle), but also to anticipate social change (see chapter 5).

If this information is available, and increasingly it is, computers can now easily overlay it drawing on numerous interactive databases and come up with not just a profile of your most likely targets but also a list of their names and addresses.

As mentioned previously, charities when targeting should be paying particular attention to 'the new old', the healthy, vigorous and often affluent younger end of the 50+ market who own so much of our country's disposable wealth and control so much of its enterprise.

Segmentation

The idea of segmenting a database is not new (so few ideas are) but it is one that can pay enormous dividends for those charities who do it properly. As yet, few charities in Britain have got round to it, but it makes

This takes us into a difficult area ... the obvious potential for cynical abuse of information.

enormous sense.

People are different. While many donors will conform to your typical profile, you'll have some who are young , rather left-of-centre working women and you'll have some elderly retired ex-army types. It doesn't make much sense to treat all these different people in the same way, particularly as modern technology has given you the means to individualise on a large scale.

Effective segmentation is the key to making personalised marketing work because while we can't (yet) write truly individual letters to everyone, we can write different letters to each segment. (After targeting I'm not going to attempt to define segmentation – we've all eaten grapefruits and we all know what a segment is.)

In the past, we have divided our lists into crude historical segments based on how people performed in the past: by their most recent gift, by the size of their last gift, by how often they've given, by what they've given to. This is immensely useful information. But it is also possible to segment by interests, by personal attributes, such as lifestyle and beliefs. All this information can be gathered with your donors' permission and can go on to your database.

Perhaps in the future a Third World development charity will be segmenting its donors into groups such as well travelled or lived overseas, young family, change the world, the old sentimentalists, lonely seekers of friendship, and so on, and writing to each of them different, more appropriate letters.

This takes us into a difficult area. I feel comfortable about technology's ability to enable us to write fewer, better, more relevant letters to our friends. But I feel uncomfortable about the obvious potential for cynical abuse of information.

This is a dilemma all fundraisers will have to address

in the near future – how far do we take segmentation and at what point does personalisation become deliberate deception?

When preparing reciprocal mailings, for example, most charities will run a de-duplication programme with the other charity's list. This is good commercial sense, but few organisations keep a note of which of their supporters also support other charities. Would it be useful to know which of your donors are also donors to other charities? I think so. Taken to its conclusion, you could then build a list of superdonors who appear not just on two charities' lists but on three, four, five or more. You could then swap your three-charity supporters with another charity's three-charity supporters, and expect correspondingly better results.

In fact, reciprocals could be much more segmented than they generally are at present. Instead of the simple swap of donors, you could also suggest swapping your three-time givers with another charity's three-time givers, and so on. (This assumes, of course, that reciprocal mailing will continue to be a permitted option – see page 177.)

How long will it be, I wonder, before someone constructs a national database of charity donors with all this information on it? Then it would be possible to select all the 'little old ladies from Tunbridge Wells' from one central source.

Alarming thought, isn't it?

Product – first of the Ps

'Give a man a fish and you'll feed him for a day. Teach him to fish and you'll feed him for life', the old adage says, probably attributable to Confucius, as most of them are. It is, of course, true and has been quoted *ad infinitum*. The sage didn't say, 'Ask a supporter for a donation and

They guarantee the long-term involvement of the purchaser, who can be sold other things now he's 'in the store'.

he'll give you a low-value one-off gift. Present your request as a product and he'll regularly give you larger amounts over several years.' But he could have and it would have been just as true.

Fundraising 'products' are of increasing value. Sponsoring a child or adopting a granny are examples of high-value ongoing needs. Sponsoring a brick or joining a low-cost membership scheme may be the other end of the scale. Recognition and reward schemes are also products. For £104 per year (covenanted) you can become a cultivator sponsor at Ryton Gardens. For £20 per year you can be a friend of the NSPCC. Such schemes may not be huge money-spinners themselves, but they do guarantee the long-term involvement of the purchaser, who can be sold other things now he's 'in the store'.

I know of one charity which encouraged its supporters to give monthly gifts by regular banker's order. As these donors were already giving so substantially and so often the fundraising staff felt they couldn't ask for any more. In fact the opposite turned out to be true. These good regular donors responded very generously to special and emergency appeals, proving what most retailers know very well – your most likely new customer is your existing customer. And the easiest way to extend your customer's involvement is to offer a new product, provided it is appropriate to their needs or desires.

When designing your product, consider what its benefits will be to your customer. Will the product sell? You can only find out by testing. More often than not it's the product, not the marketer, that determines success or failure. At ActionAid we couldn't fail with child sponsorship but, whatever we tried, we couldn't succeed with 'Village Neighbour', a lower-cost scheme where donors were linked to a village project rather than a particular child.

Those charities that have priced their proposition competitively are among the most successful charities today.

We failed because 'Village Neighbour' was a product the public didn't want to buy, even though it was a brilliant idea and entirely appropriate in development terms. Design your product to fit the marketplace, rather than expect the marketplace to fit your product.

Product is one of the key marketing considerations know as the five Ps. The others are price – what your product costs; place – which really means distribution but that doesn't start with a p; promotion – which is all your advertising, etc, and includes packaging, ie the physical appearance of your goods or services; and people, perhaps the most important 'P' in marketing. People are mentioned throughout this book and promotion and packaging are covered in other chapters but the others are each worth a mention here.

Price

Few charities are used to thinking in terms of price in the way that trading companies do. Most commercial organisations have come to realise, often painfully, that the real secret of success is not sales, supply or service, it is getting the price right.

Charities generally could benefit from a review of their pricing policy. At worst there is no guidance on price and donors are left to fix their own giving level. This usually results in low gift value and lowered response as potential donors are afraid to offend by giving a gift which the organisation might think too small. In membership and similar schemes, where there are fixed price levels, charities tend to aim low so as not to discourage the poorer end of their market.

This is ideologically commendable but not very sound commercially. Those charities that have priced their proposition competitively, such as the child sponsorship agencies, are among the most successful

Ten pounds a year or ten pounds a month, it makes little difference finan- cially to most donors but it will make an enormous difference to you.

charities today. A sponsor's minimum annual contribution nowadays is around £120 (most covenant and make one-off donations on top). The average donation for many other charities that aren't asking for a specified amount tends to hover around the £10–£12 mark. Think about the implications of that for a moment.

In many cases charities seem to be in quite elastic markets and their products are often not noticeably price-sensitive. When I was at ActionAid we increased the cost of sponsorship several times, but it seemed to have little or no effect on recruitment rates. In some areas there is price sensitivity, as between various membership schemes. Supporters might not expect Greenpeace to charge more than Friends of the Earth, for example, although I can find no logical reason whatsoever why what they charge should be affected in any way by, say, what the National Trust charges or the National Asthma Campaign.

I have also found that when the reasons behind a price increase are explained in detail to donors they invariably understand and respond positively. Ten pounds a year or ten pounds a month, it makes little difference financially to most donors, if they believe enough in what you are doing, but it will make an enormous difference to you. (See also pages 259 to 263, where price is discussed further as a major opportunity for fundraisers.)

Place

Place, although important to most commercial marketers, is really of limited importance to relationship fundraisers, unless we consider the importance of taking our marketing out of the office and into the homes of our donors. While fundraisers continue to do much of their marketing by mail, place has little importance because

What a shame we can't send volunteers round to visit our donors, rather than mailing them – we'd do up to 16 times better.

the postal service gives us almost immediate access to all corners of the globe. So it is with the telephone.

There are just three principal ways to approach your prospects – by mail, over the phone, and in person (eyeball to eyeball, as the Americans say, or belly button to belly button). According to some American fundraisers, the mail is 16 times less likely to be effective than a personal visit. Many charities already do lots of individual visits, but these tend to be organised on a regional or field basis so are often overlooked by head office, which so far has probably not even considered marketing in person, because of the prohibitive costs (and inconvenience) that would be involved. What a shame we can't send volunteers round to visit our donors, rather than mailing them – we'd do up to 16 times better. Now there's a thought ... Perhaps place *is* important after all.

Ten marketing questions

While we are in the mood for asking questions, here are ten marketing questions all relationship fundraisers need to ask themselves.

1 How many different types of prospective donor can I identify and describe?

2 How can I reach these donors and persuade them to support my cause?

3 How many 'offers' could I make?

4 How can I save wasting money on current promotions?

5 How can I test my promotional messages?

6 How good is my organisation at answering enquiries (test this one yourself, see page 113)?

7 Do we save names? What do we do with them?

8 How can existing supporters help us find new supporters?

9 Can I think of ways to get my advertising to do 'double duty'. This is where a single effort is used to accomplish two or more different jobs. That is, can you promote organisational or brand awareness while recruiting donors, demonstrate your commitment to a particular campaign while raising funds, and so on? In certain circumstances this multifunctional approach can make a limited advertising budget very much more productive.

10 Do we have ways of ensuring that we listen to what our prospects are saying?

These questions should be considered alongside those previously raised in the planning stage (see page 144).

Search for the URG!

Marketing is full of jargon. But often there's a good reason why a new word is created to express a hitherto unknown idea or process unique to a particular business area. Most professions have their jargon – from prostitution to the clergy. So it pays to understand some of marketing's jargon and to borrow it for your own purposes. But don't allow your donors to hear you are doing it, for they are hardly likely to approve. The best way to avoid the risk is to create your own jargon appropriate to your own individual business area.

One of marketing's most powerful pieces of jargon is the notion of the USP – the unique selling proposition. Finding your USP involves searching your product or service to find the one thing no one else can offer and projecting it as unique to you. Polo Mints achieved this remarkably with their 'mint with the hole' concept. Imagine buying a sweet because it has a great big hole in it! People did, and still do. The mint with the hole has been market leader for years, largely thanks to its unique

The term USP is not appropriate for fundraisers even though the concept certainly is.

selling proposition. The term 'unique buying proposition' might be more appropriate, because that expresses the concept from the customer's point of view.

An example of a fundraising organisation that has exploited its USP is Greenpeace, those people in inflatable boats who put themselves between the harpoons and the whales. Their USP is not the slogan 'Thank God someone's making waves', it is the idea of peaceful direct action to protect the environment.

Donors respond to Greenpeace because secretly they'd love to be in that fragile inflatable themselves, taking action to save the planet. Greenpeace offers them the opportunity to be there from the safety of their armchair. (A substantial proportion of their supporters, however, actually do volunteer for active service and this gives Greenpeace quite a logistical problem in handling all these would-be rainbow warriors with tact. Or perhaps it's an opportunity.)

But the term USP is not appropriate for fundraisers even though the concept certainly is. I prefer to use a term that says the same thing but is directly relevant to fundraising – URG – the unique reason to give.

I advise fundraisers to search for their URG.

Personality problems

Another piece of marketing jargon that fundraisers might usefully adopt after suitably changing its name is the concept of brand image. Imagine what your donors would think, if they heard you talking about that! But the concept of brand image is important for fundraising organisations. It is your personality as a cause amongst all the other charities they might support. A strong and even unique brand image might be the only hope of your organisation distinguishing itself from other apparently similar charities operating in the same field. Some

A logo is important, as is consistency of style and colour, but you don't get personality from a snazzy suit of clothes.

charities – for example, the Royal National Lifeboat Institution and Save the Children Fund – have very strong personalities, or brand images, while others have not. Greenpeace, Amnesty, Oxfam and Care are all truly international brand names – the number of which is growing as more and more organisations set up fundraising programmes as well as projects overseas.

Has your charity, or organisation, got a personality? Or is it bland, anonymous, or just as yet largely unknown? Could it benefit from a strong, clear personality? How might it go about getting it?

At this point, cue the charlatans from corporate design division who'll descend with a whole load of baloney about positioning, market profile, identity research and the need for massive investment in a new logo. Fine, if you can afford it. A logo is important, as is consistency of style and colour, but you don't get personality from a snazzy suit of clothes. That is not to say that brand image doesn't have any value. For example, it is the big 'brand name' charities that attract most of the floating legacy income.

My favourite bit of logo nonsense is the story of Pirelli, the tyre (and calendar) people, who, apparently, commissioned a top international design consultancy to make recommendations for the change of their logo worldwide. Off went the top design agency and several months later back its executives came to air their proposals. Pirelli's management were apparently shocked to be presented with a very slender document, not much thicker than the invoice which was underneath. The shock deepened when they read that the agency's recommendation was that their current logo was doing a very good job and shouldn't be changed at all. Rigor mortis set in when they read the invoice. It was for £1 million.

Pirelli paid, of course, or so the story goes. In fact, their design agency had conducted extensive research in the 139 or however many countries where Pirelli was represented and no doubt they tested a lot of alternatives and did a lot of work. It still seems like rather an expensive piece of self-indulgence.

The Pirelli story is now part of advertising folklore and may or may not be true. Some version of it probably is, and there are a few equally cynical stories going around involving the amounts spent by different charities on their logos.

Some organisations have got great logos which are a real asset to their cause, but the best logos are simple and immediately clear. Creating a new logo is rather like creating a new letter of the alphabet. Imprinting it indelibly on the public's consciousness is a rare achievement, a task that should only be attempted by those with substantial resources of time and money.

Fundraising by phone

Telefundraising (or, preferably, fundraising by phone) is another of those areas that has such an impact on relationship fundraising it transcends all the artificial divisions of any chapter headings, so I mention it briefly here and also come back to it in more detail later. I've already outlined some of its pitfalls and problems in chapter 6. As with direct mail I didn't wish to give telefundraising a chapter on its own because it has a relevance in almost every aspect of donor service and development.

Telephone fundraising is yet one more of those marketing techniques that a little while ago almost everyone in fundraising said would never happen in the United Kingdom, despite the spectacular success it was enjoying on the other side of the Atlantic.

Calling to sell is only a part of the story – the telephone has many more uses than that.

Events have proved almost everyone to be wrong. Telephone fundraising is alive and well in the UK and, in fact, is doing rather nicely for a growing number of quick-off-the-mark charities and universities.

The telephone is the third largest advertising medium, by expenditure, in the United States after television and magazines. (That's not all that impressive actually – how many other media can you think of?)

There's no doubt that the growth of telemarketing *is* impressive, even frightening. In 1980 it was estimated that just 4,500 people were employed in telephone marketing in the United States. By 1985 that figure had grown to 300,000. If growth continues at the present rate, and there is no obvious reason why it should not, then eight million people will be working in telemarketing by the year 2000.

The reason for this growth is that telemarketing works. Calling to sell is only a part of the story – the telephone has many more uses than that. Like many other useful techniques or tools, telemarketing can be dangerous in unprepared or misguided hands, but undoubtedly the telephone offers enormous benefits to fundraisers. So it pays to collect your donors' phone numbers. How to communicate with donors via the telephone is covered in detail in chapter 9 .

Relationships with companies and trusts

Clearly it is just as important to develop strong, lasting and productive relationships with commercial donors and trusts as it is with individuals. The techniques, prices and products may be different but the same principles of relationship fundraising still apply. The people who work in companies and trusts are, after all, just individuals doing their job.

Some of the differences are worth considering.

Don't under any circumstances be apologetic when asking for a donation from a commercial organisation or trust.

People at work don't have as much time as most people at home. Therefore, make your communications shorter and more to the point. Do your homework beforehand to ensure you don't waste your time or theirs. The decision-makers in these places are also not likely to conform to any of your typical donor profiles, so you may have to work a lot harder for them. For one thing, senior managers are still most likely to be men. They will also often be younger than the average individual donor and their motivation for agreeing to their organisation's support of your cause will most probably lean towards self-interest and mutual benefit rather than pure altruism.

So don't under any circumstances be apologetic when asking for a donation from a commercial organisation or trust. Companies only give when they want to, and most have a budget specifically for that purpose. A trust's sole reason for existence is to give money away to organisations like yours.

Your function as a fundraiser, therefore, is to help them do their job.

Show them your marketing plan (or offer it). After all, the people you are talking to do business plans. They'll be impressed to see you do as well.

Companies and trusts get very many applications for funds. Those with very specific areas of interest will tend to get fewer. Allied Dunbar, perhaps Britain's most philanthropic company, receives just 1,500 requests each year because it has carefully publicised its procedures and requirements. But that's still six different proposals to consider every working day. The Carnegie Trust gets twice as many. The Boots Company gets 15,000 requests each year – that's roughly one request for money every seven-and-a-half minutes. Even that is small beer compared to many companies. In the USA the Atlantic

The most important part of any appeal to a company or a trust is the idea.

Richfield Corporation reckons that on average it receives one application for philanthropic support every *second*.

Of course, the smaller, local companies and trusts don't get nearly so many requests and it's there that fundraisers will be most likely to find opportunities.

To stand any chance of success against such a volume of competition you have to be very good.

Read out loud the first paragraph of your letter. Does what's different about your proposal stand out clearly? Or could that first paragraph have been written by just about anyone else? If you can make a good, relevant individual application and follow it up efficiently by telephone, make an effective impression at a meeting and, once given the donation or grant, follow that with well-documented, well-presented and supported feedback on the progress of the project, then you have the beginnings of a successful relationship with that company or trust. But you must provide regular, relevant feedback and, to maintain the relationship, you must have a constant need of sufficient size and type to merit their further support.

The most important part of any appeal to a company or a trust is the *idea*. Before you apply, be sure your idea is properly thought through and fully worked out in all its detail before you go anywhere near the potential donor. It must be an idea relevant to the organisation you will present it to. Then your application must clearly, simply and persuasively present the idea. Explain in human terms what their support will achieve, not just the millions of pounds you need for a large-scale project. The people that will be involved, the work they will do, the children they will help, the kind of land that will be reclaimed, the pain that will be replaced by smiles, or whatever ... Make it human. Most of the applications that compete with yours will be boring their

In this case, the idea was rather an unlikely one.

prospect's pants off with endless reams of statistics and impenetrable pages of grey type. If your application sparkles with individuality, achievement, illustration and human interest it will stand out, and that's more than half the battle.

Many trusts and companies expect very considerable after-sales service so find out what information is expected from you and only go after the grant if you can be sure to meet those conditions.

Publicity and public relations

There are many good books on the subjects of publicity, public relations, advertising, and the communications mix so I will only touch on these here, as the focus of this book has to be concentrated on the direct relationship between donor and fundraiser. But I can't resist relating one example of a publicity campaign because the charity involved raised a great deal of money, the publicity that was generated lifted the charity's profile considerably and lots of people had lots of fun. It is also a good example of how a lot of planning, initiatives and hard work led to a classic success story.

But I particularly like the National Children's Home Birthday Campaign story because it involved an idea – what advertising guru David Ogilvy would term 'the big idea'. And in this case, the idea was rather an unlikely one. In fact, NCH's then director of fundraising, John Gray, whose idea it was, told me about it before the campaign was launched and I remember thinking he was crazy – it seemed such an obvious and simple idea I didn't think anyone would latch on to it. I should have known better.

A few years before, John had attended a CASE Convention in America. That's where he picked up the idea, and that single idea certainly would have paid for

*Everybody has a
birthday, every year ...
What better reason to
give a thank you gift?*

his trip many times over. At the convention John was in a group that was asked to come up with some long-term objectives for their organisations, things they would like to see their organisations doing in two to three years time. John realised as he thought about it that in 1989 his organisation would be celebrating some significant birthdays – the organisation itself would be 120 years old, it was 150 years since the birth of their founder, Dr Thomas Stevenson, and the eightieth birthday of their eminent and much-loved chairman, Lord Tonypandy, better known as George Thomas, former Speaker of the UK's House of Commons, would take place.

'Right then,' thought John. '1989 will be NCH Birthday Year.'

Then John uncovered the most startling piece of overlooked obviousness. Everybody has a birthday, every year. That made his campaign relevant to everyone. All companies have anniversaries. For many, their special anniversary would coincide with NCH's series of birthdays. What better reason to give a thank you gift?

By sheer good fortune, NCH's three birthday dates were evenly distributed throughout the year – one in January, one in June, one in December. Each would be the cue for a host of linked publicity and PR events. Now John had a campaign. All he and his team of fundraising professionals had to do was get behind it, maximise and take advantage of all the opportunities they could create, and wait for the public's enthusiasm and generosity to do the rest. (Of course it sounds easy with hindsight.)

The Birthday Year did succeed in involving huge numbers of people, in mounting a vast array of publicity events and in achieving enormous national and local coverage – all for something as everyday (or every year) as a birthday. NCH is a family charity and they appealed to family businesses, particularly those with families as customers and the link of supporting a charity that helps the family could be most easily seen or was most obviously beneficial. They produced and sold mugs, T-shirts and other memorabilia, all marked with the birthday year. They persuaded supporters to stage events on their birthday – from the man who raised £25,000 by cycling on his birthday to the man who abseiled down a mountain on his birthday. A nationwide chain of chemists pledged themselves to raise £150,000 in their tenth anniversary year. British Telecom, which was 21 that year, held a birthday party for children hosted by singer Stevie Wonder at the top of London's Telecom Tower. And lots more birthday-linked events were organised. In a remarkable direct marketing initiative NCH sent all its donors a birthday card, asking them to send it on to Lord Tonypandy, with a gift. Despite the fact that this mailing went out just six weeks after the charity's traditional Christmas appeal mailing, 32,000 people responded and sent £180,000 with their birthday good wishes.

To crown the year NCH launched a special 'super-donor club' – the NCH George Thomas Society – which raised a further £500,000 and the launch was attended by many of the most eminent stars of stage, screen and politics. A major feature of NCH's publicity success was its ability to involve celebrities, from all the major Royals down to, and including, current, past and even future Prime Ministers (the year straddled the change over from Margaret Thatcher to John Major, and both supported NCH).

So although the Birthday Year was described as a publicity event, NCH involved many different facets of relationship fundraising which all contributed to its success.

Publicity and public relations are inextricably linked with fundraising. There is never any reason for separating the two.

In all, NCH's birthday campaign raised over £1.2 million extra income and a research survey showed that the enormous publicity that had been generated had raised the charity's prompted awareness from 51 per cent to 78 per cent. Not a bad result from a single idea.

Success in any publicity event depends on being in the right place at the right time – and knowing the right people.

Having left NCH John Gray was later instrumental in bringing a major publicity event to his new employer, The British Red Cross Society. When author and politician Jeffrey Archer decided to launch the Simple Truth concert appeal for Kurdish refugees it was John Gray he rang for help, having worked with John in the past.

Fundraisers are frequently faced with the need to respond very quickly to emergency situations which arise completely out of the blue. Another necessary quality of the fundraiser at times like these is the ability to seize initiatives, to take risks, to get others enthused and involved and, of course, to drop everything and work round the clock until the campaign's success is assured and the need – or the opportunity – is no more. These are high adrenalin times and can be the most exciting and rewarding of any fundraiser's career.

One further point – publicity and public relations are inextricably linked with fundraising. There is never any reason for separating the two. They must both be related parts of the same division within any fundraising organisation.

ACTION POINTS

▲ **Recognise that marketing to raise funds is entirely different to marketing washing powder, motor cars or any other product.**

▲ Carry out a marketing audit and create a marketing plan. Make it part of your organisation's strategic plan. If you haven't got a strategic plan, find similar-sized organisations who have and ask them how to go about it.

▲ Turn change into innovation. Avoid complacency and see change as an opportunity.

▲ Find the right person or people to lead change. Involve everyone and get them to change their behaviour as a prerequisite to change.

▲ Identify whether you are a supermarket or a speciality store. Exploit your niches.

▲ Don't neglect the views of your non-customers.

▲ Encourage individual choice. Tailor your fundraising programmes to give donors maximum choice and opportunity for participation.

▲ Design your product to fit the marketplace, rather than expect the marketplace to fit your product.

▲ Get the price right.

▲ Don't use marketing jargon when speaking to donors.

▲ Identify your 'unique reason to give'.

▲ *Everybody* in your organisation is part of your marketing strategy. Make sure they all know it and know their role.

▲ Every time you get a donation try to get a phone number too. Give the opportunity to add a number in your coupons and reply forms.

▲ Don't be apologetic when asking for corporate donations.

▲ Make sure your proposals are professionally presented and well written. Make them sparkle with originality and powerfully presented needs.

▲ Look for the big idea.

▲ Cultivate the right contacts. You never know when you will need people but at some time or other you certainly will.

DONOR PROFILE

Marsha Robbins

'If I get another one of those charity mailings, I'll scream.' It was at least the third time this week that Marsha had found herself saying or thinking something similar. She seemed to have got on every single mailing list there had ever been and she couldn't understand how.

It bothered her. She disliked being written to by charities or anybody else trying to sell her something. Nowadays it just seemed as if all the mail she got came from somebody trying to sell her something.

She remembered the time she used to get letters from her boyfriend – when she used to look forward to getting letters. A young woman should look forward to getting letters, she thought. Because so many of them came from charities seemed to make it worse. She told her friend Elaine down at the dance centre that she really hated getting so many requests for money and felt bad that she had to say no so often. Also, she thought they all looked too much alike. None of them were very believable. Elaine hadn't a clue what Marsha was going on about – she never got any letters, not from anyone. 'I'll pass you on some of mine,' said Marsha.

Marsha was still thinking about it as she came home. Even before she removed her key she could feel the post piled up against the door, crumpling as she pushed it open. 'More mailings, I expect,' she thought and stopped to gather them up.

Later that evening Marsha went for a walk as usual, just to the postbox. She posted just three envelopes and as usual they were rather similar. On the front of each one some text explained 'This letter does not require a stamp but if you stick one on it will save us money'.

8

Finding new donors

'I thought that our government couldn't fail to listen to us when so many people were insisting that something should be done ... We may never have met, yet I think we all showed the same aim, worked together in the same spirit and shared the same joy the day John was released.'

Jill Morrell
The Friends of John McCarthy

All fundraisers appreciate the importance of finding new donors. Some indeed seem to spend more time and money trying to recruit new blood than in developing the potential of the donors they've already got.

But every fundraising organisation needs to be recruiting new supporters constantly, if not for reasons of growth then to replace those lost through natural (or unnatural) wastage.

What is a donor worth?

What constitutes a 'donor' differs from charity to charity. For some organisations receipt of a single gift qualifies the giver as a donor. For others it is receipt of a second gift, of any size, that differentiates the genuine donor from the casual, spontaneous, uncommitted responder.

As only about 50 per cent of first-time givers go on to make a second gift when left to their own devices,

However successful you are at extending the donor life cycle, as sure as they joined you, donors will one day leave.

adopting this second definition would immediately cut many fundraiser's recruitment statistics in half.

This seems to me to indicate a need to split the warm file in two – responders and donors. New responders should then be encouraged (via a welcome pack, thank you letters, mailings, newsletters and telephone calls) to move as quickly as possible on to the donor file. Responders that didn't give a second gift would be subject to various reactivation approaches before ultimately being rested on a dormant or 'once a year' file if justified.

Reactivation – don't lose your friends!

At ActionAid I learned the value of each new donor through the sufferings of a sister organisation in America. At that time we were a young, developing organisation and we had discovered that we could use press ads and inserts cost-effectively to recruit sponsors (donors who give a substantial gift, usually monthly, to sponsor a child overseas). Through adroit use of direct marketing techniques we were adding between 10,000–12,000 new sponsors a year and because we hadn't been going long enough (or our administration wasn't alert enough) we hadn't yet noticed any significant drop-outs. But my counterpart in the USA's Foster Parents Plan, George Ross, told me his agency had just spent $750,000 on advertising to recruit 6,000 new sponsors, during a year when they'd lost over 6,000 sponsors who had dropped out. So they'd spent three-quarters of a million dollars and hadn't even managed to stand still.

A fundraising product such as sponsorship clearly has built-in problems with drop-outs. However successful you are at extending the donor life cycle, as sure as they joined you, donors will one day leave (unless you can persuade them to pass their commitment to donate on to their children).

*Don't give the impress-
ion that they have already
left you. Most of them
haven't. They just
haven't got round to
renewing.*

The time in between joining and leaving is the 'lifetime' of your donor and that average figure is vital for you to know. (The ideal donor gives to a large-scale proposition over a long period of time – or in other words has a high lifetime value.)

For some organisations that time, naturally, will be very short, just a year or two. For others, like ActionAid, it will naturally be much longer. But whatever the donor's lifetime is, there is a lot any organisation can do to extend it.

A new lease of life
The first rule in finding new donors is, in fact, to do everything you can to extend the life of your existing donors. First remove anything which might make them want to leave you in the first place. Then discover through research every conceivable reason there could be why anyone might want to leave you – so you can eliminate them. Finally introduce a series, up to five or even more, of reactivation initiatives. These might range from personal letters through to a phone call, even to a personal visit from you or your chairman and may include a letter direct from one of your projects either at home or overseas. Whatever you do, don't talk about 'previous' supporters, lapsed members, departed donors. Don't give the impression that they have already left you. Most of them haven't. They just haven't got round to renewing.

Like most people, I rarely pay bills until I get the red reminder and I don't renew magazine subscriptions until I get at least three calls for renewal. This is not a deliberate policy – it's just that like most people there are some things I only get round to when I have to. Once, however, I failed to fill in the first renewal reminder for my favourite magazine, *New Scientist*, and they never

Through my own inertia, I lost out, through doing what lots of people do. But so did New Scientist.

sent me another. My subscription lapsed and I haven't got round to going into a newsagent to buy a copy so I can get a new subscription form even though I'll probably get a 33 per cent off introductory offer. So, through my own inertia, I lost out, through doing what lots of people do. But so did *New Scientist*.

In theory you can keep on sending reactivation mailings to a given section of your lapsed donor file until responses to that segment become unprofitable. Political organisations in the United States have been known to send 40 or more reactivation letters to one donor over a period of months. I wonder what kind of an impression that gives the recipient?

One kind of reactivation initiative that I'm less than enthusiastic about is the approach that suggests 'make a once-only gift of £100 and we won't ask you again'.

I dislike this on two counts. Firstly, it implies that by asking a former donor you are bothering them, so runs against the basic principles of relationship fundraising and, secondly, organisations that say they won't write again almost invariably do: the 'I know we said we wouldn't ask you again, but you'll never guess the latest disaster that has hit our programme in Guatemala' syndrome.

Any reactivation programme has to be sensitive to the donors' wishes and each communication, however presented, should allow them a comfortable way out. It should even give them the option to remove their names from the file.

A cold mailing to lapsed donors often works very well, which shows that donors frequently don't think of themselves as donors.

Finally, if every practical initiative has been tried and nothing has worked, accept it and say goodbye nicely.

That often works.

If it wasn't their favourite charity at the start of the day it probably will be by the end.

Recognition and rewards

Without doubt donors like their support to be recognised. The simplest, most usual and most important recognition device is the thank you letter (see pages 215 to 218). At the other end of the scale, a lifeboat or even a building can be named in a donor's honour. In between these extremes there are many other valuable ways of recognising a donor's contribution (and thereby increasing their loyalty and commitment). Some are surprisingly easy and inexpensive to introduce.

Recognition devices come in many forms. Several charities are already using privileged phone lines (only promoted to one particular group of donors), commemorative plaques in appropriate sites (for example, a day centre), the award of voting rights, listing in the annual report, access to privileged information and so on. Some organisations have created specialist societies or clubs for larger donors, such as NSPCC's Benjamin Waugh Foundation and National Children's Home's George Thomas Society (see page 164).

Special events that recognise donors' substantial contributions can be both interesting and rewarding. One charity I know invites all its donors to an open day. Most cannot come and many write declining the invitation but saying how pleased they were to be asked. Some enclose a cheque simply as a gesture of goodwill. Those that do attend enjoy a fun day out, see their charity at first hand and meet the people involved. If it wasn't their favourite charity at the start of the day it probably will be by the end. And many valuable donations are made as a result.

Another charity hosts regular receptions for donors and staff. Drinks are served and modest refreshments provided, usually underwritten by one of the charity's suppliers. The director makes a short speech. Those

Donors went home highly motivated and recharged but, equally importantly, so did the staff.

donors who come usually go home with their batteries recharged and the staff who attend have had a perfect opportunity to talk to donors and find out what they think and what makes them tick.

One charity I worked with used to hold regional supporter conferences on Saturdays, one every six to eight weeks on average, in different parts of the country. Every supporter in the local area was invited. Ostensibly the purpose was to explain the charity's policies and activities but inevitably those who came brought friends (attendance was always remarkably high) and we enrolled many new supporters on the day. Again donors went home highly motivated and recharged but, equally importantly, so did the staff. We never had any trouble recruiting staff for these information days, despite their being held on a Saturday. They enjoyed it.

Donor recognition events should be planned into your agenda for the coming year just as frequently as you can manage them. Renewal schemes will also help you to hold on to your donors. Donors like their support to be recognised. Why not introduce long-service awards for people who have supported you for, say, 5, 10, 15, 20 years? Choose intervals that help to extend the 'lifetime' of your donors. Structure your awards so that reaching one level automatically encourages the donor to go on to the next, as in bronze, silver, and gold schemes. The 'club' concept is well proven in fundraising terms and although recognition for long service needn't be so formal – it could be just a personal letter from your patron or president – it can be just as effective in extending and upgrading your donors.

Clearly the use of different levels of certificates or tokens depending on the amount raised will have wide application in local group and volunteer fundraising.

Most fundraisers in Britain are still a little reticent

about using incentives or rewards although these have been shown to work in other countries and can be very helpful in finding and motivating new donors.

According to Ted D Bayley, author of *The Fund Raiser's Guide to Successful Campaigns*, as few as one in a hundred people might object to donor recognition pieces, but research proves the other 99 are genuinely motivated by the recognition. Some will even increase the value of their gift if it is tied to larger, more attractive or publicly visible recognition.

One area where rewards are appropriate is in 'member-get-member' (MGM), where your donors find other friends and neighbours who are just like them and who might also be interested in your cause.

If you want to know how effective this is ask American Express. They recruit thousands in this way, but then they do offer genuinely valuable rewards such as half a dozen bottles of wine or a leather-bound personal organiser. One American Express cardholder introduced over 100 friends in one year. He either leads a very organised life or has a bad liver.

Charities have to think what incentives might be appropriate to them. Perhaps a gift of merchandise from your catalogue, or something small made by one of your projects, or a badge or lapel pin, or perhaps a certificate of recognition for special achievement – possibly for introducing five friends – and so on. If every supporter were to bring in just one new friend you'd soon double your donor list virtually without cost. Try inserting a simple member-get-member leaflet in your next mailing. Test it on a segment against the remainder of the list to see if it (a) has any impact on the basic levels or values of gifts and (b) if it covers its cost of inclusion.

To do this properly, of course, you'll have to have a clear idea of what it normally costs you to recruit one

Contrary to popular expectation there are few howls of protest from over-exposed donors.

donor. Surprisingly, many charities don't know this figure, just as they don't know what a donor is worth to them. Yet without this information the only way you can build a donor list is by accident.

Member-get-member schemes are widely used by charities but I know of few that work really well. I suspect this is something to do with donors' feelings of privacy and reticence about telling others about their generosity. Most prefer to support their favourite causes in relative anonymity and few are prepared to evangelise for their charity.

About ten years ago, when we devised loose magazine inserts using built-in reply envelopes for an overseas aid charity, I found that we had a bit of white space left over on the inside of the coupon. (Normally we have to squeeze information on to coupons, but in this case the way the paper folded meant that we had more space than we needed.) We added some address panels for 'introduce a friend', more in hope than anticipation. Response was surprisingly good. Of the thousands of people who completed the coupon about eight per cent gave the names of others, providing us with a large pool of potential new supporters. When we sent our (specially prepared) follow-up welcome pack, a very encouraging number converted, giving us one of our cheapest recruitment methods.

Reciprocal mailings

Reciprocal mailings are the simplest and most cost-effective ways of increasing your donor base. Contrary to popular expectation there are few howls of protest from over-exposed donors. They get lots of other mail anyway and generally have little idea or interest in whence it comes. Nor is there any sign that it reduces your supporters' likelihood of responding generously to your next appeal.

Reciprocals work because charities are not usually *directly* competing with each other, not even similar causes. This is another difference between us and most other kinds of business. Of course this is only true up to a certain point. Donors do feel that they can't support every cause, and will stop giving or give selectively if they think they are getting too many requests.

Reciprocal mailings produce response levels somewhere between what you would expect to get from your cold mailings and your warm (one charity I know achieved 17.5 per cent response to a reciprocal). Whereas cold mailings rarely break even these days, reciprocal mailings almost always make a substantial profit. For one thing there's no list rental cost and with every response you add a new donor to your list, which of course you don't get from warm mailings.

Donors recruited in this way will be worth more because they tend to make higher than average donations and to stay with you longer. And, as these donors cost less to recruit in the first place, reciprocal mailings tend to be good news for fundraisers.

It is, of course, important to give donors the chance to opt out of reciprocal mailings if they don't wish to participate. In Britain there is a code of practice on reciprocal mailings which can be obtained from the Institute of Charity Fundraising Managers which explains the care and precautions fundraisers must take to protect list security, to avoid upset, and so forth.

The threat of restrictive legislation looms particularly large over reciprocal mailings and this avenue for finding new donors may be closed to fundraisers in the very near future. Few of the remaining alternatives will be as affordable or as attractive.

Reciprocal mailings continue to increase in

There's very little that the current generation of direct mail fundraisers has originated ...

popularity with fundraisers in the UK thanks to the almost universal decline in response and increase in cost of 'cold' recruitment mailings. Nevertheless, despite its rising cost and increasingly unacceptable image with the general public, cold direct mail still remains one of the most cost-effective methods of recruiting significant numbers of new donors, donors that you can be sure will be mail-responsive.

Cold direct mail

There are many proven techniques to increase the effectiveness of your direct mail, both cold and warm, and most of them are not secret. The subject deserves a book of its own and its pages would quickly fill with practical hints and guidance for fundraisers. I don't have space to go into that amount of detail now. However, it would be impossible to look even superficially at the fundraiser's relationship with his donors without considering the extraordinary impact direct mail has had on the fundraising business in recent years.

Fundraising by direct mail is not new. In 1887, Dr Barnardo's Homes were mailing 200,000 appeal letters a year using very emotive, well-written letters, well laid-out with indented paragraphs and lots of underlining. They also used quite sophisticated member-get-member mechanisms, leaflets, even handwritten postscripts.

There's very little that the current generation of direct mail fundraisers has originated, but we did certainly help direct mail to proliferate.

In chapter 6 I looked at the dangers of the direct mail explosion and the potential damage badly prepared, formula-driven and badly targeted direct mail might do to a fundraiser's relationship with his or her donors.

So in this chapter I will try to restrict discussion on cold mail to considering practical ways of amending

"I THANK GOD FOR AN EVER OPEN DOOR!"

22nd March, 1888.

*To the Friends of Christ's work among the
Waifs & Strays of our Streets.*

Dear Friend,

The winter we have almost passed through has been the severest and most arduous, so far as work among the children of the poor is concerned, that I have ever known. In fact, so great have been the unceasing demands upon our resources, that these have been taxed to their very utmost in the attempt to respond to the unprecedented calls for relief which every hour brought to our doors.

Still, I thank God for an ever open door !

Dealing each month with <u>800 or 900 fresh applica</u>tions of apparently Destitute and Homeless Children, every one of which had to be searchingly investigated before a final decision could be given, involved such severe physical and mental labour (not unfrequently from twelve to seventeen hours daily) as made it often difficult to find time even for needed repose, much less to prepare and issue our Magazine, "NIGHT AND DAY," in whose columns I am able, as a rule, to communicate the story of the Lord's work in my hands. Something <u>had</u> to be left undone. I judged

it better rather to delay the Record of the work than to stop the Work itself.

As a consequence, our funds have suffered not a little, and my large and growing family, now numbering **2,432 children and 150 adults**, has been maintained chiefly by the supplies so lovingly and generously sent in about Christmas time. But these are now all haustd, and although "NIGHT AND DAY," I am nkful to say, is at last going to press, it cannot h my readers' hands for about a fortnight from date. Meanwhile <u>£100 a day for food alone</u> a moderate computation of our most pressing monts, and I feel sure I am

arving — utterly and hopelessly
y **were all admitted.**
l for an ever open door !

oo, for His own gracious help, not
e almost exhausted minds and
, but also for pecuniary supplies
tous season, through numberless
the world; these often arriving
reed, to the cheer of drooping
ce of failing hope. On my
bruary—when the treasury
I had been constrained, al-
ithin me at the thought of
eplorable little waifs whose
id most pressing character
-there came from the far-
ted "Thank-Offering for
00 to replenish our ex-
ure me afresh of our

thank God for an ever

I trust, whatever may
he face of any really

362 girls
ruary
the profound
t-five hildren of
ren, ching our
were uits to YOU
nd; our hearts !

to y ponder the
or paragraphs 5,
the i., and then, if
of <u>help me quickly</u>
es <u>with food,</u> and
s, st fighting God's
little Ones.

worker among
Children,

T. J. BARNARDO.

dy stream of child
course it is understood
ut enquiry to be really destitute), we must "swarm off"
like an overfull hive of bees. Accordingly if sufficient
money comes in to pay the cost of outfit and passage,
I am hoping that <u>200 trained boys</u> will (D.V.) sail

e one such Little Child
receiveth Me."
MATT. xviii. 5.

Long before the arrival of the computer and mailsort, Dr Barnardo was employing professional techniques to send apparently individual urgent appeals to hundreds of thousands of people in Victorian Britain.

Why not? People like to receive letters. They don't like to receive mailings.

current practice to limit any negative effects it might have on your prospects and to increase its chances of getting your relationship off to a good start.

That's not easy.

The most obvious way is to avoid slavish adherence to any established formula even though you know it, at least, has a proven track record. The trick is to devise an original or individual approach – more individual at least than the formulae that most other fundraisers follow – but it has to be one that you can show, through testing, works at least as well as or better than the traditional direct mail approach.

Difficult though this may be, it's not impossible and some charities have done it.

One way is through the facsimile letter.

The Muscular Dystrophy Group of Great Britain and Northern Ireland has been doing this effectively for several years. It all started because the chief executive of MDG at the time, Paul Walker, felt mailings failed with him because they were immediately recognisable as a direct mail appeal – and were treated accordingly. So the Group's agency devised a mailing pack that didn't look like a mailing but instead looked like a real letter, the kind you or I might send to a friend. Why not? People like to receive letters. They don't like to receive mailings. That is good relationship fundraising thinking.

The main letter wasn't on MDG letterhead. Instead it came from a well-known and much-loved supporter, television celebrity Richard Briers. It was handwritten on cream-coloured personal stationery and Richard Briers, a third party speaking on behalf of children with muscular dystrophy, was able to invest his appeal with far more urgency and emotion than many MDG staff would have felt comfortable with. And as a third party it was also more credible coming from him.

There was a discreet lift letter from Paul Walker. This was folded so recipients simply read on the outside 'if you have decided to help ...' Of course once they opened it they were hooked because Paul was already thanking them for their positive decision to support the charity. A photo card with Richard Briers' handwritten message was also included and a handwritten reply form

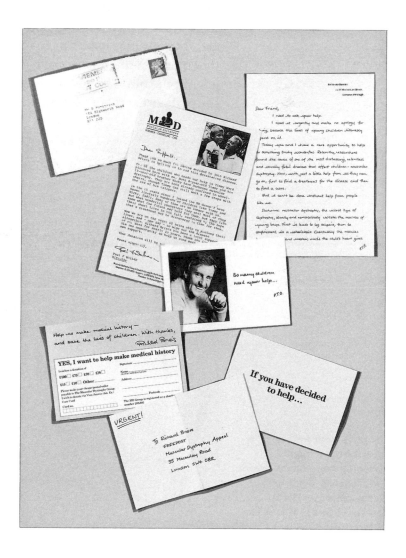

The Muscular Dystrophy Group's readers receive an interesting, moving and involving story.

The public tend to regard the mailsort symbol as junk mail's logo.

completed the pack.

One of the most controversial aspects of this mailing was the outer envelope. This was high-quality stationery, C6 with a closed face (no window). Addresses were typed by hand. Instead of the ubiquitous mailsort symbol, a real second-class postage stamp was affixed. So on arrival MDG's appeal mailing looked just like a real letter, the kind you or I might get from granny or a chum. (I hate the mailsort symbol. It so clearly identifies letters as mass mailings – as soon as that mark distinguishes the content the whole package goes in the bin. The public, I regret to say, tend to regard the mailsort symbol as junk mail's logo.)

Mailings from a machine or letters from a friend? Potential new supporters for the Muscular Dystrophy Group clearly prefer to receive letters that look like letters.

Yet fundraisers persist in sending out appeals that look like mailings.

Once opened the nature of the appeal was obvious, but its authentic and compelling presentation guaranteed readership and response to this pack substantially exceeded previous cold mailing efforts. It is still the Muscular Dystrophy Group's banker pack.

To test whether the personal touch of the individually typed and stamped letters was worth the extra cost, MDG's agency carried out a carefully structured five-way split test. Segments of several mailing lists were sent identical contents inside five different versions of outer envelope: a window envelope with mailsort symbol (the conventional fundraising letter); a window envelope with a stamp; a non-window laser-addressed envelope with mailsort symbol; a non-window laser-addressed envelope with a stamp, a non-window hand-typed address with a stamp – the conventional letter you or I would send to a friend.

Since it was prepared I have asked many groups of people which envelope they felt would most likely achieve the best response. The answer has always been the same – the one that looks most likely to contain a letter from a friend.

Yet fundraisers persist in sending out appeals that look like mailings.

In fact the typed and stamped envelope did achieve a much higher total response than all the other segments. Even when the increased cost was taken into account, the banker pack still worked best. So now all MDG has to do is find machines that can affix stamps at low cost – they do exist – and find ways of creating a hand-typed effect in large volumes. It will be done.

Different from the herd
Many organisations have now put thought and effort into making their warm and cold appeal mailings

different from the herd. One of the most effective departures in recent years came from the Henry Doubleday Research Association, for Ryton Gardens, the National Centre for Organic Gardening. Their appeal to members (all organic gardeners are likely to be fiercely opposed to junk mail) raised eight times its target, largely because it broke almost every 'rule' of the direct mail industry.

The appeal package consisted of a plain brown envelope inside which was another (reply) envelope and a single, large (A1) sheet of brown wrapping paper which was printed on one side only. The mailing immediately addressed recipients' assumed aversion to direct mail by explaining that, once read, the entire sheet could be recycled as seed pots for use in the member's garden. The rest of the sheet was taken up by some letter

Cultivating good relationships starts with seeing things from the donor's point of view. Ryton Gardens' original direct mail appeal could be recycled as seed pots in the recipient's garden.

Members seemed to appreciate that their interests and concerns had been taken into account, so they were glad to help.

copy, a map of the gardens, a list of the problems and immediate needs at the centre, and a structured hierarchical offer inviting members to become either gardeners, cultivators, seedsmen or sponsors (at different price levels). This unusual mailing was completed by a reply mechanism consisting of donation form, banker's order form, deed of covenant and a panel describing how to assemble the seed pots, *after* it had been read, by simply folding sections of the sheet.

But innovative though it was, the Ryton Gardens mailing had a built-in flaw. If the reply forms were detached the HDRA member could make six seed pots, but if he used the reply forms also, he could make *eight*. Despite this disincentive the response far exceeded expectations and generated the kind of enthusiastic fan mail that direct mail fundraisers dream about. Most of all, HDRA members seemed to appreciate that their interests and concerns had been taken into account, so they were glad to help.

If the beginning of success is to be different and the beginning of failure is to be the same, then it will pay fundraisers in the future to ensure that all our mailings are individual and different, not clones from a formula.

I think we owe that to our supporters.

Off-the-page

Press advertising does bring some direct response but nowadays the cost usually far outweighs the income.

This means that, apart from a few rare exceptions, press or off-the-page advertising is not a practical way of finding large numbers of new donors. This wasn't always the case. Nearly 40 years ago, when charities in the UK first started to raise money by paying for advertising space in their national newspapers, the process for the fundraiser seemed relatively simple.

- All one had to do was prepare a simple, highly emotive and urgent-sounding appeal, which shows people what their donation will achieve.
- Pay – at whatever discount you could obtain – to have it inserted in the better class of national newspaper.
- Then simply wait for the donations to come flooding in.

With advertisements like this Oxfam led the way in fundraising advertising in the early 1950s, setting standards many charities now neglect.

In the UK more charities than ever before continue to spend more money than ever before on press advertising.

And with reassuring predictability they did. The advertisement on the facing page appeared in British newspapers in 1953, inserted by the Oxford Committee for Famine Relief, the forerunner of Oxfam. Although it looks very dated now, it actually embodies many of the ingredients of a good fundraising press advertisement – newsy style, use of newspaper setting, listing of well-known supporters, mention of specific amounts to give, and so on.

Today's fundraiser might find this advertisement naïve, but ads like this really worked. Oxfam achieved returns of up to £31 for every £1 it invested in press advertising. Even in those far-off days, Oxfam's pioneering press ads showed an understanding of off-the-page fundraising techniques that is frequently lacking in today's ads.

Nowadays, few charities can claim to recover even their direct costs from fundraising press appeals.

Yet in the UK more charities than ever before continue to spend more money than ever before on press advertising.

According to MEAL (Media Expenditure Analysis Ltd) figures for October 1990–September 1991, just 74 UK charities spent a total of over £26.3 million in the year. That's a lot of money. And these charities are using the press in an increasing variety of ways for fundraising and fundraising-related purposes, including donor and member recruitment, image-building, campaigning, promoting events and much more. But, I wonder, how many of them are getting value for money, or anything like it? (MEAL figures fail to pick up the savings and discounts many charities achieve against rate card costs but this is compensated for to a large extent by the many specialist media that MEAL leave out.)

For the majority of charities the most practical and

*How much awareness
can you create for half a
million pounds? Not a
lot, as many charities are
now realising.*

measurable use of the press is to recruit new supporters, albeit often at high cost. But millions have been spent trying to create awareness and much of it has been wasted. How much awareness can you create for half a million pounds? Not a lot, as many charities are now realising.

Conversely, some hard-headed charities are giving clear instructions to their agencies – find us new supporters at x pounds per response. The agency's brief is to buy space accordingly and tightly monitor results. In the UK charities such as Help the Aged, Sightsavers and ActionAid have all used this system effectively. More charities should follow their example.

Many of the lessons Oxfam learned in the 1950s and 1960s still apply, although if you look through a selection of Britain's daily papers you'll quickly spot how many charities are unaware of them. Here are a few of these 'basics' of press advertising.

- Fundraising ads only work in the 'quality' press.
- They work best in special positions.
- Small spaces are generally more cost-efficient.
- Short, clear, readable copy gets best results.
- Make an offer, make it in the headline. Eighty per cent of your investment should go into picture and headline because four out of every five readers will read no further.
- Show where the money goes. The simple proposition linked with the sensible use of funds works every time.
- Make response easy.
- Clever buying in space, timing and position are certainly more important than cleverness in copy.

Most newspapers need to fill odd spaces in their page make-up from time to time and will offer very special terms to charities which can provide appropriate copy as a filler. This is usually referred to as 'distress' space.

Perhaps expenditure in press advertising will fall in coming years as more charities realise the long-term nature of press advertising.

Perhaps the specialist uses to which fundraisers put the press will become sharper-edged and more clearly focused in terms of measurable results achieved, as more and more charities realise that press advertising is just too expensive for anything short of absolute precision.

Do I sound cynical? I am a bit. Charities misspend more of their promotional budgets on press advertising than on anything else. With a few exceptions the only quantifiably justifiable use of off-the-page advertising in the UK at the moment is new-approach legacy marketing (see page 296). But perhaps in the future, as direct mail acquisition costs increase, off-the-page advertising will re-emerge as a cost-effective way of finding new donors. That would open up some new potential but if so it is unlikely to stay cost-effective for long.

For me the advertisement from Help the Aged on the next page is an excellent example of the classic fundraising ad which works as well today as it ever did.

'Make a blind man see – £10.'

What an offer! Where on earth could anyone get such value for money? These simple, clear ads from Help the Aged get straight to the point. The typewriter setting looks as if it's been put together by two old ladies working in a leaky garret. What comes across is that they passionately believe in the urgency and rightness of their appeal.

Fundraising ads *must* work. They've got to. After all, for the cost of the advertisement at full rate card price in one issue of a newspaper such as *The Daily Telegraph*, Help the Aged could have restored sight to 264 people.

If the media buyer has done his stuff, that price could

be reduced by 50 per cent or more. Still, even at that cost the ad has to work hard because, instead of buying the

Few advertisers could make such a powerful offer and those that can will almost certainly be other fundraisers. If press ads are to work they must make a clear, direct and relevant proposition, followed by an easy way to respond.

... instead of buying the ad, Help the Aged could have chosen to restore sight to more than 100 people.

ad, Help the Aged could have chosen to restore sight to more than 100 people.

That kind of thing puts quite a responsibility on those of us who would use the press to raise funds.

Inserts

Magazine inserts fall somewhere between direct mail and off-the-page advertisements. An insert can be thought of as unaddressed direct mail delivered via your prospect's reading matter rather than through the letter-box. Or it can be considered a loose advertisement which rather than being fixed to the page falls out immediately the magazine is picked up, thereby at least increasing its chances of being noticed.

Inserts were very popular in Britain a few years ago, with many charities using them extensively in weekend newspapers and specialist magazines. The development of the technology to create the all-in-one mailer complete with reply form and envelope transformed direct response advertising for some charities, as inserts provided a cost-effective way to deliver a detailed message to a specific audience *and* gave an immediate and easy way to respond. But here again the donating public showed its sales resistance. Inserts became overused in the UK, lost their novelty value and now are only effective for high-priced fundraising propositions or, exceptionally, for a membership organisation such as the Royal National Lifeboat Institution, who promote their low-cost membership scheme successfully using very simple and inexpensive inserts.

Inserts are something of a shotgun approach when compared to well-targeted direct mail, but they have some advantages including high impact, opportunities for creativity and originality and the chance to tell a detailed story through long copy and good photographs.

Some charities are reporting that donors recruited via press advertising are more rather than less responsive than those found through cold direct mail.

In addition they provide cost-effective opportunities for testing different formats and copy (one insert my company prepared involved ten simultaneous format and copy tests and a print run of 1.3 million). Inserts are also very flexible and will offer challenging opportunities to whoever designs and produces them. The disadvantages of inserts include high unit cost and quite high minimum quantities, so they can be expensive particularly in the development stages. RNLI's annual campaign in 1991 totalled 18 million inserts with 50 different copy and design tests. Production and organisation can be extraordinarily complex so it is important to know what you are doing.

Gathering names

There are other methods of recruiting potential donors than those you have to pay for. Names can be collected in a variety of ways but if a donation hasn't been given, or even if it has but not through the mail, then that new name is unlikely to be as productive as that of a new donor recruited by direct mail. They will not be as likely to be 'mail-responsive', in the jargon of the direct marketing industry.

However, even this accepted wisdom may not be standing the test of time. Some charities are reporting that donors recruited via press advertising are more rather than less responsive than those found through cold direct mail. The theory is that people on mailing lists are now over-exposed to appeals, whereas those who respond via the press are often new blood, not to be found on anyone's database.

This seems to me to be another sign of the times, yet more of a clue to the limited life-expectancy of cold direct mail.

But fundraisers have to be careful. You can't gather

names from just anywhere.

Some names will be a liability rather than an asset and may respond less well than if you had mailed the telephone directory. Of course, names can be tested at low cost and common sense will probably guide you as to what will work and what will not.

If you do house-to-house collections an effective way to gather names for free is to print a space for name, address and telephone number on the back of your collecting envelopes. The resulting names are already responders and if you add an offer of further information describing your work then the hook can provide useful members or new supporters. By flagging their source on your database you can then track these names over a period of time to see if they are cost-effective additions to your list. Even if they don't respond to mailings, it may be worth trying a telephone call.

You can try collecting the names of swimmers, walkers and runners from sponsored events and even the people who have sponsored them. However, some charities I know who have done this are not very enthusiastic about the results they achieve. This doesn't surprise me as so often runners and their sponsors are reluctant donors and may feel they've done enough already. They may, however, simply be a different kind of supporter and may well help you again if treated appropriately.

A friend of mine recently told me about a barbecue party he went to, given by a friend he used to go cycling with. Midway through the party the host was called into the house to take a phone call and left his guests for about half an hour, which was rather longer than he should have. On his return the host explained that the call had been from an environmental charity for which he and my friend had recently done a sponsored cycle

My friend's host wasn't put out by this interruption of the feast. He was delighted and very flattered to have been asked.

ride. They had telephoned to see if he would consider becoming a member.

My friend's host wasn't in the least put out by this interruption of the feast. He was delighted and very flattered to have been asked. His pleasure at the prospect of joining this group was evidenced by the length of the phone call, but he would never have joined if left to his own devices.

Names can also be gathered via the telephone. This can be done through direct recruitment off the page, as in Greenpeace's small-ad campaign which rode on the back of the 'green revolution' of the late 1980s. This surge of public interest in all things environmental allowed the charity to place tiny single-column five-centimetre ads which simply said 'Join Greenpeace' and gave a phone number. No explanation or selling message was needed and hundreds phoned in to join.

Even small ads can be costly in the national press, however, and results have to be measured carefully. Despite their high profile, name getting by telephone wasn't particularly cost-effective for Greenpeace when compared to other methods.

Unfortunately for Greenpeace, a few years later some of these spontaneous joiners are proving quite hard to renew by mail, but recent tests in telephoning renewals have produced very encouraging results. According to Rich Fox of telefundraising specialists Facter Fox, this is not surprising. Their experience in telephoning lapsed subscribers in the USA and in Europe indicates that the telephone is particularly effective at overcoming the biggest inhibitor to subscription renewal – inertia.

You can do a local variation of Greenpeace's small-ad campaign by sticking up posters or getting free or concessionary coverage in your local paper. Names can also be gathered by phone if you have an advice or

... and while you have them on the line you have a chance to discuss your work, find out more about them and perhaps increase the size of that donation.

information line – provided you let callers know that's what you're doing.

The telephone is also an indispensable means of taking credit card donations in the simplest and most convenient way. Callers can simply read their card number, expiry date and amount they wish to give over the phone and while you have them on the line you have a chance to discuss your work, find out more about them and perhaps increase the size of that donation.

If you don't offer donors the chance to support your cause in this way you are almost certainly losing both money and potential donors. Note also that credit card givers tend to give up to 25 per cent more than those who just send in their cheque.

Membership

If you work for a cause, consider launching a membership or similar type of scheme. People who join as members will often quite happily pay an annual membership fee (covenanted) and respond regularly to warm appeals for funds, as well as buying merchandise, leaving legacies and doing all the other things good donors do.

Just because you call them members doesn't mean you have to grant them voting rights. (Check your constitution first.)

But for many people the word membership has connotations so an alternative may be preferred, such as key supporter, club donor or friend, although these are often not felt to be as good. One thing about members is that they do belong. It's that sense of belonging that your scheme needs to cultivate.

You can offer a hierarchy of members (or supporters), recruiting ordinary members at, say, £15 per annum, family membership at £25, lifetime

It helps donors to find their ideal giving level.

membership at £150 and so on, with special concessions for students, old age pensioners and people who are unemployed. These amounts are roughly typical of those charged by national membership charities in the early 1990s and are probably a lot lower than they ought to be in terms of relevant value for money. Getting the price right is obviously crucial – too high and you'll put people off, too low and you'll lose money and also give out the wrong signals in terms of value for money.

It is quite possible to further subdivide your membership and create usually purely nominal sub-levels. The Americans are adept at this, successfully dishing out meaningless titles that sound slightly more grand the more you are prepared to pay. But it helps donors to find their ideal giving level and, of course, the member who pays you most in membership fee is the one most likely to give you most in other ways such as special appeals, capital gifts and legacies.

The information line
An information service, of course, doubles as a very convenient avenue for supporters' complaints, doubts and criticisms. By advertising your hotline, action line, or information line you appear anxious to please and donors respond very positively to this. You are therefore able to smoke out any concerns and anxieties among donors easily and, as I said earlier, many charities have found that complaints often turn into valuable donations. Once established your hotline service can be easily advertised at no cost in all your promotional materials, newsletters, and even in your direct mail (see page 239).

The video party
In the mid-1950s an enterprising American company

What has really lasted is the memory of those parties and Tupperware's distinctive and successful marketing method.

with an overpriced and ordinary product range hit on a marketing idea that transformed its fortunes and turned both company and products into a household name. The firm was Tupperware Inc and they sold their plastic airtight containers by the million at Tupperware parties.

These were no ordinary sales demonstrations, no mere repetition of Avon calling. Tupperware parties were major social events. Just to be invited was an accolade and to be allowed to buy was almost a privilege. Women went along just to touch Tupperware's plastic containers and talked about it for weeks afterwards.

Well, it seemed like that to me, a mere boy at the time. A friend of my parents was awarded the position of South West Scotland regional representative for Tupperware and she introduced my mother to this elevated social activity. Somehow in time Tupperware disappeared from the scene – they were too expensive and overtaken by cheap imitations. The product lingered on, however – many of my mother's original Tupperware containers are still in use and I'm sure some pieces, particularly the zany salt and pepper set, are now collectors' items. But what has really lasted is the memory of those parties and Tupperware's distinctive and successful marketing method.

In the UK naughty nightie queen, Ann Summers, revived the idea in the permissive 1970s to market far more salacious products in the privacy of the prospect's own home, where intimate items could be demonstrated and bought in the company of half a dozen raucous and not quite serious friends and neighbours.

Does this strange concept have applications for the fundraiser in the 1990s? I think it does.

Hence the video party. The concept is delightfully simple and essentially is the Tupperware formula. You need to find competent and willing hostesses/

For the most successful, their XYZ party will soon pass into local legend and attendance at the next will be a must.

volunteers recruited from your donor file who will agree to hold an XYZ (insert the name of your charity here) party in their own homes. They provide the tea and scones, you provide a suitable short video of your work (10–15 compelling minutes) along with supporting leaflets, enrolment, membership, or covenant forms and some guidance notes for the hostess.

She (or he), the host, selects and invites suitable friends, some of whom will already be XYZ donors.

The objective for the evening is clear and single-minded. Your hostess wants to recruit at least five new donors to the cause. That'll make sending the video and support material worthwhile. Some will organise it brilliantly, recruit lots of friends and go on to host lots more XYZ parties. Others will do less well and may need encouragement.

For the most successful, their XYZ party will soon pass into local legend and attendance at the next will be a must. But don't neglect their effectiveness at recruiting new donors and even as a way of thanking and encouraging existing ones. Everyone will enjoy the video.

The President's Task Force

The following case history makes a fitting end to this chapter, for it really is recognition par excellence; proof that donors really do like the hierarchical schemes that I mentioned earlier. Even if they clearly understand it as a device designed to secure their involvement, they appear not to mind at all.

Donors want to be involved in their favourite causes. The joining of a structured scheme gets them in on the inside, usually at a very modest cost. Fundraisers should capitalise on this compulsion to belong. Voluntary organisations have a clear and very desirable product in involvement schemes, one which is so far underdeveloped in Britain.

A classic example of how completely this can work in practice was the launching of the President's Task Force, an elite donor group established by Ronald Reagan's office shortly after his election in 1981 as president of the USA. Of course, the qualification to join the President's Task Force was that you should give a minimum donation – $10 each month – to campaign funds. Large numbers of patriotic Republicans rushed to do their duty, trading a small amount of their disposable cash for the recognition and reward that went with being able to tell friends and neighbours that they were a member of the President's Task Force.

Various pieces of commemorative paraphernalia were produced and distributed in case members had to prove their status to doubting acquaintances who needed physical evidence of their friend's important role in the affairs of state. These included a 'presidential medal of merit', a presidential medal of merit lapel pin, a model American flag, which was dedicated en masse at a special ceremony in the White House, and inscription of the donor's name on the 'presidential roll of honour'. There was even an exclusive 'members only' Task Force telephone hotline.

Donors, of course, loved it. For just $10 a month this was real value for money. Most of all to encourage the authentic feel of the campaign the fundraisers had produced stationery that was the exact facsimile of the President's writing paper. Colour printed and embossed, laser personalised and signed it looked exactly as it would had the President himself taken time out from his busy schedule to write a personal note to Elmer E Rosenblum, or whomever, to acknowledge his individual contribution and stress its importance to America.

More than a few of these letters were framed and hung in a prominent place in the family home.

More than a few of these letters were framed and hung in a prominent place in the family home so that visitors could be easily subjected to an hour or so's dissertation on Elmer's sacrifice for his country.

Across the length and breadth of the entire United States, thousands of Republicans took their membership of the President's Task Force very seriously indeed – and the dollars rolled into the President's office as a result. Sustained by a brilliant direct marketing campaign of record and reward, the President's Task Force gave its donors something beyond price – the prestige of practical involvement in something they believed in. As such it simply used the best of technique and technology, plus a forgivable amount of kitsch, to establish the ideal relationship fundraising proposition, an ongoing relationship where both donor and recipient could benefit in equal amounts, at the end of which a clear financial and practical target could be reached.

In relaying the case history of the 'President's Task Force' at the International Fund Raising Workshop in Holland, John Groman of Epsilon Data Management provided an anecdote which summed up the power of the campaign.

Late one evening a motor-cycle patrolman flagged down a speeding motorist on one of America's interminable inter-state highways. With customary leisurely grace he strolled up to the driver, who appeared to be in something of a hurry, and proceeded to ask him to provide his driving licence and evidence of insurance. Without a word, but inwardly seething at the delay, the driver – it may even have been Elmer E Rosenblum – got out of his car and led the patrolman firmly by the hand round to the back of the car, to the enormous boot (or trunk) of his Cadillac. Still without a sound, but with a gesture of magnificently righteous indignation, he flung his hand dramatically down to point out the large and very official-looking bumper sticker which prominently proclaimed the 'President's Task Force' and indicated that the driver was, in fact, nothing less than a member.

The patrolman was astounded. He stammered a fulsome apology, saluted, swore it wouldn't happen again and waved his distinguished visitor happily on his way.

I don't know that the patrolman escorted Elmer across the state line with lights flashing and sirens wailing, but I like to think he did.

ACTION POINTS

▲ **Don't overemphasise finding new blood unless you are already doing all you can to keep your existing donors.**

▲ **Find out the average cost of recruiting a donor for your organisation. Then find out how much, on average, each donor is worth. Costs will differ according to recruitment method, but you may also find that, for example, a donor recruited by a press advertisement will, on average, be worth more to you than a donor recruited by direct mail.**

▲ **Differentiate between donors and responders. Prepare material to upgrade responders speedily.**

▲ **Set up a logical programme of reactivation for lapsed donors. Test it.**

▲ **Introduce appropriate schemes of recognition and reward, where relevant.**

▲ Hold a donor recognition event at least once each year.

▲ Test your donor-get-donor recruitment methods. See if you can offer an appropriate incentive.

▲ Exploit reciprocal mailings. Follow the reciprocal code of practice.

▲ Consider whether you can make your appeal mailings individual to you and different from the rest, while retaining their effectiveness. If you must rely on formulae, try not to make it too obvious.

▲ Test the value of gathering free names, such as event participants.

▲ If you haven't already got one, consider the benefits of setting up a membership or similar scheme. Choose membership price levels carefully. Try to structure the scheme so that members' activities are purely charitable, enabling you to invite them all to covenant their subscription (up to 80 per cent will).

▲ Make your involvement schemes special and worth joining.

▲ Establish a telephone information line.

▲ Try organising some video parties.

DONOR PROFILE

Molly and Don Patterson

There are six different charity stickers on the back window of Molly Patterson's car. Her husband, Don, hates them and would throw them all away but he doesn't say anything because it is easier that way. In their family Don makes the big decisions, like whether America should invade Afghanistan or what will happen when world demand for oil slumps, and Molly makes all the small decisions, like which programmes to watch on television and what to do with their money.

Molly and Don are not rich but they do support several well-known charities. Molly does all her Christmas shopping from about a dozen colourful charity gift catalogues she receives each June. She even acts as an agent on behalf of her bridge ladies, rounding up all their orders and sending in one large cheque, often with a donation thrown in for good measure. She doesn't need any more fridge purifiers or plastic potato racks but will probably order some again this year, just to make up the order. Most of the charities Molly deals with have earmarked her as a substantial donor/buyer and she's beginning to notice they're starting to treat her rather more personally, which she likes. When their premium bond came up last March, Molly sent more than half of it to an animal welfare charity that had recently sent her a harrowing letter about cruelty to cats. Don had sulked over this for a week.

Although she treats him severely, Molly is really quite dependent on Don, particularly as her health isn't good. In her will she has named Don as her sole beneficiary, but if he should go first then she wants all her assets to be divided equally between her six favourite charities.

Unfortunately for them, Don is in excellent health and he hates charities.

9 Communicating with your donors

'We cannot create feelings. We must learn how the tide is running in people's minds, and float our messages on the surface.'

Drayton Bird
Commonsense Direct Marketing

Floating our message on the surface of people's minds is an extremely expensive business. It's also too often hit and miss. To ensure we get a reasonable return from our limited promotional resources, we fundraisers have to be more than a little circumspect in our choice of promotional media and our choice of messages. Most important for fundraisers is getting our messages regularly and consistently to our 'warm' lists, our established and newly recruited donors. But it's also important to promote our messages to less proven audiences – the cold general public – and inevitably there will be considerable overlap between the two. Don't forget that the most demanding critics of your donor recruitment advertising will be your existing donors.

I learned this early on from public reaction to the first fundraising loose insert inserted into one of the UK's leading Sunday supplements, *The Observer* colour magazine. I was involved in organising this innovation for a Third World aid/development charity. Our insert was a, then, unique-format leaflet with built-in reply

... most fundraising organisations simply haven't got the resources to make any noticeable impression.

form and envelope. The response was quite over-whelming but most strident amongst it were comments from the charity's existing supporters (the majority of whom were recruited via *The Observer*) who, along with nearly a million other people, had seen the insert fall from their Sunday magazine. Thankfully all the calls were overwhelmingly favourable. Donors were greatly encouraged to see such a surprising, positive promotion. Although our new insert had been entirely directed at potential new donors, its impact on existing supporters was considerable.

The effect applies equally to all forms of communicating with donors – direct mail, press, television, posters and everything else.

General awareness advertising

Donors will certainly see your press advertisements and posters, as will volunteers, staff, even trustees. So, of course, will you. This may be regarded by some as sufficient justification to make up for the desperately poor response and income that most charity off-the-page advertising generates. I find that hard to accept. In the absence of direct response many fundraisers justify press advertising through its indirect benefits, although these are usually vague and notoriously hard to measure. Advertising does put the organisation's name about, it does help to pave the way for other initiatives, but press advertising now is so expensive, the public's consciousness so hard to penetrate and the competition for your reader's attention so substantial and sophisticated that most fundraising organisations simply haven't got the resources to make any noticeable impression.

Therefore they can very easily waste a great deal of money. All but a very few charities have extremely

An example of this is the British Red Cross. Their logo is one of the most distinctive in the world. Their name is universally known. But few people know what they do.

limited budgets for advertising. By limited I mean that anything less than an advertising spend of £1 million per annum these days is almost certainly not enough to sustain an already established brand image on its own, or make any lasting impression on public recognition. Not that public recognition is any indicator when it comes to ensuring a charity's continued income. A perfect example of this is the British Red Cross. Their logo is one of the most distinctive in the world. Their name is universally known. But few people know what they do.

Many charities are established household names but few, if any, have achieved this solely through press advertising campaigns or similar vague attempts at achieving awareness, even though press advertising may have played a part.

Selling like soap

People sometimes complain that charities are 'being sold like soap powder, or cornflakes, or margarine'. Well, in 1990/91 Radion the soap powder spent just short of £10 million on advertising in the UK, Kellogg's cornflakes spent £5.82 million and Flora margarine spent more than £4 million. (My son Joe, who is nine, thinks there's something seriously wrong with his family because we don't use Radion, so I suppose advertising must work to some extent.)

Against this kind of expenditure, how can charities compete? The figures I have quoted are for single brands only, not organisations. The advertising spend of their parent companies is vastly more. The total advertising expenditure shown by MEAL for all washing liquids and powders in the UK is £86 million per year. These figures show that really charities are not being sold like soap at all – nowhere near it.

I know that much of this expenditure goes on

... it is a mistake to equate expenditure with value.

television. Charities have already shown that they can't spend enough to make television work for direct response.

As costs escalate and responses fall it seems likely that most other national media will become equally uneconomic. Recruiting new donors via paid-for national promotion as we know it – television, press, direct mail – may soon become a thing of the past, except for very special propositions.

Support for field fundraising activities, to inform and announce, to raise money, to recruit members are all valid uses of advertising. But while paid-for advertising still has a place in many large charities' marketing mix its role is a generally supportive one. It should never be seen as a panacea for all messages, covering fundraising, image, identity, information, education, *et al*. Fundraisers often think advertising will solve all their marketing problems because the amounts of money spent appear to be so large, but of course it is a mistake to equate expenditure with value.

And broad awareness alone will not make an appeal successful. Several London-based medical charities seem to have been led down this particular garden path recently. They have spent millions of pounds on awareness campaigns in the press and on posters in the hope that they could buy into the public's consciousness or create some kind of donor 'brand awareness'. Sadly, almost all this money has been entirely wasted, public consciousness has hardly been stirred, far less shaken, and when the money has run out these charities have been left with next to nothing to show. You can't bank a five-point temporary increase in awareness.

Most charity 'brands' have been created over many years. To short-cut the process, if it is possible, would take more money than is likely to be available, yet many

Remember David and Goliath. Perhaps it's just a question of getting the approach right.

charities attempt awareness advertising with pitifully limited resources. For most fundraising organisations it is like firing a peashooter at a battleship, the budgets just don't match the objective.

But remember David and Goliath. Perhaps it's just a question of getting the approach right, of deploying your limited resources with cunning and strategy so that a very little can go a very long way. That's what most effective charity advertisers do. Press, poster and even television advertising is seen as a reinforcement of other methods of keeping the charity and its messages in the public mind, including local and national publicity, public relations including media relations, special events, regional staff and volunteers, and so on. And, of course, your own direct communications with supporters.

Disaster advertising

Direct response off-the-page advertising plays a very important part in how many international charities respond to a disaster overseas. While public attention – and sympathy – is focused on the plight of the victims, the fundraiser has a brief chance to be of immediate and practical help. But he or she has to react with extraordinary speed, implementing a probably prearranged plan of action at a pace that would be unthinkable in normal times – information to be gathered, advertisements written, copy approved, positions negotiated and space booked in hours rather than the usual weeks.

There are several other important aspects to successful disaster advertising.
• Judging the scale of the disaster. Ads will only work if they are supported by major press and television coverage.
• Courageous booking. Media owners and their

representatives have to be persuaded to displace already booked advertising, often from regular customers, to make way for your appeal. For some unknown reason disasters usually seem to happen at weekends and this means finding the personal phone number of senior advertisement sales staff and ringing them at home.

• Good media selection and appropriate copy are crucial. An urgent, newsy style usually works best. And media owners, even at short notice, will discount space for charities at times of disaster.

• Sustained TV and press coverage. If the disaster is dislodged by subsequent news, ads can die.

• Absence of any conflicting disaster. Two simultaneous disasters tend to cancel each other out.

Communicating by letter

As with press advertising, my purpose in this book is not to look in detail at the different procedures and techniques of fundraising by direct mail. No other fundraising subject has been given so much attention or interest in the past decade as direct mail and it has been covered in many books, umpteen articles and in every fundraising seminar or conference that's ever been held.

Despite some of the problems and dilemmas of direct mail that I've outlined in chapter 6, the subject will continue to be described and debated enthusiastically throughout the 1990s because we can't do without direct mail and because direct mail can still work very well for our needs. I think it is the most challenging of all media, creatively and organisationally, and it can and should be a lot of fun. It may be in the future that some other and more effective means of floating our messages regularly before our donors will be found but I can't imagine what it will be, unless the technology can be found to beam fundraising messages via our prospects' central heating

Bleary-eyed and expectant your donors shuffle towards it.

systems, or something equally unlikely.

I am sure somebody is working on it, but meanwhile we have to make effective use of the postal service to deliver in reasonably good time and shape the unique messages we can create, print and insert into letter-box-sized packages. Direct mail remains our most frequent and most important communication with donors.

So I want to use the space within this section not to belabour the basics of direct mail fundraising but to consider how fundraisers can approach their use of frequent postal contact so as to best develop and exploit their relationship with donors.

Let's switch away from marketing theory and abstract concepts to perceiving direct mail the way our donors see it – as it arrives, uninvited, through the letter-box, tossed in indifferently by the postman to land in a jumbled heap on your welcome mat. Bleary-eyed and expectant your donors shuffle towards it, generally containing their mounting excitement at what wonders the postman might have brought.

Most people I meet are excited by the receipt of mail, particularly if it's unexpected. So the fact that your communication is uninvited can even be a plus. But excitement can easily turn into disappointment and even dismay if the unexpected message is a bill, or a tax demand, or bad news of any kind.

We all know this. What's the point of going over it here? Just this: most fundraising marketers plan their communications by thinking of themselves, what they need, what they want, what they have to say. The relationship fundraiser starts by thinking of his donors, what they want, what they need and what will interest them.

So perhaps our first objective should be to bring only good news. Something which is good for them, rather

If it looks like a sales pitch, the same negative applies. You don't sell to your friends.

than good for you. They're already irritated by having to get up in the morning. If you can brighten their day rather than add to the irritation, your communication will have a much better chance of working. If not, then first glance is all you'll get.

But be aware, as with everything else, there are exceptions to this. Some people will *always* respond to the cause, however the message is packaged.

Every fundraiser should have the hallway scene in mind when preparing any mailing. Whether it's an appeal, a questionnaire, a thank you letter, an invitation. Whether you're writing to thousands of people or to one individual. Stand beside them in the hallway and imagine how your letter will arrive and will be received. Watch how your partner receives his or her mail. Go and stay with friends, and watch them. Know what it's like when the mail arrives. Build the presentation of your package around this activity.

It's at this point that your understanding of your donors will be really valuable. You can then write to your donors where they are, not where some marketing agency thinks they should be, or wants them to be.

You cannot claim any depth of relationship with your donors if when you write to them your letter has the appearance of a mass-produced, mass-mailed communication employing obvious computer technology and techniques. You don't write to your friends like that. If it looks like a sales pitch, the same negative applies. You don't sell to your friends.

And you don't write to friends at well-spaced, convenient intervals that fit in with your marketing plan and preconceived notions of when to write. You don't write ritually on quarter days – you write when you have a good reason for doing so. So that tends to negate Easter appeals, and Christmas appeals and so on. I'm not

Try not to let donors see that as your reason for writing. Otherwise their response may not be what you wanted.

saying these are not the best times to write, they probably are. But try not to let donors see that as your reason for writing. Otherwise their response may not be what you wanted.

AICDA: attention, interest, conviction, desire, action. This is one of the first aids I learned as a copywriter. It used to be AIDA, and still is for most direct marketing copywriters, which might be a more memorable mnemonic. However someone who knew a little about fundraising clearly felt attention, interest, desire and action were insufficient for fundraisers, so added conviction. I don't know what an 'aicda' is, but I find it just as easy to remember. You need to give that kind of directed structure to all your communications. I also learned a lot of other things, sometimes the hard way, about what does and doesn't work in direct mail.

I'm going to make the rather risky assumption that you, the reader, have also had these tenets of fundraising-by-post thrust at you in various parts of your training and education for your fundraising job, so I will just go through the checklist very quickly. It always pays to remind ourselves of the basics and the checklist may even be of more use to you without the usual verbiage to describe what's often fairly obvious.

Like every other aspect of direct mail, the addition of a message on the outer envelope should be rigorously and regularly tested. In cold mail a message on the envelope almost always reduces response largely because it acts as a signal that an appeal is inside and so reduces opening. Any exception to this is usually a singularly clever or appropriate message, and these are rare. Or perhaps something which is intriguing and almost demands that the recipient opens the envelope. In warm mail the envelope message usually makes little difference either way, presumably because most donors

Constant testing of every aspect of direct mail really is essential because society is changing so dramatically ...

are prepared to hear from organisations they've supported before. However this is not tested often enough. (I would be interested to hear from fundraisers who have information on envelope tests.)

Constant testing of every aspect of direct mail really is essential because society – and our donors in particular – is changing so dramatically and people's understanding and opinions are evolving rapidly. What worked two months ago won't necessarily work next month. I especially advocate that you test concepts such as letter length, use of a leaflet or lift letter, the almost obligatory use of a postscript on a letter (surely donors are beginning to see through such devices?), underlining, use of a Johnson box, salutation and so on. It pays to keep testing constantly so that your message is as sharp as possible.

I advocate anything which makes your message seem individual to you and them – to your relationship. Start with 'you' and not 'we' and don't start by asking for money. Treat them as family. Let them recognise your need as their need. Share the problem. Tell your donors what you want them to do, give a clear and easy course of action (see reply coupons, this chapter). Remember that emotion always outsells intellect and get in plenty of little human details, action, case histories and first person quotes. Use simple, everyday language and write in an informal, friendly tone. Avoid all jargon and don't assume that your readers know all that much about what you do, or will have read your last letter or even any of those that went before. Make all your materials stand alone. Type your letter on a typewriter, don't have it set on any kind of typesetting system. And don't justify type. Remember that, in fundraising direct mail, neatness costs money.

Decide also not to refer to your written communications as mailings or even appeals. Mailings

What kind of a person writes to their friend as 'dear friend'? What kind of friend can't be bothered to use my real name?

and appeals are impersonal and presuppose a request for funds. Instead, talk about letters, news and special messages.

Personalise your warm letters. Of course you can test this against a 'dear friend' letter, but the personalisation will almost certainly cover its cost. Even if it didn't I'd still advocate its inclusion as worth the money. What kind of a person writes to their friend as 'dear friend'? What kind of friend can't be bothered to use my real name? Sending a circular is not what relationship fundraising is about.

The key word in regular letter writing to donors is *relevance*. Make your letter relevant, interesting, appropriate. Don't appear to take it for granted that they will respond every time. Talk about what their involvement enabled you to achieve last time, why it was needed then and who benefited. Let third parties tell their own stories of what that benefit meant. Give them many different ways to help. Keep it interesting, short, readable, structured. Remember the hallway. Make it a letter you'd like to receive yourself.

The ideal thank you letter

I think thank you letters are a much underestimated fundraising tool. Many fundraising organisations might benefit from paying them a little attention.

A short while ago I set myself the task of writing a multi-purpose thank you letter for one of my company's clients, and you can see the result on the next page . It is probably far from ideal. In true copywriter style I borrowed several components from other letters I'd seen, most noticeably from a superb new customer welcome letter I came across from a firm of UK publishers called Wyvern Books. Their letter, although addressed 'dear business manager' rather than

SPINAL RESEARCH
INTERNATIONAL SPINAL RESEARCH TRUST
NICHOLAS HOUSE · RIVER FRONT · ENFIELD · MIDDLESEX EN1 3TR
TELEPHONE: 081-367 3555 FACSIMILE: 081-366 7999
CHARITY NUMBER 281325

Mr and Mrs J Walsh
25 The Drive
St Ives
Cornwall
PL29 6DF   28 March 1992

Dear Mr and Mrs Walsh

I was delighted to receive you generous donation
of £75.00 towards helping us make the break-
through to a cure for paralysis caused by spinal
cord injury.

Donations like yours are the lifeblood of our
search for a cure. Now that scientists are making
such exciting and rapid progress, thanks to recent
leaps forward in medical research, your support
is having an even greater impact. We know it
will lead to real steps forward, making paralysis
caused by spinal cord injury a thing of the past.

Imagine what that news will mean to a young person
contemplating a lifetime in a wheelchair or to
those people who have been paralysed for years.
Your support may well mean that in the not too
distant future they will stand up and walk again.

We would like to thank you for your contribution
to our work by updating you from time to time on
the progress our scientists are making. Should
you prefer not to hear about our work, please
let me know. Meanwhile, if you have any queries
about research or fundraising questions, I'd be
delighted if you would
call me on the number
opposite.

Thank you once again.

Yours sincerely

Suzanne Yull
SUPPORTER SERVICES

**DO YOU WANT A WORD
WITH SOMEONE?**
Please call us if there's anything you'd like
to discuss.
● Elizabeth Liddell is our director.
● Suzanne Yull looks after all correspond-
ence with our supporters.
● Jacqueline Van Der Veen-Brown is our
financial manager.
We are all here to help you. Please call us on
081–367 3555.

Royal Patron
HRH THE PRINCESS OF WALES
Patrons
DUKE OF BUCCLEUCH AND QUEENSBERRY   BARONESS MCLEOD OF BORVE   LORD CRAWSHAW   LORD ENNALS
THE RT HON LORD PORRITT GCMG GCVO CBE   LORD WALTON OF DETCHANT   MR WILLIAM BUCHANAN   LIBBY PURVES
Trustees
DR H L FRANKEL MB FRCP   BARONESS MASHAM OF ILTON   LADY CULLEN OF ASHBOURNE
MR P EDMOND CBE TD FRCS   DR L S ILLIS MD BSc FRCP   S YESNER (FOUNDER)   J W A HICK   P M CLEMENTS
M P CURTIS   SIR CHRISTOPHER LEAVER

HOW THE INTERNATIONAL SPINAL RESEARCH TRUST WORKS

Until recently everyone believed that if you broke your back or your neck you'd be paralysed for life. Now scientists believe we're on the threshold of finding a cure. That's why we're here. To raise money to fund carefully chosen research to make this break-through. Quite simply, to enable people with spinal cord injury to get up and walk again.

WHY OUR WORK IS SO IMPORTANT

Breaking your back or your neck is easy. It can happen at work, at school, in the car or in the home. The effects are devastating. Some people lose all feeling and movement from the waist down. Others are paralysed below the neck – they can't hug anyone. That's why the search for a cure demands our fullest commitment.

WHO ELSE SUPPORTS ISRT?

Lots of people. Thousands of men, women and children with spinal cord injury, their families and friends and many more thousands of ordinary, concerned people. Sports personalities, celebrities and politicians are all helping us towards our goal. Our patron is HRH The Princess of Wales.

WE NEED YOUR REGULAR SUPPORT

Research is, by necessity, a long-term undertaking. That's why your regular support is particu-larly valuable. Because it enables us to plan very effectively for the future. A deed of covenant in-creases the value of your support by a third at no extra cost to you.

HOW WE CAN HELP YOU

We'd be pleased to send you our free newsletter and ideas and advice for fundraising events. Let us know the help you need and we'll try to make sure you get it.

OUR FRIENDLY COMPUTER

Our computer tries to get details of your name and address right, but if anything is incorrect, please let us know and we'll correct it immediately.

OUR MAILING LIST

From time to time we agree with other carefully selected charities to write to each other's support-ers. We only do so with charities whose aims are in sympathy with our own. If you would prefer to be excluded from this process, please tick this box ☐.

[...] YOU INTRODUCE A FRIEND TO US?

[...]ve or colleague who might also like to help spinal research, please add their [...] provided below. Of course they will be under no obligation to support our [...]nds we can get!

[...]rm in an envelope to Suzanne Yull, ISRT, FREEPOST, Nicholas House, River [...] you.

[...]*ends who may be interested.*

| Name |
| Address |
| | Postcode |

[...]TRA HELP THAT COSTS YOU NOTHING

[...] support to ISRT through a deed of covenant. This means that if you are a [...] the Inland Revenue the tax you have already paid. This increases your [...]esn't cost you a penny.

[...] how often you wish to give (it must be for a minimum of four years to be [...] send them to us at the above address. If you're already giving to ISRT by [...] fill in the deed of covenant, dating it to start on the date of your next banker's

[...]R FORM

| *(your full name in caps)* |
| *(your address)* |
| [...]de |

[...]ternational Spinal
[...]c (Enfield Town
[...]N2 6LY (20-29-77),
[...] of

£ _____   *(amount of each payment in words)*
every month/quarter/year* on the same day until
cancelled me in writing,
commencing on _____   *(1st payment date)*
(Please date this form about one month from today.)
and debit my a/c no. _____   *(account no.)*
accordingly.
To the Manager _____
_____   *(your bank name)* Bank
Branch address _____
_____   Postcode _____
Signed _____   *(your signature)*
Date _____   *• Delete as applicable.*
For office use only
When making each payment please quote no. _____

DEED OF COVENANT (TAX RECOVERY FORM)

I _____   *(your full name in caps)*
of _____   *(your address)*
_____   Postcode _____
hereby covenant with the International Spinal
Research Trust that for a period of _____ years*
from today (or during my lifetime whichever shall be
the shorter) such a sum as will after deduction of income tax at the basic rate amount to (write here the
amount you wish to donate)
£ _____   *(amount in each payment in words)*
each month/quarter/year**
Signed and
delivered by me _____   *(your signature)*
this _____ *(day)* day of
_____ *(month)* 19 _____ *(year)†*
in the presence of _____
_____   *(Witness's signature)*
_____   *(Witness's full name)*
_____   *(Witness's full address)*
_____   Postcode _____
* Your covenant must run for a minimum of four years to be valid.
** Please delete as applicable.
† This date should be the same as the first payment.

**International Spinal
Research Trust's thank you
letter is virtually a welcome
pack on a single sheet of
paper.**

That's brilliant relationship marketing. I'll buy their books again.

personally, struck me as a really well thought-out user-friendly communication that clearly told me everything I needed to know about how Wyvern Business Library could help me and my business. A summary of their service was included with details of their mission, their administration, mailing policy and even the chance to introduce a friend. It was almost a mini-welcome pack on a single A4 sheet. The bit I really liked – so much so that I copied it – was the box that asked, 'Do you want a word with someone? We are just a phone call away'. Then it listed who's who at Wyvern Books and what they did, and their final line before the number said, 'But we're all here to help. Call us.' The whole thing was very comprehensive and businesslike, yet it was done in such a friendly, helpful tone of voice that I decided to plagiarise it mercilessly as its approach is so appropriate for fundraisers. It is an example of brilliant relationship marketing. I'll buy their books again.

The other inspiration I borrowed was an idea Oxfam had many years ago of simply printing a covenant form on the back of their letter stationery. It costs next to nothing yet is a constant reminder of Oxfam's need for funds. I wonder how many of Oxfam's suppliers and business and trade contacts have covenants with Oxfam as a result.

In my example the text of the letter is individually laser-printed for each donor. What the illustration on page 216 doesn't show very clearly is that the stationery is in two colours and the information panel on the right is printed in grey, so the letter text really stands out.

These letters work hard for the cause. They look the part. Yet so many charities have pompous and impenetrable stationery, on which they write pompous and impenetrable letters.

That doesn't help the welcome mat in our imaginary

The newsletter is an automatic reason to write to your donors.

hallway to do its job. How welcoming are your thank you letters?

Newsletters and magazines

Several charities I know have tested the bottom-line value of including a newsletter or magazine with supporter mailings. Results have been mixed. Sometimes a newsletter adds interest, increases readership and lifts response. Sometimes a magazine seems to make little noticeable difference or may even distract from the appeal, and its costs of preparation and insertion clearly indicate that the charity is losing money including it. To be reliable these tests have to be done on a large scale over some time against a control group and even then the results can be misleading. Nevertheless, as a result of this kind of research, some organisations have stopped sending their newsletter or magazine and so have cut an important means of communicating with their donors in the interests of immediate cost-saving.

In relationship fundraising some form of regular platform for communicating with donors is essential. It needn't be a frequent full-colour magazine. It can be a low-cost four-page A4 newsletter printed in two colours and sent out just three or four times each year.

The newsletter is an automatic reason to write to your donors. You need no other excuse. It must be interesting, relevant, exciting, short ... an attractive and highly readable summary of what the organisation is doing, thanks to your – the donor's – help. It can have features of value and interest to the reader, as well as reporting on the charity, such as tips on exercise or health from a medical research charity, news on legislation and advice services from a disability group, and so on. In a relationship that can easily seem one-sided – you asking and them giving – the newsletter is a

Donors don't want waste paper. But they will really appreciate a good newsletter.

gift from the charity to interest and involve its supporters in the work they believe in.

From the organisation's point of view a quality newsletter repays its investment as it serves as an effective low-cost way of involving people in your organisation's mission.

But so many charity newsletters are appallingly done. They either neglect their readers entirely, drown them in too much information, or subject them to archaic or virtually absent design and unimaginative copy. A good newsletter will have a range of stories of different lengths and styles. A typical A4 four-page newsletter might have 10 to 14 different pieces from a short feature to 'snippets', including a strong lead story taking two-thirds of the front page. And, of course, it will use several, only excellent, photographs.

Donors don't want waste paper. But they will really appreciate a good newsletter and you will be able to use it for all sorts of productive purposes – to explain your philosophy, your new ideas, your latest campaign, how you use legacies, your helpful new booklet, to report on the last appeal, to give a brief trailer for the next appeal... The list of uses is endless.

Magazines more elaborate than the four-page A4 newsletter are perhaps more likely to fulfil a role for the charity, at a cost, than to make any direct contribution to fundraising income. However, that doesn't mean to say the informative, well-designed colour magazine cannot be readily justified. Many organisations need to keep donors informed of the detail, the people and the stories that make up their work, and a regular magazine can be the ideal vehicle. It can also pay you to inform your supporters in detail and to educate them in the issues and dilemmas that your organisation sometimes faces. But magazine production is demanding and expensive

This is one area where the accountant's cold logic needs to be balanced by the fundraiser's flair.

and too many charities do it badly. A bad publication does a lot of harm. Yet a really good magazine can make a unique contribution to relationship fundraising.

This is one area where bottom-line considerations certainly apply but where the accountant's cold logic needs to be balanced by the fundraiser's flair, imagination and enthusiasm for the long-term benefits of good donor communications.

A good newsletter or magazine form just a part of your communications with donors, but it is a crucial and highly versatile part. If it's well done it gives you unique opportunities to float your messages on the surface of your donors' minds, and ultimately into their consciousness.

The annual report

I won't say too much here about techniques and methods of annual report production except to refer readers to *The Complete Guide to Charity Annual Reports*, published in the UK by The Directory of Social Change. Although many of the examples seem quite dated now, much of what I would wish to say about the role and value of the annual report is contained in that publication.

The annual report is the one chance you have each year to present the entire story of your organisation, its news, its philosophy, its character, its commitment, its style and its methods of working. Your annual report is your case statement – for staff, for volunteers, for your trustees, for all your different types and levels of supporter, for other charities, for businesses and trusts, for the media and for suppliers and for many other specialist audiences. Consequently, its content, design, text, illustration, presentation and use are all vitally important.

Any publication without a covering letter is just a circular and will be treated as such.

The annual report can be very valuable for donors, particularly larger donors. You need to assess its cost-effectiveness for smaller donors and if you do decide to send it they will need to be told why it is being sent to them. It is also worth considering research into how your most important publication is viewed and used. Training is essential for all staff who will use the report.

Whatever you do, don't send your annual report to any donor without a personalised covering letter. You must also provide some means of response and some compelling reasons to do so. Any publication without a covering letter is just a circular and will be treated as such.

Reader response doesn't just prove that your message is getting through, it can pay for the whole publications exercise – and even show a profit.

The Royal Star and Garter Home, located at Richmond in Surrey, England, is a residential nursing home for disabled former members of the armed forces. Each year, it produces an illustrated annual report – a moving document full of dramatic human interest stories which is well-written and well-designed. In 1987 the report carried a shopping list of high-value items the Home needed. Within days of sending the report out, the top gift – £20,000 for an ambulance – had been pledged. Encouraged by this success the 1988 report contained another shopping list, this time with a top gift of £60,000 for a day centre. This time, within three days of sending out, one generous supporter pledged to give the Home that large amount.

To test further the value of their publication the Royal Star and Garter Home ran a split test, the only difference being that one half of the test segment received the annual report, whilst the other did not. The results shown overleaf speak for themselves.

Significantly, inclusion of the annual report didn't increase the number of donations, but it did encourage donors to give more.

This is not conclusive evidence of the value of sending a good report, but an efficient annual report or review can do a lot to encourage response as the points listed below show.

RSGH Mailing test results	
Without Annual Report	*With Annual Report*
Total mailed 1,473	*Total mailed* 1,473
Responses 379	*Responses* 368
Percentage 25.73	*Percentage* 24.98
Total income £15,917	*Total income* £22,383
Average donation £41.99	*Average donation* £60.82

Encouraging a response
1 Always send your publications with an explanatory covering letter.
2 Include a reader enquiry form listing multiple ways to help.
3 Encourage response in your editorial at every practical opportunity.
4 Include a coupon/donation form.
5 Enclose a freepost reply envelope.

Perhaps there is no ideal reply form, but certainly some are more appealing than others and many suffer from being downright unfriendly to the user. These discourage response so are expensive and wasteful.

6 Include a named individual to write/send to.
7 Invite calls to a telephone hotline/information line (ideally manned, not an answering machine).
8 Use a hook, if appropriate – a relevant incentive device, such as closing date, free offer, draw, competition, introductory subscription, invitation to a special event/reception.

The ideal reply form
Perhaps there is no ideal reply form, but certainly some are more appealing than others and many suffer from being downright unfriendly to the user. These discourage response so are expensive and wasteful. The following checklist may be a useful general guide, which you can adapt to suit the particular needs of your individual mailings. Please don't stick rigidly to any formula you may find in this list. The worst thing for all of us would be if all fundraising appeal forms were identical. We already suffer from this to some extent.

Reply form design considerations
The reply form has to be the hardest working piece in any fundraising communication. Its function is to provoke the most generous possible response from the potential or existing supporter. It is up to the design and copy to make this possible.

The objectives of the form are straightforward
• to reiterate the appeal
• to confirm the action the donor should want to take, including suggesting clear gift amounts
• to guide the reader easily through all aspects of information both on the front as well as on the reverse of the form
• to allow for the fact that the majority of the donors are middle-aged to elderly.

The appeal message should be a concise, emotive reiteration of the appeal.

(I have taken the following list from a more detailed version my company uses to ensure that when we prepare a reply form no important detail is left out.)

Size of form
It must be large enough to feature the information but tie in with the size of the outer envelope. Normally it will be the same size or double the size. If the form is folded it must be along the bottom so that it can be inserted mechanically. It must fit the reply envelope or should not have to be folded more than once to do so.

Appeal message
This should be a concise, emotive reiteration of the appeal described in the accompanying letter.

Action to be taken
There should be a line saying 'Yes, I want to ...' or some appropriate variation.

Donation values
Have a line saying 'I enclose my donation of ...' before tick boxes (with descending amounts if you prefer) in a large typeface.

Method of payment
This can be by cheque or postal order with the cheque made out to the charity's name. Make sure the charity's branch (if applicable), bank and account number are shown. Donors can also pay by credit card (check your organisation accepts credit card payments and which ones) – specify Access/Visa, etc and leave sufficient room for at least 16 digits for the card number and four for the expiry date. Then leave space for the signature, name and address of the cardholder.

Address label

Ensure sufficient space is left for the address label to be placed or for laser printing. Do not print corners or a rectangle as when the label is affixed mechanically it does not always cover the position guides and looks unsightly. Make sure there is enough white space around the label so that if the form moves in the envelope the print never shows through the window. On a warm mailing ask the donor to notify you if any of the details on the label have changed or are incorrect. You can include space for the donor to add their home phone number, if you wish. If you wish to carry out reciprocal mailings the form needs an appropriately worded clause allowing donors to opt out if they don't want to take part in reciprocal mailings.

Additional giving options

The donor might be motivated to give by the following:
• A shopping list explains what the donation values featured can either buy or achieve. Remember, the question most often in the donor's mind is, 'How much should I give?' Make sure that the tick boxes on the donation form correspond to your shopping list.
• A photograph of the appeal subject will round off the message. Unless the identity of the person(s) is obvious the picture should be captioned.
• A directional instruction also to complete the reverse of the form. UK charities usually put banker's order and deed of covenant forms side by side on the back of their reply forms. Together these somewhat forbidding instruments can enable UK charities to ensure donations are received reliably and regularly and to increase the value of each gift by reclaiming tax already paid on the donation.
• The words 'deed of covenant', the official name of the

Would your grandmother fill in this form? If your answer is yes then you have the right reply form.

form, must appear somewhere at the top of the form, but adding the more user-friendly title 'tax recovery form' helps to make it more acceptable to the donor.

• Both forms should have a friendly explanation of how easy they are to fill in, what benefit they give and that completion of the deed of covenant costs the donor nothing. It may be signed off by the person who has made the appeal in the letter. It is important to check the wording of the deed of covenant form against Inland Revenue guidelines.

• Always allow sufficient space for an older person to fill in information which has been requested. Reversed panels can help guide the reader to the sections which need to be filled in.

• The charity's name, address and registered number must always be featured on the reply form.

• If the address is not on a label affixed on the reply form codes must be added to identify the various list segments to be tested. This is most commonly done as a scratch-off code (ABCDEFG etc).

• Don't forget to say thank you.

• Would your grandmother fill in this form? If your answer is yes then you have the right reply form.

The function of the form is firstly to sell and secondly to make buying easy. In a way it is unfortunate that in order to do this it has to be written and designed. Neither of these requirements entitle it to be regarded as a work of art. You don't buy from a salesman because of his pithy delivery of lines or because of his gestures, you buy because you are convinced by what he says and because he facilitates your purchase on the spot. Think about that before you write or design your next form.

The coupon

The least helpful coupon I ever came across was in a

A reversed coupon implies either a terrific sense of humour from someone who wanted to resign anyway, or an agency that deserves to lose the client's account.

French magazine. The ad appeared on the right-hand edge of an early right-hand page – a very good position, from a response viewpoint. The problem was that the entire ad, including the coupon, had been reversed white out of black. Now, reversed type is a bit silly for any ad, because it's more difficult to read and should only be used for effect in short, bold copy in magazines. But a reversed coupon implies either a terrific sense of humour from someone who wanted to resign anyway, or an agency that deserves to lose the client's account. Unless, of course, French people all walk around with pens with white ink, for writing on black paper ...

Many fundraising ads do fall down at the coupon and again lose response and waste money as a result.

The advice given above for reply forms also relates to coupons but of course with the coupon you have much less space. So only the absolute essentials can go in as you still have to leave enough room for handwriting. And of course coupons should only ever appear at the bottom outside edge of the page for access and ease of removal.

Creative use of the phone

Talking to your donors on the telephone is the next best thing to being there. Without doubt, the potential of the telephone for fundraising is only just beginning to be realised and the coming months and years will see considerable and continuing expansion both in the extent of its use by fundraisers and in their methods of using it. I have no doubt this will be true, whatever legislation might do to curb telefundraising.

Whenever anyone mentions telemarketing, both fundraisers and donors in the UK tend automatically to think of invasions of our domestic privacy, some intrusive, pushy student stumbling through an ill-

If fundraisers generally are held in low public esteem, then telefundraisers have sunk out of sight.

thought-out script in an embarrassing attempt to pressurise us into buying something we don't want.

'I always hang up on them', we say, and wonder how on earth they can possibly make a decent living.

If fundraisers generally are held in low public esteem, then telefundraisers have sunk out of sight. I felt enormous sympathy with Robert Leiderman when I read the opening chapters of *The Telephone Book*, his entertaining explanation of how to use the telephone to find, get, keep and develop customers. It seems Robert can clear a room at parties even more quickly than I could, just by announcing his line of business.

Yet most objections to being telephoned are apocryphal or imagined. People think they don't like telemarketing calls because that's what they think they should believe or they've been led in the media to believe. If someone receives a call that is relevant to them, then he or she will not consider it to be either unsolicited or telemarketing. The calls people object to are almost all the classic – and objectionable – pushy telesales calls.

Why is it, I wonder, that so many charity trustees consider the telephone to be intrusive and unacceptable but have no objections at all to collecting house-to-house? In practice house-to-house is far more intrusive and more difficult to deflect. Yet I've never known a board of management object to house-to-house solicitation in the way so many object on principle to using the phone. The method of approach is neutral. It is how it is done that is either good or bad. The key is relevance. In that regard, telefundraising is no different from direct mail.

No sensible fundraiser concerned with the building of long-term relationships would wish to jeopardise her relationship by making unwelcome junk phone calls. But short-term opportunists might. The potential for

When it rings, it's answered. That's the power of the telephone.

considerable damage and distress obviously exists.

It's for you

One piece of professional conduct that might be enshrined in a code of practice for the telephone is that fundraisers should not make calls to any potential donor at home unless they have had a previous relationship with them. Another is that as soon as the phone is answered callers should be required to ask if now is a convenient time to call – and should politely and promptly end the conversation if it isn't.

When it rings, it's answered. That's the power of the telephone. It's a power that has to be wielded with great respect.

Some years ago I saw a presentation Robert Leiderman prepared for fundraisers to demonstrate the potential of the phone. When comparing the phone to direct mail he said, 'When did you last get out of the bath to answer a direct mail letter coming through your door?', meaning you would get out of the bath to answer your phone.

This didn't convince me. I enjoy my bath. I would try to drown the sound of the phone ringing, perhaps by singing more loudly or by splashing my rubber duck. If the caller persisted then I suppose, very reluctantly, I would get out and, dripping wet, clutching my towel, I'd trot downstairs to answer the wretched thing. How do you think I would react if the caller was someone trying to solicit a donation? Few things could be more calculated to dent my relationship with that charity, believe me!

So this power also has to be wielded with caution. Every time the phone is answered, telefundraisers should think that it might be me, or someone a lot bigger than me, who's just got out of the bath to answer it.

Scripting is just preparing what you want to say in advance.

But Robert's point is a good one.

When did you last stop a meeting to read a magazine ad? You did, to answer the phone.

When did you last tell someone to ring you back because you were watching a TV commercial?

When it rings, it's answered.

That makes the telephone the most intrusive advertising medium. Visiting by phone is exactly like visiting in person. As Robert Leiderman says, why should we be any less respectful of our hosts just because we are visiting by telephone?

The key is to ring the right people on the right subject at the right time with the right offer.

Relevance.

Just as it is an irresistible method of contacting donors, the telephone can also be irresistibly persuasive in the hands of an effective user of the medium. A good telefundraiser raised on relationship fundraising knows just when and how to use that power to develop and extend donor relationships. Fundraisers too often think they are dealing with yeses and noes. Most donors and potential donors haven't thought it out so clearly. The telephone is an ideal vehicle for approaching the maybes, the nearlies, and the lazies.

Don't be afraid to prepare a detailed and comprehensive script. Scripting is just preparing what you want to say in advance. Like any publication or direct mail shot, what you want to say to potential donors will be more effective if it is carefully structured and well presented. A good telefundraiser will use the script as a base, departing from it effortlessly as the need and the conversation dictates, returning to it when required to keep the focus of the call and avoid lengthy expensive and unproductive chats. If you use outbound telefundraising to any extent it will pay to have your script prepared by experts.

Robert Leiderman gives delightful advice about scripting in his book, such as, 'Write the way you talk, not the way you write', 'Cut the first three paragraphs, because almost inevitably it takes about three paragraphs to get the rubbish out of your brain' (that's also often true for direct mail), 'Forget the rules of grammar', 'Ask your granny if she understands the script', and lots more.

Inbound or outbound?

So far I've only mentioned outbound telefundraising – where you call them. Telefundraising can also be inbound, where they call you. And you can also use the telephone for events, research, lobbying and for other important purposes.

A word of caution: if you store research information on a database, be careful to let your donors know. You may be infringing the Data Protection Act if you don't. Similarly, if any research information is to be stored for later use in sales or fundraising, that would be infringing codes of practice. This doesn't mean you can't use research information for fundraising purposes, but you have to let donors know beforehand that this is what you are going to do.

I said in chapter 8 that one of the best uses of outbound telefundraising is in reactivating lapsed donors. Most donors fail to renew or continue their support simply through inertia. But however inert they may be, when the telephone rings, they answer it. As the calling charity already has a relationship and if the caller can represent their case cogently and compellingly, the donor will agree to renew, and will accept and sign the completed donation form that the caller will send to them the next day (note that to close the deal the

Even the most optimistic of pundits, however, is aware that these spectacular results won't last.

telefundraiser still has to rely on the post to get confirmation, unless the donor has given a credit card number). Often donation averages pledged by telephone are much higher than those achieved by mail. Many recipients of phone calls can be persuaded to take out covenants. And where reactivation mailings are achieving percentage response levels in low single figures, a well-conducted donor reactivation campaign by telephone can achieve reactivation rates of 60 per cent or more of successful contacts.

Each outbound telefundraising call will cost around 10 to 15 times as much as a direct mail shot, but provided an established relationship exists the results can easily be 10 to 15 times as successful. The benefit for the telefundraiser is that at the end of the campaign he or she will have more donors and as many times more net income, providing the campaign has been successful.

Even the most optimistic of pundits, however, is aware that these spectacular results won't last. As it did in the United States, responses in the UK will decline as more charities employ this method and donors become increasingly used to it and increasingly resistant. It may only last for a few more years, so if you wish to use the telephone for reactivation – get cracking!

I just called to say I love you
The phone is also a useful way of thanking important donors or of personally communicating some important news or information. For years Guy Stringer, when at Oxfam, used to ring larger donors (in the evening, at cheap calling rate) to thank them on the day that a particularly large gift had been received. This personal touch, he found, was widely appreciated and often brought in more, equally large donations. But one evening his call was answered by a particularly irascible-

What better way to bring hot news personally to the really important people in your organisation.

sounding gentleman. Guy asked for the lady of the house and the husband (for it was he) not surprisingly wanted to know who it was that was calling.

'Oh I'm the director of Oxfam', breezed Guy, 'and I wanted to thank your wife for her very generous donation of £200.'

Well, it transpired that the good lady had been making these gifts without her husband's knowledge or approval, and Guy got the impression that he was a little annoyed about it.

The telephone does have to be handled carefully, and Guy was in the perfect position to pour oil on troubled waters, to offer tactfully some comfort and reassurance to mend matters, while remaining at a safe distance at the end of the line.

This experience taught Guy the first and most important lesson of telefundraising – always speak directly to the donor. He also found you have to say immediately who you are, you have to be patient, subtle and you have to listen. Many donors welcome the chance to talk and will really open up to an interested caller, so the whole process can be taxing, if not exhausting.

But Guy also found that those donors who were telephoned far exceeded those who were not, in their interest, involvement and contributions to Oxfam.

News by phone

Charities live on news. They create it, they thrive on it. Fundraisers have access to newsworthy subjects in a way that is unthinkable for most commercial organisations. Charities deal with big issues, life and death subjects. You just have to watch the TV news bulletins, listen to radio news or look in your daily paper to see how effective fundraisers are at exploiting what's news.

Why not on the telephone? What better way to bring

If a disaster occurs overseas, you wouldn't think of writing to inform your key field staff.

hot news personally to the really important people in your organisation or to those people who can respond to the news with positive financial contributions.

If a disaster occurs overseas, you wouldn't think of writing to inform your key field staff whose response you hope will be to get to the disaster scene as quickly as possible. You'd telephone them to tell them immediately and avoid any possibility of delay.

So it should be with donors, whose response can be to provide the funds that you need to make your emergency operation possible.

Most donors would appreciate that call more than anything else you can do. We all like to be needed. Donors particularly like to see what their contribution can achieve. So if it's warranted, call them. You can hardly get closer, and their involvement can only increase.

The power of the lobby

Unity is strength and power. Many charities realised years ago that the combined voice of their supporters could be an irresistible force for change. Supporters' opinion can influence politicians and so alter legislation or create new laws. Often described as charity politicking, it is usually independent of any party politics and is simply a visible demonstration of a charity's potential to make the world a better place. Charities almost invariably lobby against injustice and oppression and for a better lot for mankind.

Both warm and cold direct mail have long been used to find potential dissidents, giving recipients who agree with the charity the chance to lobby either their own MPs or other figures of influence, usually by signing and sending pre-printed postcards to previously targeted individuals. Greenpeace has used direct mail to encourage supporters to lobby governments that have

Almost everyone tele-phoned agreed to do so.

transgressed the rules of the International Whaling Commission; Amnesty International has used it to lobby countries with particularly bad records of human rights violation; in Britain the Royal Society for the Prevention of Cruelty to Animals (RSPCA) has used it to encourage their supporters to press for national dog registration.

Now the telephone offers campaigning charities a much more effective, immediate and accessible means of encouraging committed supporters to take direct lobbying action.

The RSPCA has used the telephone to dramatic effect to support a parliamentary bill against the tethering of sows (female pigs). They called just over 6,000 people who had helped in a previous lobby to persuade them to contact their local MP to ask him or her to be sure to attend Parliament when the bill would be voted on.

Almost everyone telephoned agreed to do so.

Then, as a parting request, the charity asked for a small donation to cover the cost of the campaign. The results were staggering. The RSPCA raised almost enough money to cover the entire cost of the campaign but, more importantly, the sow tethering bill was easily passed. In fact, one Government minister told Gavin Grant, then RSPCA's Director of Public Relations, that never before had he heard of so many calls generated on a single subject. To give some idea of the scale of this success, it happened in exactly the same week as the deadline date given to Saddam Hussain of Iraq to get out of occupied Kuwait or face war, yet this same Government minister reported that British MPs had received five to ten times as many letters and phone calls on the subject of sow tethering as they did on whether or not Britain should go to war.

Other valuable uses of outbound telefundraising include helping upgrade current donors by explaining schemes such as deed of covenant, banker's order and Gift Aid, getting introductions to potential new donors from existing supporters and discussing other methods of helping with non-donors where an already established relationship exists – for example, petition signers, catalogue customers, etc. One fundraising sector that is making particularly good use of the telephone is education. What better way of approaching alumni than person-to-person, via the phone?

Just a call away

Inbound telefundraising is not likely to be nearly as contentious as outbound, but it is just as challenging and offers as many possibilities for the relationship fundraiser.

We are all already familiar with inbound telefundraising and, although they may not know it, most charities are using it already. Inbound telefundraising includes the use of a telephone number in a poster campaign, the 'freephone' number that appears at the end of a TV commercial or in the credits of a television programme (if you are lucky) and, increasingly, the press advertisement that has a phone number within the coupon.

You can encourage enquirers either to ring in to your switchboard, to ring a dedicated number that is manned at certain times, to ring in to a pre-recorded message/answering machine, or to ring a professional outside call-handling agency. Inbound telefundraising also includes your 'helpline' service or your customer service number that you advertise to encourage donors to ring in to discuss concerns, raise issues or even to complain.

Free or reduced-rate telephoning as a way of encouraging business is a relatively new concept for the United Kingdom. Advertisers at present can offer two free sys-

When you are using the phone as a response vehicle you are actually talking directly to your customers, your donors.

tems (freephone and 0800) and one nearly free (0345). Of course these are only free or nearly free for the consumer (0345 costs the consumer the same as a local call). The advertiser has to pay fairly steeply for each call. There is also the 0898 option, where callers pay a premium for every unit and the recipient can earn a useful sum from each call. Whichever system you use is largely a question of preference, of economics – I won't go into those here – and also the type of campaign you are planning.

For general customer service and answering complaints I recommend you try to secure the resources to do the job properly in house. When you are using the phone as a response vehicle you are actually talking directly to your customers, your donors. I wouldn't feel comfortable about leaving that responsibility in the hands of an anonymous outside operator. If an agency was involved it would have to be one that I could closely oversee and that I know to have first-class experience of fundraising and the donor/charity relationship. There's not too many of those at present.

In off-the-page advertising it is relatively easy to test the value (and the cost) of including a telephone number. The advantages are that your skilled and trained telefundraiser can refer callers to the benefits of covenants, to the convenience of credit card donations (where gift averages are almost always higher) and to discuss any other relevant scheme. And he or she can also discuss with callers the follow-up material that they will be sent.

The telefundraiser must be a skilled and highly trained operative, carefully prepared with a good, imaginative script that can be departed from whenever necessary and will never be spotted by the caller. As in every fundraising use of the phone, the basic approach has to be customer care, not pressure.

Fundraisers don't want dissatisfied donors out there in the cold. You want them on the inside, where you can work on them and change their minds.

The call of the wild

The telephone, with follow-up, is the best method of handling complaints. Then the complaint is immediately and personally acknowledged. Convincing the donor that their complaint is taken seriously is the most important component of complaint handling. According to some research in America only five per cent of dissatisfied customers actually complain. In my experience of talking to donors that's not an underestimate. In fact it may be much less for fundraisers because, by and large, donors really don't like to complain. So at least 95 per cent of the people who think you are awful won't actually let you know what they are thinking, but, according to this same research, they will each go out and tell between 10 and 12 other people how horrible you are – friends are like that.

That's bad news. You need to stop that. You need to increase the percentage of dissatisfied customers calling you – sounds weird, doesn't it? But think about it. Fundraisers don't want dissatisfied donors out there in the cold. You want them on the inside, where you can work on them and change their minds.

How many people stop buying a product because they've had a problem with it which, very easily, the manufacturer could have fixed if he'd known about it?

The phone is quicker than the mail for handling complaints and may be just as cheap. And it's more effective and you can be sure your customer is satisfied.

This is another area where first-class training is paramount. Operatives need to be trained in how to use the phone (there's far more to it than just knowing which end to speak into), how to answer questions, how to handle objections, the techniques of telephone sales and the use of scripts. It's just as important as training them in what your charity does. And really good people should be encouraged to depart from their script and do their own thing (within reason). Part of that training has to be to keep exemplary records of all phone calls and to record details of complaining donors, as they will be useful for further research.

When charities get round to establishing dedicated customer service departments, a donor service line will be an essential component. Of course not all calls will be complaints. Many will be from satisfied donors ringing in for a chat.

Encourage your donors to talk to you. Promote your helpline vigorously. The number to call should be clearly displayed on annual reports, on appeal reply forms, on everything you print and distribute to donors and potential donors.

If you can, offer an answering service that is always on hand to help – 24 hours a day, each day of the week. Some of the larger charities may be able to do this. Smaller organisations will find it is forgivable to offer an answering machine that promises a human response within 24 hours, so it has to be checked daily.

You might find that potential new donors will ring in also. You should encourage them. The telephone then would have a sales function.

Report back regularly to donors on how the phone-in service is being used. Describe its benefits and successes. Make a big thing of it.

You'll soon wonder how you ever managed to fundraise without it.

Even closer encounters
The closest you can get to your donors within the bounds of decency is to visit them in person.

Clearly charities already do this on quite a large scale, particularly in big gift fundraising or at a regional level.

We mustn't forget the potentially enormous benefits of encouraging donors to come and visit us.

With the exception of some of these campaigns, however, not many have planned the visiting of donors into their marketing strategy, have worked out cost/benefit equations for visiting or have established individual annual targets for visits.

As yet most face-to-face fundraising in the UK at least is for small change. Why is this? I predict a major shift here. Visiting donors is inevitably an expensive and time-consuming activity, but it has unique value in many areas of fundraising. I also predict that the first fundraising area to develop the potential of visiting general donors will be legacy marketing.

Once fundraisers start thinking seriously about their donors' needs, a range of fundraising products will follow which can best be promoted in person, such as investments, insurance and other individual propositions.

And, of course, we mustn't forget the potentially enormous benefits of encouraging donors to come and visit us. Again many charities are already doing this, but few are doing it in any planned or structured way.

This is the future, so inevitably there is some overlap with the next chapter, on opportunities, and with my final chapter, for which I have consulted my crystal ball. So I won't go on at length about visits here, but will come back to the subject later.

The benefits of face-to-face contact are considerable and largely obvious. I learned this in my first few days as a fundraiser, when my predecessor at the charity I worked for, who was showing me the ropes, was invited to a well-known seaside town on England's South Coast to meet two elderly single ladies who had given the charity substantial support in the past. I went along too.

In anticipation of further large gifts we had prepared a shopping list of goodies because, like most donors,

... I wanted to persuade these two donors to pay some of our press advertising costs.

these good women liked to be able to see where their money was going and to be able to imagine what it would achieve. Not surprisingly all our tangible products and propositions involved funding projects in our overseas programmes, but I had discovered on my arrival that the charity's real and immediate need then was for unearmarked general funds. So more in hope than in anticipation I had added a general fund project to our sheaf of overseas ones – I wanted to persuade these two donors to pay some of our press advertising costs.

We motored down to the South Coast and enjoyed a very civilised if rather formal afternoon tea with the ladies who were pleased to see us, happy to hear of the success of past work they had supported and quite prepared to hear of our further needs.

Over a toasted muffin and between sips of tea I had the chance to explain my rather unusual proposition, that a gift of the cost of an advertisement could repay itself many times over as the donors who would be recruited as a result would pay in far more over the years, for direct use overseas. Furthermore, if we could add a panel to our advertisement to explain that all costs of the advertisement had been donated by a generous supporter, that would generate further increased response. I had worked the whole thing out, including the cost of the ad, likely response and likely donation level. I could show that every pound they gave for advertising could be turned into three pounds for the charity's overseas work. It was a complicated and novel proposition. I doubt if I could have made it by letter or even by phone. The two ladies nevertheless appeared rather coy about volunteering their generosity there and then and we left our proposals with them. Later we received a cheque for £15,000, including £6,000 to pay for advertising in two national magazines.

Television is the instant medium. It is the reality substitute that sits in the corner of the living-room of every prospect you'll ever want to reach.

Unfortunately at that time the charity had no strategy for dealing with larger donors and I quickly became so absorbed in our general marketing that in my time there I failed to implement one. I regret to say that I never visited those two ladies again.

However, I believe the fundraiser who accompanied me, Ian Kerr, did. Ian went on to become a very effective independent fundraiser and is neither as young nor as foolish as I was. He is also considerably more skilled and experienced at visiting donors.

A few years later I visited the charity's programme in Burundi, in central Africa, and was driven around that impenetrable country in an enormous Chevrolet truck – one of our shopping list items that had also been bought thanks to the donation from our two ladies. If I had been a good relationship fundraiser I would have taken pictures of it and on return used that reason for another visit to the South Coast to show my donors the direct results of their generosity. They would have benefited and so would I. Oh, lost opportunities ...

Television

Television is the instant medium. It is the reality substitute that sits in the corner of the living-room of every prospect you'll ever want to reach. Almost without fail it is used and listened to and watched every day of the week.

How can anyone ignore television?

Most fundraisers have managed to – consistently. Many of those who have treated it rather more seriously since the IBA regulations in Britain were relaxed to allow charities to advertise on television are now regretting their interest. They have learned the expensive and rather painful lesson that television comes nowhere near likely to cover its costs when used as a fundraising

Direct response fundraising is likely to be the least successful use you can make of television.

medium in the same way as Unilever uses it to sell washing powder or Kellogg's to sell cornflakes.

Charities haven't begun to invest the necessary millions to build brand image by television and there's a good chance now that they never will.

In any event that seems to me to be the least interesting aspect of television for fundraisers: it was never likely to turn out to be a practical fundraising medium, certainly not for commercials of under two minutes' duration. Anything as long as that, of course, was equally doomed as prohibitively expensive.

As I write, however, one national charity is experiencing a direct payback from its TV ads, perhaps because it used a direct marketing agency with fundraising experience to produce the ad, rather than the head-in-the-clouds types who usually do these things.

I hope the response lasts and I'm proved wrong, but I still believe that direct response fundraising is likely to be the least successful use you can make of television. But it can be used for other purposes that are very important to fundraisers. Some of these other purposes require sophisticated back-up such as banks of telephone operators, response and information packs or retailer networks because, however powerful it is, television is one of the most transient of media. It is intangible. It is not a good medium for direct response.

John Hambley of Euston Films, London, says that television can create for you an informed and emotionally prepared audience, but you need to use methods other than television to turn the information into action and the emotion into giving. From fundraisers television demands advertising that seeks to inform rather than to persuade. It should make fundraising easier from a mass audience. It is fundamentally awareness advertising and it will only work if it can be sustained on a scale that is

For a brief time millions of people are unavoidably involved in doing something for the needs of others.

outside the reach of almost all fundraisers.

To get worthwhile exposure on television fundraisers have to take advantage of the programme makers' increasing need for good material. What interests the viewing public – drama, human interest, emotion, tales of advantage out of adversity, courage against the odds? What have fundraisers got if not access to all these things?

The fundraiser's skill is to seek sensible opportunities to promote his or her concerns and issues as usable material for the programme makers. This can often be done with great success, particularly by campaigning charities. The Sympathetic Hearing Scheme, a consortium of charities promoting care for the deaf in our society, managed to place a sticker displaying their distinctive 'ear' logo on the door of Alf Roberts' shop in Granada Television's *Coronation Street*, one of Britain's longest-running and most famous 'soaps'. That was at least eight years ago and it is still there, seen by nearly 18 million viewers three times each week. Not a bad bit of free publicity.

(I have another use for Alf Roberts and his famous corner shop. I hope someone will persuade *Coronation Street*'s scriptwriters to weave the subject of will-making into their plots so that, amongst other things, when Alf makes his will, along with taking care of his family and friends, he'll include a bequest to the Grocers' Benevolent Fund – see page 287).

ITV's *Telethon*, BBC's *Children in Need*, *Comic Relief* and so forth are other worthwhile uses of television that simply couldn't take place anywhere else. They show direct fundraising action to a huge audience made up mostly of people fundraisers could never hope to reach. For a brief time millions of people are unavoidably involved in doing something for the needs of others, which has to be a better use than television normally enjoys. But this is hardly relationship fundraising so I give it no more space here.

The fact is large numbers of people do respond to telethons often just because it's the thing to do, so are unlikely to become long-term donors. The British Red Cross Society, on the other hand, has successfully used outbound telefundraising to solicit worthwhile further donations from a large part of the audience that initially responded to their 'Simple Truth' appeal. So TV donors tend to be somewhat unpredictable.

Radio

Most of what I've said about television also applies to radio. Fundraisers should be targeting local and national radio for editorial purposes because local stations frequently need more good, relevant, editorial matter. Radio's advertising possibilities are also largely unexploited by charities and some, such as charities helping blind people, have particularly appropriate messages for radio. Watch this space. I predict radio will feature strongly in future in many charities' marketing plans. Radio reaches our donors in volume. We shouldn't neglect it.

Video

Last Christmas my father was given part of an elephant. It was a Christmas gift from my sister Jane who, like me, is a fundraiser and has an unusual sense of humour.

But this wasn't any old part of any old elephant. It was part of Taru, an orphaned baby elephant in Kenya that had been rescued by an organisation called Care for the Wild.

My father was now part sponsor of Taru, and with his commemorative certificate to record this event came a 20-minute video which showed Taru at play with his

I predict a busy future for Care for the Wild just in answering enquiries from the Scottish Highlands.

other little elefriends and told his history and explained his needs.

Father proudly showed this video to me as he has shown it to many other visitors. I'd never sought to have an elephant as half-brother, but this endearing film brought the concept alive and gave Taru a personality and a reality that I would otherwise have missed.

That is the power of video. Heaven help dad now if he fails to renew his sponsorship ...

Next year he'll get another video to show him how Taru has developed and to introduce the triumphs and trials of rearing orphaned elephants for return to the wild. Our entire extended family is now hooked on Taru. And as each new visitor to our house runs the risk of meeting our recently acquired relative too, I predict a busy future for Care for the Wild just in answering enquiries from the Scottish Highlands.

Videos can also be widely used for other relationship building purposes, particularly in explaining new and complex situations and in making the organisation's work come alive. A very high percentage of donors have a video cassette recorder. Fundraisers can send videos to donors which they can keep for a small fee or can return after viewing. The fundraiser can then re-record over the tape when it is returned, for subsequent use.

But the days of video publications are not here yet. Costs are not just high, they are perceived to be very high. In real terms video production costs have dropped compared to print in recent years but the perceived higher cost still remains. When video publishing appears regularly in the bookstands, that's when charities should consider the possibilities again. It won't be long.

Meanwhile, there is always the video party (see pages 196 to 198). Or why not use video as Care for the Wild has done?

... And the rest

There will be many other ways of reaching donors that are impractical now but may work well in the future. Cable and satellite television, cinema, door-to-door, media cards, piggybacks, joint communications, and so on. All are potentially useful ways of reaching donors and fundraisers must be constantly vigilant to ensure no worthwhile avenues are overlooked.

The integrated approach or getting it all together

No single method of approach should be seen in isolation from the others. No single contact should be considered without considering all the other contacts that have gone before or will follow. The secret of donor communication is to operate an integrated total communication strategy – total relationship fundraising. This involves seeing your contacts with the donor entirely from the donor's point of view, and resisting the temptation to divide your marketing into neat little parcels, allocating one function to one department and the next function to another, and never the twain shall meet. If your communications are integrated the donor will receive relevant, coordinated and continued communication and will be informed, involved and motivated without being inundated or overlapped, or irritated by inappropriate contact.

If this is happening, with all donor contact emanating from one central point, then true segmentation can begin to be practised. Some donors will hear from you only once or twice a year. Others will hear from you every month. Some will hear on only one or two subjects, others will know about every aspect of your work. Some will get letter copy A, others will get letter copy B, and the rest will get one of the other 24 letters you now send to your superbly segmented donor file. No longer will everyone get the same mailing, in the fundraiser's version of grape-shot. In the future, each contact will be finely targeted and precisely timed. With its subject, content and tone of voice just right.

That's relationship fundraising.

ACTION POINTS

▲ Beware of vague concepts in promotion, such as awareness. Always seek ways to measure your results.

▲ See how donors react when they receive their mail. Subject all your communications to 'the hallway test'.

▲ Make sure all your letters have AICDA.

▲ Test, test and test again. Never give up testing.

▲ Don't always ask for money. Look for opportunities to give your donors something in return.

▲ Don't talk about appeals and mailings. Call them letters or messages.

▲ Always send a letter with your publications. And include a reply device too.

▲ Give your donors only interesting material. It will pay in the long run.

▲ Check your reply forms and coupons. Replace those that don't have all the essentials.

▲ Make better use of the phone, both inbound and outbound.

▲ Promote your helpline vigorously on all your printed materials, even your letterhead.

▲ Prepare an individual, appropriate and variable thank you letter. See if you can give it some of the functions of a welcome pack.

▲ Train your telefundraising staff well. Don't leave any aspect to amateurs, any more than you would assign a new recruit to manage your direct mail.

▲ Keep good telefundraising records.

▲ Encourage complaints. Use any device you can. Set up a donor complaints facility.

▲ Plan donor visits into your annual strategy. Establish targets and costs per visit.

▲ Encourage donors to come and visit you. Invite them to special occasions at your office.

▲ Exploit radio and television's increasing demand for good news stories.

▲ Consider how your organisation can make appropriate use of video.

▲ Integrate all you donor communications through one central point – your donor service department.

DONOR PROFILE

Ian Dunlop

Ian is 34 and very active. If he had been born 15 years earlier he would definitely have been a hippy or even a beatnik, but the establishment at his school simply consider him a scruff.

He is untidy. Ian drives an old VW van and belongs to a club of similarly scruffy people who go scuba diving and pot-holing at weekends. During the week Ian is a teacher of geography and a very good one. Popular with his pupils, if not with his headmaster, Ian has single-handedly started just about every conceivable type of spare-time activity in the school, from boating and mountaineering clubs to the local chapters of Greenpeace and Amnesty International.

Ian believes in education for change. He sees the organisations he supports as resources for him and his students, sources of information, display material and campaign ideas. They also give him a channel for action that Ian *knows* will work.

Ian is no passive armchair supporter. He has campaigned for recycling facilities from the local council, lobbied Parliament over the development aid budget, written dozens of letters to prisoners of conscience and pedalled 60 miles for parrots, raising money and publicity for the campaign against the live import of exotic birds. In each of these endeavours, and more, Ian is supported by an enthusiastic and growing group of young pupils from his school who have been encouraged to see that charitable support is only truly effective if backed by positive political action.

The promotional materials and education packs produced by the charities to support these campaigns are a great help to Ian. He has papered the walls of the staff room with posters and slogans, and now instead of objecting or muttering under their breath many of his colleagues come up and ask him about the campaigns and sometimes make more positive gestures of support.

Ian is now planning two major initiatives which he wants to introduce to his school when the moment is right. The first will involve bringing one of the major environmental charities into the classroom on a formal basis to provide tuition on specialist environmental themes contained within the new national curriculum. That's not controversial. The second idea may take more selling to the headmaster. Ian wants the whole school to join in an official walk against whaling, culminating in a candlelit vigil outside a certain Scandinavian embassy.

Ian's not optimistic, but he is going to give it a try. He has a fall-back option if it doesn't work – a full-scale sponsored walk within the school. Ian is banking on the fact that his headmaster hates sponsored walks so much that the alternative may even seem appealing.

10
Some opportunities

'I was seldom able to see an opportunity until it had ceased to be one.'

Mark Twain
Pudd'nhead Wilson

Fundraising is all about opportunities. Recognising opportunities, discovering opportunities, creating opportunities, developing opportunities, seizing opportunities, turning ideas into opportunities ... Mark Twain would have been a lousy fundraiser.

Despite recession, despite greatly increased competition, despite the pace and scale of recent developments, there have never been more opportunities for relationship fundraisers than now.

Some of these opportunities have been covered in earlier chapters: creative use of the telephone, meeting donors, a thank you and welcome policy, reactivation campaigns, setting up a complaints line, establishing central service facilities, and so on. The most important opportunity of all, legacy marketing, is so substantial and remarkable in the potential it offers fundraisers that I feel it deserves a chapter all on its own (chapter 11 *The Last Great Fundraising Opportunity*). But other opportunities abound and I'd like to review a few of these here.

You won't have to rent a tuxedo, hire a limo, come out on a rainy night or make small talk with all those vacant glitterati.

The non-event

Very often opportunity arises out of adversity and that is usually when the best ideas are formed. The non-event is just such an idea and it is marvellous because it involves almost no work and gives people an unchallengable excuse to do just what they most want to do – nothing!

In the United States now fundraising events have reached saturation point in some areas. There are just too many big-ticket events. For some people (presumably those strange individuals who just can't say no) charity events had become a real problem because they never had a free night in their social calendar to stay home and watch TV. For the organisers, market saturation meant diminishing returns and, of course, the ever-present danger with big events – failure to cover costs.

Enter the non-event.

'Send us your $500 and stay at home.'

That was the offer. You won't have to rent a tuxedo, hire a limo, come out on a rainy night or make small talk with all those vacant glitterati.

Just stay at home and feel good.

The non-event organisers went even further. They sent 'participants' (I use the term loosely) a bottle of rather nice champagne to help them enjoy the evening, snug in the knowledge that by taking part in this state-wide non-event they were helping to raise huge amounts of money for the cause.

And it works very well. Some charities now claim that the non-event is their most cost-effective method of raising funds. How long it will work? Who knows? How long before John Q Public and his wife start complaining that they've got just too many non-events to go to and there just aren't enough evenings in the week? Who knows? Who cares?

Grab the opportunity while you can.

Donors don't like it when fundraisers take credit for their successes. To come between the donor and the footlights is bad manners.

Getting the best out of people

Too often we approach fundraising activities as if they were a matter of technique, that all we have to do is mechanically follow procedures and all will be well.

This definitely isn't so. The greatest opportunities of all arise from the fundraiser's ability to get the best out of people. Fundraising is a people business, not a procedures business.

'If anything goes bad then I did it. If anything goes semi-good then we did it. If anything goes real good then you did it.

'That's all it takes to get people to win football games for you!'

The above quote is from an American football coach called Paul Bryant. I found it in James Gregory Lord's book *The Raising of Money*.

Donors don't like it when fundraisers take credit for their successes. So you should always take due care to remain in the background, like the football coach, taking complaints and criticisms but never the credit. To come between the donor and the footlights is bad manners.

Provide involvement

James Gregory Lord also tells his readers that the way to raise real money is to provide real involvement. Obviously there are countless different ways of providing involvement but the key word here is not involvement, it is 'real'. Fundraisers have to differentiate between tricks and gimmicks – so-called 'involvement devices' – and real, sincere involvement. Bernie Cornfeld, the insurance swindler who ran Investors Overseas Services, had a favourite question of all potential recruits to his organisation which, at first glance, seemed to provide an obvious answer. He asked, 'Do you sincerely want to be rich?' Naturally all the

Donors have a right to be involved in your charity, just as shareholders have a right to be involved in the companies they partly own.

eager young people who came knocking on Bernie Cornfeld's door answered affirmatively, but Cornfeld wasn't just asking if they wanted to be rich. Obviously everyone would answer yes to that. The key word was 'sincerely'. 'Do you *sincerely* want to be rich?' To Bernie Cornfeld this meant that chasing riches took precedence over *everything* else. Applicants had to be sincere enough to work all hours, doing whatever they were asked, sacrificing friends, family and all other interests. Real involvement, of course, needn't go that far. But it has to be real, not illusory.

Donors have a right to be involved in your charity, just as shareholders have a right to be involved in the companies they partly own. As investors both the donor and the shareholder are entitled to influence and active involvement.

Major gifts

Providing selected donors with the opportunity for real involvement gives the fundraiser a ready means of setting up a major gift campaign. I said in the introduction to this book that I would not comment in any depth on this area and I won't. But it is one of the most challenging opportunities available to the strategic fundraiser so I can't leave it out entirely. Like so many other areas of fundraising, success in big gift fundraising depends upon the development of effective donor relationships.

There is no minimum or maximum gift size that qualifies a campaign to be termed 'big gift'. The common characteristic is that all gifts in a big gift campaign are solicited face to face and the amounts given tend to reflect that personal approach.

For many campaigns, particularly specific or tangible appeals such as a new hospital wing or a university chair

The really difficult part in big gift fundraising is not in getting people to give money, it is in getting people to ask.

where general public appeal is limited, the most likely route to success is via a major gift campaign, carefully planned and targeted towards those rare individuals who can make substantial individual donations. In these campaigns often a small group of people can be so focused and cultivated that less than a hundred donors are needed to take a multi-million pound appeal over its target. On average, half of the targeted figure will come from just ten or twelve donors. The keys of big gift fundraising are careful planning and unhurried assembly of all the crucial components. The fundraiser's skills are in motivating a carefully selected group of donors to do the asking and enabling them to ask their peers for the *right* amount of money at the *right* time.

The really difficult part in big gift fundraising is not in getting people to give money, it is in getting people to ask. For no fundraiser will make any headway if he or she attempts to solicit big gifts themselves. That is a job for other people – other donors. It is the perfect example of active involvement from donors, but it is not easy.

Most people in Britain seem to have great difficulty in asking. It's a national failing. We want to ask and we know we should, but just at the crucial moment we stumble, apologise and our palms begin to sweat. No matter how carefully and diligently you have built up to this moment, if this happens, the asking is usually diluted or fudged and loses its impact.

Unfortunately, in Britain even many paid fundraisers don't like to ask for money either, so would-be volunteers often find little inspiration from the professionals.

Shyness when it comes to asking is not unique to Britain. Many other countries don't have any significant culture of asking for money so it becomes a rather abnormal and frightening thing to do. The French seem

....there's something very pleasing about the big gift concept, where one of the rich's own leaders actually does your stick-ups for you.

to abhor it. There's something in the Gallic character that rises up against the need, or even the very suggestion of the need, to ask for money for a cause.

Not so in America. The American people have been reared on fundraising. It's part of every community, every neighbourhood, every childhood. Asking for money is as natural to Americans as watching television.

One way to make asking easier is to ensure that the asker has already made a very big gift (even the lead gift) him or herself. This makes their request almost irresistible to members of their peer group, who after all are not going to be outdone by one of their own.

If you subscribe to the Robin Hood view of fundraising (see page 34), where the fundraiser's role is considered as redistributing wealth from the rich to the deserving poor, then there's something very pleasing about the big gift concept, where one of the rich's own leaders actually does your stick-ups for you.

Big gift campaigns are essentially volunteer programmes where the volunteers are usually local eminent individuals or captains of industry and commerce, what is often termed 'the great and the good'.

They are volunteers for your cause, just like the woman who stands behind the counter of your charity shop, clutching a mug of tea and looking as if she owns the shop. Volunteers work best if they feel a sense of ownership of their project. In big gift fundraising this is essential. They are the heroes. The professional fundraiser's task is to treat them well, to keep their sights high and never to let them feel anything other than vitally needed. Good relationships are paramount.

If a committee is necessary, and most big gift campaigners seem to believe it is (I can't quite understand why committees are still seen as important to the human condition – 'search your parks in all your

All potential members must earn their place all the time, work hard and be the most generous and regular donors.

cities, you'll find no statues of committees'), then it is essential that the volunteers themselves elect it and choose its leader. Let them think of it as the campaign cabinet if they wish and encourage them to have whatever fun they can while raising your funds.

However, the forming of the committee is not an opportunity to add a lot of illustrious names. This is 'real' involvement; there must be no token attenders or committee servers. Chuck them off. All potential members must believe it is a privilege to serve on this group and to help the cause in such a vital way. They have to earn their place all the time, work hard and be the most generous and regular donors. Their role must be to ask identified persons for prearranged specific sums. If they feel ownership of the appeal, they will do it. In return you have to agree with them a finite time scale, a finite number of hours they have to give and to provide them with a written list of their responsibilities. Then you can be quite certain that their contribution is defined and understood. In the politest possible way you can ask them to account for it later just to emphasise that their responsibility is real and not a token.

There are a few fundamentals to big gift fundraising:
1 a succinct, clear and persuasive case
2 accurate identification of the donor constituency
3 good leadership from sound and committed volunteers
4 immaculate direction from the fundraiser.

With the enormous escalation of capital appeals in Britain recently it seems likely that those potential donors who will do the asking, who are one of the most important cornerstones of every big gift campaign, may soon be in short supply. Meanwhile, fundraisers are establishing big gift campaigns for all they are worth and are achieving some noteworthy successes. If the

Those relationship fundraisers who have cultivated their donor/ askers over some years will still be able to mount big gift campaigns, come what may.

competition for good donor/askers does become tougher, then my bet is that those relationship fundraisers who have cultivated their donor/askers over some years will still be able to mount big gift campaigns, come what may, because the donor/askers will stick with them.

Pricing and propositions

I have already mentioned price in chapter 7 (pages 152 and 153) in terms of its importance in any fundraiser's marketing plan. It seems to me that strategic pricing represents some worthwhile opportunities for fundraisers, because in the past so little thought has been given to the price of fundraising propositions, and fundraisers have often failed to let market forces naturally fix their price levels.

The addition of prompt boxes to reply forms and coupons was one moderately successful way of attempting to influence price for general charitable donations. The average giving level, however, is still too low. When the proposition is general it seems very difficult to persuade the average donor to raise his or her sights. It is a curious imbalance but when confronted with a tragedy on the scale of, say, the famine and starvation that faced millions in Ethiopia, the typical member of the public responds with a gift of around £10. Of course, the public is constantly being asked to respond generously and does. But £10 or £15 against such a large need is a drop in the ocean and the public knows it. However, £30 can buy a plough with which an Ethiopian farmer can double the yield from his tiny plot of land, not only enabling him to feed his family but also to have a small surplus for sale in the local market.

In this example the donor can see where his money might go and what it might achieve. Many donors would prefer to give £30 to an identifiable, comprehensible goal than to give £10 to a general appeal. This technique is well understood by the international aid agencies in whose programmes small amounts of cash can achieve great things: £3 can immunise a child against five killer diseases, £10 can make a blind man see, and so on.

But is it used enough? And can some home-based charities not make better use of it than they do? We know the public likes it.

The Ryton Gardens appeal mailing, which could be recycled as seed pots, was hugely successful in financial terms, but was its success due to its intriguing format, its 'big idea', or because it got the pricing right? Ryton invited donors to sponsor their work at different levels – an ordinary sponsor at 50p a week, a seedsman sponsor at £1 a week, a cultivator sponsor at £2 a week and a gardener sponsor at £5 a week. Appropriate benefits were offered at each level. People did indeed come forward and sign on as gardener sponsors, paying £260 per annum. For them, the price was right. They could make the choice themselves. If they hadn't been given the chance, they might just as easily have given £10 only and the Ryton Gardens appeal would not have been nearly so successful.

This, of course, is as much a question of identifying the proposition as deciding the price. The two are inextricably linked. But consider again the £3 that immunises and protects a child. What a proposition! People would flock to send their three pounds. But because the unit cost is so low, it may not be worth the charity's while to service them or, to put it another way, perhaps the price could be increased without affecting overall response.

Basically there are two principal ways of fixing price. By considering the unit cost of production and adding a percentage for profit and contingencies, or by considering how much the market might bear. (There is a third option which is to base your price on your competitor's charge.) Fundraisers use all these methods but, in my experience, whichever they choose they often aim too low. Perhaps this is because fundraisers have always been badly paid, so they over-estimate the value of money. Of course, for the donor price relates to benefits and so £3 to protect against five killer diseases and £10 to make a blind man see represent almost unbelievable value for money. The price is so low I expect it puts many people off, because they find it simply incredible and they can't relate the enormity of the action – saving a life or saving someone's sight – to such a small amount. Price testing – offering the same product at two different prices – is not permitted in Britain but it would be interesting to split-run these offers against doubled or even trebled amounts to see what the difference in response would be (see page 262).

A donor's ability to pay, however, depends to a large extent on his or her perceived disposable income. As fundraisers are usually offering intangible products or propositions it makes sense to offer them across a range of prices, such as the Ryton Gardens example. Where the product or service is tangible, however, as it is with child sponsorship, the fundraiser has to find an optimum pricing level above the cost of providing the service but below the point where too many people will drop out because they can't afford it. A fundraising 'product' such as child sponsorship can justifiably be priced high as the cost of recruitment and administration is high and demand is not noticeably price-sensitive. Even if demand does fall as the price increases, the fundraiser may still find this a preferable situation as fewer donors will now be paying the same or even more money, and

Membership cost might be priced towards the lower end of their price spectrum because the organisation does not wish to deter people, purely on the basis of cost.

the costs of administration will be less.

The downside is that, in theory at least, fewer children will be able to enjoy the benefits of sponsorship.

But child sponsorship remains one of fundraising's most appealing and effective products from the donor's point of view. It has enabled charities to present a £100-a-year proposition that is bought by people from all walks of life, from the residents of mansions to those who live in council flats.

Sponsorship schemes clearly show the advantages of 'thinking monthly' when structuring product prices. Donors on monthly subscription give a lot more, with less thought and concern. It makes sense. Most people are paid monthly. And £200 seems a lots of money to give in one go, but £20 a month appears much more manageable to most donors.

At the other end of the scale, membership cost for an organisation that supports the victims of a disabling disease might need to be priced towards the lower end of their price spectrum because the organisation does not wish to deter people who should be benefiting from membership purely on the basis of cost. However, the price should not be so low that the scheme becomes a drain on the organisation rather than a benefit. That's why different price levels are so important. 'From each according to his means' is just as important for fundraisers as 'unto each according to his needs'.

The first thing an organisation must decide in developing a pricing strategy is what it wants to achieve. If you are seeking to build a large database for future development there is no value in setting the price of entry too high. Fundraisers often find a conflict between maximising their surplus (ie making a profit) and maximising their market size. This is why pricing policy is so important and why charity managements or boards

Whatever you do, don't overlook price. That would be to miss a worthwhile opportunity.

of governors must understand what the objectives of your policy are. For example, the objective of cold direct mail is to build a donor list. It is regrettable that this process will cost rather than raise money, but it is now a fact of economic life.

Raising the price would almost inevitably lower the response, so fundraisers – and their boards – have to accept this as an instance where they must speculate to accumulate, where it will take a long time, perhaps many years, before that investment is repaid.

When you have decided on your pricing objective you can then consider whether your pricing strategy should be cost-orientated, based on market tolerance, or led by your competitors. Whichever you choose, price is a potent and effective tool. You can lower it, to stimulate demand, or raise it to take advantage of high demand or donor indifference to price. You can use price to promote a particular proposition such as group membership, which might attract a lower price, or to introduce supporters to a new project, which might attract a higher price to cover start-up costs.

But whatever you do, don't overlook price. That would be to miss a worthwhile opportunity.

Creative targeting

While discussing price it is also worthwhile considering the negative and positive influences of targets. Fundraisers frequently publicise huge financial targets and often the effect of this is to demotivate rather than impress. Many donors are deterred by an appeal for millions. 'Against such a huge target', they think, 'what difference will my £15 or £20 make?'

Setting the right level of target, just like the donkey's stick and carrot, can have a major influence on your appeal.

Two examples from Britain's NSPCC illustrate this point. In a split mailing test the NSPCC selected three identical segments of its donor file and sent each group letters that were also identical but for one tiny change. The letter to the first group mentioned an appeal target of £1 million, the second group's letter mentioned a target of £100,000 and the third's just £10,000. The response was good at £1 million, but better at £100,000 and best of all at £10,000, probably because donors felt encouraged that that amount was attainable and their contribution would make a difference.

Targets can also be strategic. At the planning phase of the NSPCC's Centenary Appeal some of the charity's committee members suggested a target of £5 million. They felt that was certainly achievable and it would be good publicity for the appeal to succeed. The NSPCC's appeals director argued for a much higher target of £12 million on the basis that they might fail and only raise £8 million, but an £8 million failure was better than a £5 million success.

The appeals director's argument won the day and the appeal went on to raise £16 million.

Sponsorship of publications

One of the features of successfully grasped opportunities is that they often involve recognising when a situation has changed and taking advantage of it before anyone else has realised what's happening. I have said more than once in this book that fundraisers are surrounded by change. This leads to many opportunities.

One visible and easily demonstrable change in the UK in recent years has been the quantum leap in the quality of fundraising publications. All fundraising organisations are prolific publishers: annual reports, reviews, newsletters, magazines, leaflets, posters and

Good publications cost money, although, it has to be said, not as much as bad publications.

more. Every fundraiser relies on the printed word to communicate his or her message to large and varied audiences wherever they may be.

Good publications cost money, although, it has to be said, not as much as bad publications do. They are a very tangible and potentially attractive part of any fundraising programme.

So they can be sponsored.

A little while ago no donor in his or her right mind would have wished to sponsor the kind of publication produced by a British charity, or college, or medical centre. Of course, there were exceptions, but not many.

In the past the dismal affairs most fundraisers used to send out deterred corporate sponsors. The melancholy drabness that once characterised British charities has no appeal for their corporate counterparts. But all that has now changed. Fundraising organisations of all colours are now making efforts to present themselves in better light. Commerce and industry, surely, can be persuaded to support these efforts and to direct their largess towards financing such obvious evidence of a good cause.

This kind of support is most likely to appeal to a corporate donor who might welcome in return the opportunity to display their generosity through some kind of credit, such as their logo, and some words of thanks discreetly placed on the back page.

Some companies already sponsor charity publications and one or two can clearly be seen to prefer this way of helping. But fundraisers have not sold the opportunity very well so far.

Corporate sponsors need to see what they are supporting. They need physical evidence that you intend to produce a far superior model to their established notion of charity promotion. They will need to know who will get the brochure, how it will be distributed and what purposes it will achieve. If you have already produced a new-style report they may feel you don't need the money. If you have not, they may need convincing by a detailed plan of your proposed contents and structure for the publication, accompanied by well-presented design visuals to show how it will look.

And don't forget to include their logo in some reasonably prominent place.

Commercial partnerships

Numerous other opportunities exist within the general area of corporate fundraising, many in areas so complex and even risky as to render their description beyond the scope or remit of this publication.

A major component of corporate fundraising or joint ventures with commerce is that both parties must benefit in recognisable ways. If they do, the venture will almost certainly be a success. Here some cooperation between charities (and other appropriate causes) would certainly be worthwhile. Commerce needs to take charities seriously, to see them as valuable partners and to include them automatically when drawing up plans.

For fundraisers the most important opportunity is in establishing and developing partnerships with selected appropriate commercial organisations. These can be short-term – for example, a charity's selection as 'Charity of the Year' for a high-profile organisation – or they can be longer-term, often lasting for many years. Fundraisers need to build the kind of relationships with companies that will make more such partnerships possible.

A central service agency promoting fundraising opportunities to possible commercial partners would seem to me to have practical value. Such an agency might considerably enhance fundraisers' opportunities

It also acts as a clearing house to unite interested companies with a host of relevant suppliers from whom the customer can choose. It's a bit like a marriage bureau.

to link with big business. In practice this central agency might operate along similar lines to the Direct Mail Sales and Service Bureau, which centrally promotes the medium of direct mail to every kind of business. It also acts as a clearing house to unite interested companies with a host of relevant suppliers from whom the customer can choose. It's a bit like a marriage bureau.

Such a bureau would be invaluable for fundraisers in a number of areas: locating customers for corporate entertainment/hospitality at events, finding sales promotion partners, stimulating companies interested in employee fundraising, developing affinity marketing opportunities, and so on.

It could sort out impractical approaches and issue warnings about industries looking to use charitable partners in undesirable ways, such as to upgrade their tarnished image.

I am not advocating an exclusive system where the central service agency would take over the fundraising and relationship-building role of the individual organisations; far from it. That doesn't happen with the Direct Mail Sales and Service Bureau and it wouldn't happen with fundraising.

Employee fundraising

Many companies can boost their staff's morale and self-esteem, raise the company's profile and standing in the community, develop customer relationships *and* improve profits by running employee fundraising schemes.

A suitable high-profile, basic-need cause is selected (it could be your organisation) and made the subject of a high-visibility appeal. Targets are set within a specific time-frame. The company's management can even chip in a matching fund so that for every £1 or $1 raised an equivalent sum will be put in by the company up to a

There is an opportunity for voluntary organisations to encourage many more people to find a way to contribute to our society by volunteering.

fixed amount. The PR department is brought in. Notices and posters appear all round the workplace. Departments vie to outdo each other in yet more innovative and involving ways to reach their individual target. People have a lot of fun and feel good when they reach or exceed their targets.

Your charity raises a lot of money and builds a relationship with a corporate partner that will become a lifelong friend.

Volunteers

I briefly alluded to volunteers in the opening chapter of this book. We in Britain have a strong tradition of volunteering but we haven't taken it as far as some countries, particularly the United States and France. There is an opportunity for voluntary organisations to encourage many more people to find a way to contribute to our society by volunteering. It is something *everyone* can do. It is not the prerogative of one privileged sector, such as the middle-class, middle-aged, predominantly white, predominantly female ghetto whence most donors come.

If fundraisers could offer the public useful, productive, accessible volunteer activity and present and deliver these in customer-oriented packages, particularly those targeted towards young people, the potential benefits for our total society would be huge.

A big task but nevertheless a big opportunity and one many voluntary organisations have yet to address.

Inform your ambassadors

Imagine you are interested in a range of merchandise and you visit the local stockist, hoping to resolve some queries before finalising your purchase. What would you think if a complete portfolio describing that range

'Voluntary' shouldn't equate with 'incompetent'. In too many people's minds, it does.

was not available, or if the salesman did not have, at his fingertips, all the benefits, reasons to buy and competitive advantages ...

You'd be unimpressed. It wouldn't matter if the salesman didn't know every answer himself, but you would expect him to find out quickly by referring to a file or catalogue, or by ringing his head office, or some other immediate way of answering your enquiry.

Despite their regular and universal contact with the public through regional organisations, shops, events, local groups, volunteers and other networks, few representatives of fundraising organisations are anything like so well equipped.

Many regional organisers and branch volunteers aren't even given a copy of their employer's annual report, far less trained in its use. Too many simply don't know what their charity does.

Fundraisers are missing a useful opportunity if they fail to equip their public sales force with the basic tools they need to do their job. Loose-leaf sheets produced on a word processor are simply updated and relatively inexpensive. They'll be appreciated and will help isolated field staff feel more involved. A little training can also be inexpensive and won't go amiss. 'Voluntary' shouldn't equate with 'incompetent'. In too many people's minds, it does.

The RFM route to upgrading donors

RFM stands for recency, frequency and monetary value. It is a system of awarding points for these three characteristics and it is used in America to evaluate mail order customers. To monitor it effectively you would need a good relationship database. The purpose of RFM monitoring is to enable you to award a standard point value to every donor on your list and then to watch their progress as you try various methods of upgrading. The following example is to illustrate the system only. Points and values can be varied to suit each individual organisation, so long as they are always consistent within that organisation. It works like this.

Recency
Award eight points to a donor who last donated within the last six months.
Award four points to a donor who last donated 6–12 months ago.
Award two points to a donor who last donated 12–24 months ago.
Award one point to a donor who last donated more than two years ago.

Frequency
Take the number of donations and multiply by four points.

Value
Award one point for every £25 value to a maximum of 40 points.

So a donor who last gave £100 two months ago and has given three other gifts, bringing the total, including the last gift to £250, would be given an RFM value of 34 points.

The fundraiser's objectives then are to increase his or her donors' individual point values, the average point value and the total point values. He can do this by applying the principles of relationship fundraising.

I don't know if it works because I don't know anybody (yet) who has tried it. But targets and objectives are always valuable. It seems likely to me that if such a

Some back issues of your newsletter and a photocopied sheet are not good enough.

system can be implemented to monitor the results of upgrading it will add a new purpose and vigour to every fundraiser's efforts.

Although the calculations themselves are relatively simple, donor values would be constantly changing up and down with the passage of time, so your computer might need a nifty bit of programming.

If you know of any other system for monitoring donors' individual performance over time please let me know – apart from your organisation's bank statement – I already know of that one.

Thank you, thank you and welcome ...

The game show host's standard words of introduction always make me think of one of the postal fundraiser's biggest hurdles, converting the one-time responder into a true donor – getting the vital second gift that indicates that, perhaps, here is a real friend.

I've said all I want to say about thank you letters. An example of a thank you letter that is almost a welcome pack in itself is shown on page 216.

But the welcome package is an underused tool for fundraisers. It can provide the opportunity to convert your responders into real donors.

The welcome pack has to be appropriate. It must not be extravagant but neither should it be cheap and nasty. Above all it has to be welcoming. Some back issues of your newsletter and a photocopied sheet are not good enough. A special welcome issue of your newsletter is a worthwhile idea. Make it bright, readable, busy, visual. Explain to readers what it means to be a donor. Start at the beginning and show what their help is achieving. Assume no prior knowledge of your work but don't overburden your readers with details. Be short, dramatic and newsy. And display details of your phone service,

But if their organisations are to thrive and develop fundraisers must find effective new products.

who to call and so on. Think about the kind of welcome newsletter you'd like to receive and make it just like that.

In the United Kingdom Greenpeace has produced a welcome pack that is simply an A3 (420 x 297 mm) sheet folded over to letter size. One side is laser-personalised in several places, not just with the new supporter's name but with membership details too. The reverse side is printed with remoistenable glue. Recipients can easily cut out various labels for their address book and diary. A window sticker is even included which they can display. A reply form is also included so by removing and affixing some more stickers the new supporter can easily tell Greenpeace how he or she wants to help the organisation in future.

All Greenpeace's current campaigns are summarised too. It is very action-oriented which suits Greenpeace as they want supporters to realise that they are joining an organisation committed to action – and their action is expected too.

New products and new product development

Innovation in the design and development of new products has always been venerated. Industry and commerce depend on it so spend large amounts of time and money in researching and testing new ideas and new propositions. Some work, some don't. That's the name of the game. The essence of progress, my boy, is never to stand still.

Research and development is a very strange subject for a fundraising organisation to consider. Charities are almost devoid of any risk capital and many trustees and board members find the concept almost impossible to grasp. It just doesn't fit their notion of what a charity is.

But if their organisations are to thrive and develop fundraisers must find effective new products. Otherwise their organisations will be overtaken, will wither and will die. Just like other commercial organisations, fundraising organisations need to know when to introduce new products and when to drop, or play down, old products. An example of a new product that works well, after time, is the affinity credit card. It is run in association with an established credit card issuer and is just like any other credit card except the charity's name is printed on it and the charity gets a benefit each time the card is used. Most charities have found this an easy product to launch and promote to their existing membership. It works for me. I've never liked the exorbitant charges levied by credit card companies but it is somewhat more bearable when I know a charity will benefit even by a little bit. On the other hand, an example of a product in decline, it seems to me, is street collections, perhaps because the public no longer has sympathy for them.

But launching a new product can be hazardous and sometimes requires considerable investment, as well as skill and know-how. This is particularly true for products which apply to all charities, for instance payroll giving and Gift Aid.

Successful launch of a product is a highly specialised business and in the fundraising area, certainly in the UK, that specialism is very rare indeed. Until charities learn to treat new product launches less casually and accept the inevitable investment of money and skills that they demand, we can't be surprised that the launch of some fundraising products will be disappointing. In future charities will have to invest more in researching and developing new products and propositions. If they don't they will be left behind.

Fundraisers in other countries now have the opportunity to introduce similar products to their home markets.

Planned giving

Legacies (or bequests) account for by far the largest part of what is sometimes referred to as planned giving – the arrangement of a donor's affairs in advance to provide affordable and tax-efficient ways of helping favoured causes.

Planned giving is well developed in the United States, where donors are offered a wide range of insurance, health and investment-linked schemes and are encouraged to view substantial gifts to charity as part of their planning for retirement. Fundraisers in other countries now have the opportunity to introduce similar products to their home markets. This seems to me to be an area rich in opportunity, both for joint partnerships with appropriate financial services organisations and for developing worthwhile products that would provide value to donors during their lifetime and income for their chosen charity after their death.

The fundraiser who consults donors, finds out what they want and involves them in designing the planned giving product will be more likely to see success than the fundraiser who presents donors with a *fait accompli*.

Central promotion

The idea of centralised promotion on behalf of charities is very attractive, but fundraisers should be cautious before diving in. Rather than a treasure ship, they may land on a shark.

Certainly fundraisers could and should cooperate on certain subjects to cut out duplication and to present one strong central message which might be well beyond the means or resources of any individual organisation.

One such area is legacy marketing. Obviously each individual charity must promote its own corner, but the basic idea – the notion of leaving a legacy to a worthwhile cause – can be more effectively promoted centrally using the combined resources of all charities, than by the diffuse energies of each one, all trying to do the same thing.

I hope charities can get together – without excluding anyone – to do it. They have much to gain.

As for the central promotion of the generic concept of giving, I find that a much harder task and can't quite imagine how it could be done effectively. I am prepared to be proved wrong, but it seems to me that giving is an abstract and meaningless concept if it is taken away from the subject of the gift – the worthy cause. Why on earth would people want to give *per se*?

So I don't believe generic giving campaigns offer any worthwhile opportunity. Telling people *how* to give is not likely to be of much interest to anyone. But the successful central promotion of legacies, if it can be made to happen, may well open up other areas for useful collaboration between fundraisers on specific themes.

And donors would certainly welcome that.

What's in a name?

I mention in chapter 9 the opportunities that will arise from an integrated donor service department. The fundraiser of the future will go even further. Not only will terms such as 'mailings' and 'packs' disappear, so too will job titles such as direct mail manager and head of appeals. In their place will come much more friendly titles and terminologies to reflect the much more friendly departments they manage. Goodbye head of direct mail, welcome donor development manager.

2001 and all that

When he wrote his seminal piece of science fiction Arthur C Clarke must have felt the next millennium was

We are in for some rather sensational celebrations when the twenty-first century comes of age.

so far in the future that anything might be possible. Now it is just around the corner and soon, as we were with George Orwell's dismal vision for 1984, we'll be upon it, and past it and we'll know what it is really like. Nineteen eighty-four was such a disappointment. I remember reading the book at school and, while recoiling with horror that anyone could have such a depressing prediction of the future, was encouraged that at least it was different. Reality in the event was much more ordinary, just like 1983, which itself was not that much different from the year before. Perhaps it is just as well.

The year 2000 will probably not be very much different from 1999, except that it will most likely start with a few more, and more spectacular, hangovers. Not everybody may have realised it yet, but we are in for some rather sensational celebrations when the twenty-first century comes of age. Millennia don't come and go very often so New Year's Eve 1999 promises to be one almighty and rather prolonged bash.

A few people cottoned on to this some time ago. Tables at London's Savoy Hotel on New Year's Eve 1999 are fully booked already and have been for some time. Flights on Concorde from Paris to Los Angeles via New York (so you can have two New Year's Eves on the same day) are also already fully booked.

The Café Royal, The Dorchester, Grosvenor House, and other London celebrity spots are similarly placed and the French are already worried (seriously) that there won't be enough champagne to go round. Apparently they (the wine-growers of Champagne) neglected to plan for the millennium and it takes more than a few years to turn out a decent champagne.

Bad luck – there's always New Year 2999. Perhaps they should mark in their diaries when to start planning.

What does the approaching millennium mean for

fundraisers? Well, I don't know. I expect the imminent turning of a century represents rather a large opportunity and for rather more than a host of 'opportunity 2000' affinity clubs. The last time a millennium came and went William the Conqueror hadn't yet been born. Significantly, on the throne of England then was King Ethelred the Unready.

I'll be interested to see what fundraisers make of it.

ACTION POINTS

▲ Fundraising is all about opportunity so be prepared to grasp yours while you can, before someone else does.

▲ Try a non-event. It could be just what your expense ratio needs.

▲ Offer real involvement. See your donors as investors who are entitled to have influence *and* active involvement in your work.

▲ Look after your donor/askers. Put them near the top of your relationship fundraising priorities.

▲ Review your pricing policy and strategy. Use price to stimulate and control demand.

▲ Think monthly when pricing propositions.

▲ Set targets carefully to benefit from maximum motivation.

▲ Prepare a portfolio of your publications suitable for sponsorship so you can sell the idea to corporate donors.

▲ See if other fundraisers respond to the idea of setting up a central agency to facilitate links with corporate donors.

▲ Try to interest local employers in employee fundraising schemes.

▲ Look for opportunities to encourage volunteers.

▲ Equip your sales team (your staff and volunteers) well with information and basic training.

▲ Use the RFM method to measure your donors' support and to monitor the success of your upgrading activities.

▲ Reconsider how your organisation welcomes new supporters. Could your welcome package be improved?

▲ Invest in research and development. Keep innovating to avoid stagnation.

▲ Encourage and support *appropriate* central promotion.

▲ Consider restructuring and retitling job descriptions to reflect your new donor orientation and eliminate purely functional descriptions.

▲ Don't forget the millennium!

DONOR PROFILE

Eric Levine

Eric Levine was only six years old when he arrived at the Port of Liverpool in 1914, a refugee from the Austro-Hungarian Empire. With him were his father, mother, grandmother, two sisters and all they could carry: two bundles, some carrier bags and an old battered suitcase. The family settled in two rooms in a Manchester tenement block round the corner from the basement where Eric's father made a kind of living mending shoes, clocks and sometimes watches.

Eric didn't mix with other children, just like his family didn't mix much with other families on their street. Eric's schooling was sporadic, to say the least. At 12 he got a job as a delivery boy for a large department store. He learned the retail trade from the bottom, a training that stood him in good stead later on.

As he grew Eric realised that he had a talent for just two things: he knew how to sell and he knew how to buy. Using capital scraped together over years from any source he could find, Eric Levine went into business buying derelict run-down sites in areas with potential, turning them into general stores and corner shops. He started a down-market jewellery shop which became a national chain. By the time he was 30 Eric had made himself a millionaire from each of his business areas – jewellery, property and shops. Nobody knew how much he was worth, not even Eric.

He never married. His home was in a depressed part of central Manchester and there he stayed. He lived simply with few interests other than work.

As he grew older Eric's obsession changed from his work to his health. He began to worry that he smoked too much and took little exercise. Concern for his physical well-being developed into a kind of hypochondria and his general practitioner began to regard him as something of a nuisance.

Then Eric suffered a mild heart attack. By then he had sold all his business interests so his preoccupation with his health had the opportunity to become a full-time neurosis. He took to writing to and visiting every noteworthy authority on any aspect of personal health, particularly the heart. He assiduously collected any published information he could – booklets, posters, leaflets. His daily visits to the local out-patients clinic were treated with kindly tolerance.

In the end it was a bout of influenza that killed Eric Levine at the age of 75. After his death his estate was valued at more than £23 million. He left almost all of it to medical and research charities, including £1.5 million to develop a new heart unit at his local hospital. Some of the causes he chose as beneficiaries were quite surprising, having little or nothing to do with any known ailment of Eric Levine's. Yet two of the larger heart research organisations received nothing at all.

They never found out why, because no one could connect the down-at-heel aggressive little man who rang and wrote and constantly questioned, with the fabulously wealthy Mr Eric Levine.

11 The last great fund-raising opportunity

'I can imagine a better line, but I do not know of one.'

George Stephenson
*commenting on his great rival Isambard Kingdom Brunel's
completion of the Great Western Railway*

The marketing of legacies is without doubt your last great opportunity to get money from a donor, although in reality the seeds of the idea should have been planted some long time before the legacy might actually come into effect. As a potential source of funds it may not quite be the last opportunity for professional fundraisers but it is almost certainly one of the greatest.

Legacy marketing is, I believe, the largest and most important area of all for fundraisers. Amazingly enough it is a new area. Its potential has been virtually neglected until quite recently. That means it is still largely unexplored territory with all sorts of interesting opportunities for people like you and me. It's also an area where all the principles of relationship fundraising apply.

Let me first of all ask a question of you, the reader. Have you made a will? If you have, good. You've shown commendable foresight, but you are in the minority. If you haven't, I'll bet you have thought about it, you have no strong reservations or objections to making a will and haven't done it yet simply because you haven't got round to it.

In most cases, death prevents this inertia from ever being overcome.

That's why most people don't make a will – good old inertia, the most consistent public response to the really important things of life. As a result, in England and Wales, something like £2,100 million is left each year 'intestate' – by people who haven't made a will. Therefore the State decides for them who gets what from their estate. They are, well and truly, out of it.

In most cases, death prevents this inertia from ever being overcome. Many others, however, do decide to make a will dangerously late in life. While seven out of ten adults have *not* made a will, by the time of death the figure has dropped to just less than half. (These statistics have kindly been provided for me by David Ford of Smee and Ford Limited, that unique company which has its own room in Somerset House and whose staff tirelessly read every will that is proved in England and Wales and record, analyse, digest and distribute this priceless data to any charity that is really serious about preserving and developing its legacy income.)

Here are some more basics of legacy marketing, again courtesy of David Ford:

• Charities depend on legacy income. It accounts for about one-third of all voluntary income and is bigger than both government grants and donations from grant-making trusts *combined*.

• Legacies to charities in England and Wales total between £600 to £700 million per annum – a great deal of money. There is no evidence yet that this is growing in real terms, although the individual share of some charities is increasing and there clearly is enormous potential for growth.

• The value of all estates in England and Wales totals more than £16,000 million per annum. So charities only get around four per cent of the total , which is not a very large share, if you think about it. An increase of just 0.5

Residuary legacies are worth, generally, at least ten times the value of cash legacies.

per cent would mean a lot of new money for charities.

• Only eight per cent of wills mention a charity. That's just four per cent of the population.

• About 240,000 estates above £5,000 are proved (finalised) each year. Of these approximately one in four – 60,000 – are intestate. In total, approximately 450,000 deaths are recorded in England and Wales each year, indicating that something over half of all deaths have proved wills.

• Collectively it's the poorer half of the population that dies intestate (£2.1 billion in proved estates above £5,000 compared to £13.8 billion).

• The average age on death of someone who leaves a legacy to charity is 81 years. The chances are she is female (60:40). Females leave more residuary legacies, ie rather than a specific gift, the charity gets the whole or a share of the remainder of the estate after other bequests have been made. Residuary legacies are worth, generally, at least ten times the value of pecuniary (cash) legacies.

• The average age of a will which includes a bequest to a charity is less than five years (25 per cent are less than one year old). Therefore legacy marketing is not nearly as long term as some people suppose. This is easily proved: several charities my company started working with in legacy promotion in the last few years are now seeing substantial direct returns from their investment.

• Following on from that, it is now quite clear that legacy income can be influenced. It can even be predicted. Potential legators can be identified by their shaky handwriting, by their length of membership, by the fact that they live in a retirement area. They can be recruited from your own donor base and from the public at large. And they can be specifically targeted through the specialist press and specialist lists, and through their special interests and where they live.

All this points to a comfortably agreeable thought for the charity marketer – a clearly identifiable need exists, we know that many donors are only too happy to leave something of their estate to a favoured cause, a huge market is available for the proposition and there are many affordable ways of reaching that market. What could be better? It all adds up to a quite fantastic opportunity for fundraisers.

The average value of an estate which included a charitable gift in 1990 was £110,000. Those that didn't only managed an average value of £70,000. The average age on death of women leaving a charitable bequest was 83 that year, while for men it was 79. The average age on death of women who *didn't* leave a charitable bequest was 81, and for men 76. However, unfortunately and despite initial appearances, this doesn't constitute conclusive proof that generosity to charities in your will will ensure either longevity or greater riches in this world, any more than it will ensure greater contentment through all eternity in the next. But it might help.

Fundraisers should be aware that large legacies are not easily or quickly to be had. Legacies are the ultimate reward of a lifetime of relationship fundraising. But up until now they have probably just as often been the product of pure chance.

Different strokes for different folks

Different people prefer to leave money in different ways. Following on from the observation that residuary legacies are vastly more lucrative than pecuniary, it may appear sensible for fundraisers to promote the former strongly. This is so, but like everything else in legacy promotion it has to be done with great care.

Many charities find that a very common form of

... your deceptive financial charts will unquestionably see you left out by many of your more financially astute donors.

legacy, if not the most common, is what is known as a reversionary legacy. This is when a named person has access to the value of the estate which only reverts to the charity on the death of that person . For instance, the original will states that a friend or partner is allowed to live in the legator's house until their death, when it will revert to the charity.

Fundraisers don't like this practice for it invariably means they have to wait for their money. Therefore they rarely mention it. However, donors clearly like it very much, so fundraisers would perhaps be advised to promote reversionary legacies more strongly, along with any other schemes they can devise that will have public appeal.

The cost of bad relations

Legacy marketing is not wholly about response. Many factors can influence the decision whether or not to leave a legacy. For example, your intrusive, badly targeted and overtly commercial direct mail might easily put off a large number of donors. Your dull, uninformative publications might deter quite a few. Your impenetrable accounts and your deceptive financial charts will unquestionably see you left out by many of your more financially astute donors. And the interminable delay before that stroppy person on the switchboard managed to get some inaccurate half-answers to their questions about the charity's use of funds will have had many of your best prospects scuttling off to their solicitors to cut you off without a penny, leaving the lot to the local dogs' home.

It's amusing to imagine, but I have no doubt that some versions of this do happen just about every day.

That's why I say legacy marketing is the ultimate pinnacle of relationship fundraising, the collection of a

If fundraisers are to promote legacies widely, we should re-examine the language we use to make it more appropriate to what donors want to hear.

just reward for a lifetime of carefully developing and maintaining the right kind of relationship with the right kind of people.

A new language

One aspect of wills, bequests and legacies that charities can influence for the better is the terminology. It's an area full of arcane words and phrases such as legator, residuary, codicils, executors and so on. We have even contributed by introducing terms of our own such as pledging, which isn't a very user-friendly concept or at least doesn't sound as if it is. If fundraisers are to promote legacies widely, perhaps we should re-examine the language we use to make it more appropriate to what donors want to hear.

A collective chance

I don't see legacy marketing just as a chance for each individual organisation to increase its own income from legacies. It is a chance for all fundraisers to work together to alter fundamentally the public's perception of the concept of leaving some money to a favoured cause through the means of their will. If we can change the public's attitude to charitable legacies, enormous benefits will follow not just for charities but for universities, hospitals, arts companies, and a whole list of other worthwhile organisations and causes.

Leaving a legacy to charity must become part of our culture, as fashionable as independent pensions, retirement homes, holidays by the sea and fish and chips. Donors must be persuaded that they can afford to leave a legacy, that it will cost them nothing in their lifetime and that it is an extremely satisfying and effective way to help their favourite causes.

The concept, the idea of leaving legacies to do good

It is easy to get things wrong in legacy promotion.

work after you have gone, has to be widely promoted *as an idea itself.* So far this hasn't been done.

The commitment and compulsion that some people feel must be felt by everyone. At least they must be the norm rather than the exception.

The satisfaction, sense of purpose and fulfilment felt by some must be available to everyone. There should be nothing elite about leaving a living legacy.

We'll know we've succeeded when we get it written into the script of a national television drama . It may sound daft but this could be one of the most constructive uses of television for fundraisers as few things are as effective at getting a subject into the nation's consciousness as getting it on to the box. Editorial exposure on television is just what legacy marketers need. See page 244 for my suggestion.

Legacies already form the biggest single source of voluntary charitable giving yet we are getting all this money from only four per cent of the population. That is what I mean about a fantastic opportunity. So far, charitable legacies have only begun to scratch the surface of their potential, because the idea has not been properly presented – yet.

Suicide

Inevitably the subject of legacies is a delicate one. Any marketing initiatives have to be appropriate and extraordinarily sensitive, otherwise the opposite of the desired effect will result. It is easy to get things wrong in legacy promotion. Mostly that just means the promotion is wasted, but it is possible to create offence where really none is intended.

A few years ago a major charity sent out a legacy mailing in an envelope with the challenging message 'Do you believe in life after death?' boldly emblazoned on it.

Many complaints were received, but one I saw was returned marked simply 'deceased' across its front. It's funny, I know, but in legacy marketing this kind of insensitivity can be thought of as suicide.

I saw a similar mistake from an American charity, in one of their 'lost friend' (lapsed donor) reactivation mailings. It had splashed across the envelope 'lost friend, please come back' underneath which was handwritten 'Harry would love to but he died last fall'.

To be successful, legacy marketing has to be subtle and sensitive which is hardly surprising.

Handle legacy marketing with care as well as flair.

Donors' communications, particularly from obviously very elderly supporters, should also be treated with considerable care and a policy should be established to cope with almost any situation that will arise. Recently a charity I work with received a letter from an obviously frail elderly woman, who complained that she was too old and infirm to appreciate the publication they sent and would they please stop sending it. Her irritation was clear, the charity was obviously doing something wrong and needed to put it right. How a charity responds to the writer of such a letter could be very important. She was no doubt treated carefully and courteously, which is just as well, for she may be a legacy prospect. Every charity should be prepared to deal sensitively with situations like this.

A new approach

Until recently, charities have done remarkably little to encourage legacy income and have treated that which has landed on their plates as just that – a windfall. The only form of promotion has been a very limited type of largely unmeasurable advertising which I have taken to calling 'the old approach'. A new approach to legacy

Hundreds of charities squander their meagre resources year after year, placing irrelevant ads in ill-designed compendiums that are hardly ever read either by solicitors or by anybody else.

marketing is needed because the old approach clearly doesn't work. It never has and it never will.

By the old approach I mean the allocation of a small, but significant, part of a charity's promotional budget to buying space in the various yearbooks and journals directed towards solicitors. Hundreds of charities squander their meagre resources year after year in this way, placing irrelevant ads in ill-designed compendiums that are hardly ever read either by solicitors or indeed by anybody else.

The usual response to these ads is a resounding zilch. Yet charities continue the folly year after year because, 'Well, you never know, old boy ...' Even the apparently serious-minded try to explain this phenomenon away by stating 'legacy advertising is indirect and long term' and 'well, you can't expect to know where legacies come from'.

Piffle!

Spend half an hour or more with a collection of these publications and you'll soon find out why people avoid them. The ones I refer to are not much more than loose collections of badly designed advertisements which show limited imagination and even less individuality. I believe they have done little to promote the cause of leaving money to charity. These ads frequently feature headlines such as 'Fight cancer with a will' or 'Where there's a will, there's heart research' and so forth. I am sure most charities have better things to do with their money.

A few years ago, two national charities in the UK, seemingly independently of each other, began to try a new approach.

Instead of asking for a legacy, these charities decided to offer helpful information. Their objectives were to be helpful, to encourage more people generally to make

This database, these far-sighted charities realised, might be enormously valuable one day quite soon.

wills and to build a database of individuals who they knew were interested in either making or changing their will. This database, these far-sighted charities realised, might be enormously valuable one day quite soon.

Inevitably the first charities doing this were innovating in what was an unknown area. However, now they have been doing it for a few years and have experience of what works and what doesn't.

Here in essence are the key points of this kind of legacy marketing campaign.

1 Prepare a strategy and brief your field staff and local groups.
2 Reinvest a percentage of current legacy income in future promotion.
3 Talk about legacies with your supporters. Give examples in your newsletter and in your annual report. This is the most neglected area. Everyone wants to dig in the street without digging their own back garden first.
4 Research your supporters – know your strengths and weaknesses.
5 Prepare relevant, helpful information on how to make or change a will.
6 Offer it as widely as possible to your key targets.
7 Prepare a flyer leaflet for general use
    a) to enquirers
    b) with the annual report
    c) in the membership pack
    d) everywhere.
8 Prepare a campaign to assist professional advisers.
9 Offer incentives, if practical and appropriate. Test their value.
10 Keep excellent records.

... very few charities have considered reinvesting even a small percentage of their current legacy income in future promotion.

Creativity in legacy marketing

Having criticised the advertisements most charities prepare for the legal press, perhaps I should now describe what I believe is creative in legacy marketing.

As evidence of the extent of most charities' neglect of legacy marketing, very few charities have considered reinvesting even a small percentage of their current legacy income in future promotion. This is extraordinarily short sighted. Competition for legacies is increasing. Those large corporation charities that collect such vast unsolicited legacy income need to look to their laurels. Without doubt it makes sense for any charity to invest in developing new sources of legacy income. The expense ratio inevitably will be infinitesimally small when compared with most other sources of charity income. What follows are nine different opportunities for creative legacy marketing.

Plagiarise!

Learning from others, borrowing what works for them, is the most sincere form of flattery. It is also the least expensive road to success, so in my view it must be creative – if it is well done. Poor imitation, on the other hand, is an insult. It's like misquoting someone, or like borrowing a friend's car and returning it dented. We none of us can protect our ideas once published, so lie back and accept plagiarism without complaint. If your ideas are good, it'll happen anyway and if they're not worth plagiarising, well ...

Creative targeting

If 50 people left you a legacy last year it would be really creative to find another 150 or more just like them, each and every year.

The key is research. Who leaves you legacies? What

The easiest target to reach, of course, is in your own back garden. Talk to your existing supporters first.

are their previous connections with your organisation? Where do they live? What characteristics do they have in common?

The easiest target to reach, of course, is in your own back garden. Talk to your existing supporters first. They're the most likely group to react favourably to your legacy proposition. Identify those who live in known retirement areas, those who have been on your list for many years and those whose handwriting is a bit shaky. Flag your donor base with details of these prospects and keep a record of their activity. Treat them accordingly.

Then go outside your own list to target people with special interests or hobbies, who belong to clubs specially for older people or whose lifestyle indicates that they are likely to be elderly. Target readers of the 'grey' press, such as *Saga* magazine and *50+*. Target people on certain commercial mailing lists, for instance gardeners, particularly those that live in the known retirement areas. In this way you can cut out the traditional donor pyramid and talk directly to people who might be legacy prospects, most of whom may have had no previous contact with your cause. If resources are limited, prioritise your targets.

Creativity in approach
The new approach involves the charity positioning itself as a helpful source of information. Its aim is to encourage more people to make a will and its objective is to build a database of people that it knows were considering either making or changing their will at the time when they were recruited on to that database. From this point, the key to the new approach is in successfully developing a relationship with these enquirers which will, in time, become mutually beneficial.

If you have a regional network you will be able to use them to spread the legacy message throughout the country ...

Creativity in strategy and objectives

Any organisation undertaking legacy marketing needs to be clear about its proposition and its objectives in making it. You need to be very sure about what you want to achieve and you need to know all you can about your organisation and its supporters. Any legacy marketing initiative must include sufficient resources for research into donors and legators.

Next, your strategy has to take account of your available staff and deploy them wisely. Similarly with volunteers and local groups. If you have a regional network you will be able to use them to spread the legacy message throughout the country through the ripple effect, but you will need straightforward easy-to-use training materials to ensure they know what they are doing and why. Full briefing is essential preparation for anyone involved in legacy marketing.

Preparing the right materials is important. One national charity that has been very successful in generating new pledges for legacy income has developed organised training sessions for its field staff and volunteers. Amongst other things they have prepared 25 overhead projector slides summarising the potential and importance of legacy income, the strategy of their campaign, the benefits for donors, the materials available and the back-up help they can provide to stimulate discussion particularly among groups of donors 'at home'. A short video has been prepared, featuring the key points about making a will and the benefits of the charity's helpful information. Combined with special leaflets and a detailed booklet describing how to make or change a will, this equips the charity's regional staff and volunteers with all they need to go out and talk to their supporters about legacies.

Sometimes an incentive helps to encourage local

When they see how increased legacy income can transform their figures, they won't need to be told twice to go forth and evangelise for the cause of making a will.

groups to promote legacies. Usually it is quite a simple piece of internal accounting to credit them with a percentage of legacies received from their area. When they see how increased legacy income can transform their figures, they won't need to be told twice to go forth and evangelise for the cause of making a will.

Creativity in language

Like most fundraising communications, simple, direct, everyday language is what is needed in all legacy promotional materials. Avoid any complex descriptions, solid paragraphs, weighty text and long words. Harold Sumption, who taught me much of what I know about charity marketing, had a phrase which I've never forgotten. 'Talk to people where they are, not where you want them to be.' This sums up the task for the copy-writer perfectly. Know your reader. Make your copy relevant to him or her. Make it accessible, make it interesting. Tell them what they want to know, not what you want to say.

Simplicity always works, and this also relates to image. Show homely, familiar situations using real people that the average older donor can relate to – not bewigged lords, millionaires or young trendies.

I mention lords in their wigs and robes because a legacy advertisement that frequently springs to mind is one that featured the former Lord Chancellor Lord Hailsham, and was run by I forget which charity. This was, I believe, ill-advised and an inappropriate use of his high office but I'm not oblivious to the power and impact that such senior and imposing figures can have. I will digress a little here to relate an anecdote about the said lord, which confirms my point.

One day Neil Kinnock, leader of the UK's Labour Party, was showing a group of his constituents around

Eventually, of course, they all had to pay for advertising space to generate the volume of enquiries they required and to build that all-important database. Here the key word is 'negotiate'.

the imposing halls of Westminster, Britain's Houses of Parliament. En route the party happened to meet the then Lord Chancellor thundering along the corridor in full robes and regalia.

'Neil!' boomed the eminent statesman in friendly greeting – and meekly half of Kinnock's constituents dropped to their knees in obeisance. Like most political tales it may not be entirely true, but I hope it is.

Creative use of media

If you have a promotional budget for legacy marketing, most of it will probably be spent in press advertising. Media costs are so high that even the bravest have to be very careful.

One short cut is to go for free publicity. There is tremendous editorial interest in matters financial and that includes will-making and legacies. Most newspapers and many magazines have a money section, which from time to time will focus on the needs of older readers and advise them on issues relating to their financial health. Your initiative on will-making, therefore, might well be considered newsworthy, particularly by local papers or radio if you can bring in a local angle or get the piece placed personally by your local group secretary. Sometimes you may need to link an advertisement to the article to secure the kind of coverage you need. If you are using a celebrity to introduce the campaign he or she will be particularly useful in ensuring you get the free column inches.

This is not pie in the sky. I have recently worked on five major new approach legacy campaigns and all the organisations involved gained valuable free publicity.

Eventually, of course, they all had to pay for advertising space to generate the volume of enquiries they required and to build that all-important database.

Successful space negotiation will have a far more immediate and beneficial effect on your cost per reply than any number of clever headlines.

Here the key word is 'negotiate'. Cost per reply is the crucial equation in legacy marketing and nothing improves that so much as your ability to pay only 40 to 50 per cent of rate card for your advertising space. Successful space negotiation will have a far more immediate and beneficial effect on your cost per reply than any number of clever headlines in your advertisements. If your current agency doesn't get those kind of discounts, change your agency.

Off-the-page advertising in the quality national and specialist press has proved extraordinarily cost-effective for new approach legacy campaigns. But all media should be tested and rigorous records of each insertion kept in your campaign guard book. Direct mail has frequently been tested against press advertising for new approach legacy marketing but generally it works less well because of the higher unit cost per reader. Magazine inserts too can be used. One charity I know has tested legacy ads on the radio (it is a charity that helps blind people so there's some logic here) and it won't be long before the first telephone legacy marketing campaign (telelegemarketing?) will be launched.

Creativity in offer
The cornerstone of most new approach legacy campaigns is the offer of an informative and helpful legacy information booklet, of which the key ingredients are simple and straightforward text covering 'why and how to make a will?' The booklet will describe the benefits of making a will so that you can ensure that your money goes to those you really care about (including, of course, your favourite charities) and how you should set about it – choosing a solicitor, gauging how much you are worth, appointing executors, types of bequests and the advantages of reducing the gross value of your estate to

This gives the charity a perfect excuse to write again to its legacy database every time the inheritance tax thresholds are changed.

avoid inheritance tax. But this publication should not be an ostentatious promotion of your organisation. It's only valuable if the advice it gives appears independent and unbiased. I recommend that your charity's involvement should take a very low profile, at this stage at least.

In the back of the booklet you should accompany your information with several loose inserts, either to be filled in by the recipient, such as a list of personal assets and liabilities which will save time when visiting a solicitor, forms of codicil and so on, or information that needs to be updated frequently, such as inheritance tax levels, etc. This latter document naturally gives the charity a perfect excuse to write again to all legacy booklet enquirers every time the inheritance tax thresholds are changed.

The final loose inserts are of course the inevitable reply envelope and the detailed pledge form (reply card) so that supporters can confirm that they have included the charity in their will and indicate the kind and size of legacy planned.

Some charities have included incentives to encourage return of the pledge form – for instance, tie-pins or free books – but there is little evidence that these tokens increase response. What does seem to have an effect, although it is difficult to quantify, is the prospect of a kind of immortality that is offered by such devices as the 'book of remembrance', a permanent inscription of your name in a leather-bound record, or the 'tree of life' when a metal leaf inscribed with your name is added to a symbolic tree, probably attached to the charity's boardroom wall. One charity I know has several such trees as over the years the leaves have filled up. Perhaps eventually they'll have to have a forest of remembrance. These ideas seem American in origin and audiences in other countries may feel uncomfortable with them. But it is a matter of choice and I doubt if the existence of such a device would put many people off. Clearly it can turn some people on.

From the existence of a helpful booklet to the additional trappings of a tree of life – all these form part of the offer to potential legacy donors in new approach legacy marketing. Recently a consortium of Third World development charities called WillAid came up with an additional offer which also worked remarkably well.

The WillAid scheme simply involved the commendable participation of a large number of solicitors from around the country. Its objective was to encourage more people to make a will and its means was to promote a special discount of £25 off the cost of drawing up a will, that sum to go to the charities that make up WillAid. The scheme was a success and proved to be an excellent example of creativity which worked in five different ways.

- It got substantial publicity nationwide.
- It gave solicitors a useful PR boost.
- It encouraged lots of people to make a will.
- It raised lots of money for the member charities.
- Ninety per cent of solicitors said they would do it again.

These are only the immediate benefits. Of the new wills made through WillAid, how many do you think will contain a legacy to charity?

The British charity RNIB (Royal National Institute for the Blind) recently launched a new approach legacy campaign and successfully linked it with their URG (unique reason to give, see page 155). The charity had a splendid opportunity to change the offer relevantly because their legacy marketing materials were largely directed towards older people and, they reasoned, as people get older they often start to experience eyesight

If the ads create a positive image with this large group then the charity will receive a further significant benefit ...

problems, many have difficulty reading and some lose their sight altogether. So RNIB produced their legacy information booklet in four different formats: standard print (A5), large print (A4), tape and braille. Readers could choose whichever format suited them. No one was denied access to the information because of their visual impairment, which suited RNIB very much, and interestingly one out of every five requests specified their preference for large print, tape or braille.

Such a relevant offer would also have done the charity's image no harm at all. The large majority of readers of their advertisement will not respond to the ads simply because at the time they are not in the market for legacy information, but the message will certainly create a good impression with many current and potential supporters. If the ads create a positive image with this large group then the charity will receive a further significant benefit from its new approach legacy promotion. This is an example of the importance of communicating with those who *don't* respond, that I mentioned in chapter 6 – the impression your advertising has on non-respondents (see page 115).

Creative advertisements
Position, media used, the offer, competition from other sources: these are all more important, in terms of their effect on response, than the so-called creative content of the advertisement. This is a terrible admission for a copywriter to make, but it is true. Anyway, varying the offer and packaging of the proposition is every bit as challenging for the copywriter. However, the appearance and wording of the advertisement can have a negative effect if badly executed. Again the watchwords must be simplicity, clarity and ease of reply.

In their press advertisements RNIB featured actress

'Quite why not is a mystery to me, but it is a fact that Henry, her husband, simply <u>did not make</u> a will. He just hadn't got round to it. In fact most people don't make a will – I really haven't a clue why. It's quite easy and not at all expensive. Anyway, of course, there were <u>lots</u> of complications for his poor dear wife, what with tax and duties and so on. She was so angry when she found out. I do believe she'd have done away with him, if he hadn't been dead already ...'

SOLVE THE MYSTERY OF MAKING A WILL

Send for your free guide today

All versions contain
- why you should make a will
- how to save tax
- what to do before you see a solicitor
- how to leave a legacy
- all the forms you need.

Send to Miss Joan Hickson, c/o RNIB, Freepost BS528/74, Bristol BS3 3YY.

Please send me my free copy of *How to Make or Change your Will*.

Name _____

Address _____

_____

_____

_____ Postcode _____

Tick your choice

☐ standard print

☐ large print

☐ tape

☐ braille

914ST1B

Royal National Institute for the Blind

Reference: 914ST1B

An original and relevant offer gives the Royal National Institute for the Blind an edge in legacy marketing.

If more people make a will solicitors get more business, so present your campaign as good news for them.

Joan Hickson, well known as Agatha Christie's Miss Marple from the popular TV series of that name, and the ads were headlined 'Solve the mystery of making a will'. The response was very much higher than expected, partly I believe because of the positive response to the offer of different formats and partly because of the fortuitous choice of celebrity to introduce the proposition.

Coupons in particular must be clear and easy to complete. The YMCA advertisement (see next page) worked particularly well because it was one of the first but also its offer is absolutely clear, reader-oriented and unambiguous. Again a good choice of personality contributed, as does the use of Sir Harry Secombe in the NSPCC ads (see next page also). Celebrities should be of the right age group, well known and well liked by all your audience, inoffensive – don't include any politicians – and cheerful.

These are early days for the new approach to legacy fundraising and doubtless fresh creative ideas are even now in preparation. Watch this space.

Creative response and follow-up

You might now consider launching a more individual campaign aimed at the advisory sector, particularly solicitors. Explain the thinking behind your current public campaign and your purpose of encouraging more people to make a will. If more people make a will solicitors get more business so present your campaign as good news for them. You can also offer quantities of your helpful information for them to pass to their clients. That's good for both them and you. Get them on your side. If you can, make sure your network of volunteers is trained to visit their local solicitors to make sure they are well stocked with the latest materials from your

All you need to know about making a will

'I found this leaflet practical, helpful and informative. It's clearly written – and it's absolutely free!' Vera Lynn

At last, there's a concise new booklet that will help you to make your will efficiently and painlessly.

As well as explaining how to make sure each of your loved ones is well looked after, **Seven important points to consider when making or changing your will** shows you how to keep your legal expenses to a minimum.

There's also an important section on how, with careful planning, you may even be able to reduce the tax you pay! And if you ever doubted whether you needed a will at all, the booklet has an interesting section on what could happen to you – and those you love – if you die without making one. This new YMCA booklet has been written to be of general interest to anyone making a will, as well as those considering a bequest to the YMCA.

Write for your free copy today.

▽ YMCA

To the Legacy Department, Room 50, National Council of YMCAs, 640 Forest Road, London E17 3DZ.

Please send me my free copy of **Seven important points to consider when making or changing your will.**

Name ————————————————

Address ————————————————

———————————— *Postcode* ————

Leave it to us to continue your care.

HOW TO BE A PROPER GOON

Forget to make a Will

NSPCC

Making a Will is the only way you can be certain your wishes will be carried out after you die.

If you don't make one, your family could face many worries when, especially just after your death, they are at their most vulnerable.

By making a Will you can be sure your loved ones are cared for. To help you do this the NSPCC has prepared a helpful **free** booklet called *Caring For Their Future*. It's simply written and tells you all about making or changing your Will.

So don't be a Goon. Send for your free copy today.

Please complete and return this form to the NSPCC, 67 Saffron Hill, London EC1N 8RS.

Please send me ———copies of *Caring For Their Future*

Name ———————————————
(Mr/Mrs/Miss/Ms)
Address ——————————————

————————————— Postcode ————— Ref. 910328

Clear copy, a straightforward proposition, easy response and the endorsement of a trusted personality combine to produce effective legacy promotion for the NSPCC and YMCA.

After that the keynote is involvement. The list should be mailed regularly, whenever a practical and valid reason presents itself.

organisation. You may be able to use retired solicitors for this purpose who will find it much easier to make contact at peer level. Oxfam did this some years ago, recruiting a team of retired solicitors who were known internally as 'the death squad'.

Recruiting names and addresses for a legacy database is just the start. Some research, both initially and ongoing, is paramount. What do these people want? What is their profile? What do they think of the work you do? Research should enable you to sort out the serious prospects from the rest. After that the keynote is involvement. The list should be mailed regularly, whenever a practical and valid reason presents itself. The most obvious is the need to keep these potential supporters informed of any fiscal changes which might alter or affect the information you sent them earlier.

Your objective is to build a relationship with these people. All the techniques and practices of relationship fundraising apply. Perhaps you can develop a twice-yearly newsletter. You might wish to invite them to a special open day, or set up a legacy planning event (to complement the donor recognition events you were planning). At some stage, as the relationship develops, you may wish to telephone or visit them or to offer a telephone call or a personal visit from one of your tax or legal specialists. This is a sales operation, of course, but it has to be very soft-sell. I believe that legacy solicitation will have to be regulated and guidelines should be prepared soon. The potential for abuse is obvious.

This risk must be minimised and considered against the potential benefits. The opportunities for legacy marketing are almost limitless, once charities – and universities, hospitals and arts organisations – realise that they can naturally and easily occupy the position of helpful counsellor and source of information on everything to do with estate planning.

In this way charities will begin to change the public's attitudes to and perceptions of charitable legacies – and there will be no looking back.

Charities really do need to campaign to change the *culture* of our society to alter people's attitudes to making a legacy.

Too many British people still believe a legacy to charity is only for the very well off, or that they have done enough during their lifetime, or that their responsibility to their family and friends precludes a charitable legacy. The current status of a charity legacy is too low. We need to raise its desirability, to give it a cachet that is all but irresistible.

No single fundraising organisation will achieve this on its own. It will require collaboration, careful strategy, perseverance and substantial investment.

But it *is* possible to alter radically the public's perception of charitable legacies just as the insurance industry did for personal pension schemes about 30 years ago.

And the possible benefits for charities are simply staggering. By comparison, Aladdin's cave would look like Mother Hubbard's cupboard. There is no greater challenge or opportunity for fundraisers today.

Two ideas
The will-making clinic
I was hosting a session on legacy marketing at an ICFM seminar once and someone in the audience came up with the idea of organising a series of local clinics on making a will, using his charity's local office – there's one in almost every town – and inviting people in for free advice and a cup of tea (and a short presentation from the charity). Handouts would be made available.

Does that sound like a crazy idea to you? To me it sounds like a potential gold mine for someone.

I am sure that if it followed up the idea, this organisation could build its legacy base more quickly and at less cost than most others.

The one-per-cent club

'I'm on umpteen charity mailing lists', said a friend of mine one day, 'but no one has ever written to me and asked for a legacy.' My friend also happens to be quite well off. He went on to say that of the myriad requests for money he gets from charities, sometimes for quite large amounts, not one charity had ever suggested that he give them a small percentage – say one per cent – of the residue of his estate.

'I wouldn't miss it, because I'd be dead,' said my friend. 'And frankly neither would my estate. I think a lot of my friends would agree with that.'

Put in these terms, it really doesn't seem a lot. Who could refuse such a moderate proposition? But my goodness, it would soon mount up!

Does that sound like a crazy idea to you? To me it sounds like a potential gold mine for someone. Imagine if every charity could successfully encourage all their supporters to leave just one per cent of their estate ...

ACTION POINTS

▲ **Read this chapter again (this really is the most important subject in this book).**

▲ **Make a will.**

▲ **Make sure no other promotional activity is jeopardising your legacy income.**

▲ **Prepare a strategy for recognising and dealing with obviously elderly people.**

▲ Take care not to waste money in unproductive legacy advertising.

▲ Invest a percentage of your current legacy income in initiatives to develop new sources.

▲ Adopt the new approach to legacy marketing.

▲ Start to build a legacy database.

▲ Learn from others. Copy their successes and avoid their mistakes.

▲ Research your legators. Ask your donors what they feel about legacies and whether they intend to include your cause in their will.

▲ Encourage legators to leave money to your cause in ways that are most suitable to them, rather than in ways convenient to you.

▲ Target new potential legators already on your donor file.

▲ Write down a concise description of your objectives and your offer. Train and equip your staff and volunteers. Provide them with practical incentives to promote legacies.

▲ Use simple, direct, everyday language.

▲ Negotiate hard for discounts on press space.

▲ Test different media. Keep a guard book of results.

▲ See if you can introduce an offer or adaptation of offer that is unique to you and valuable to donors.

▲ Test any relevant incentives.

▲ Consider a suitable celebrity to introduce your campaign.

▲ Launch a campaign to cultivate solicitors and other advisers.

▲ Research your new legacy database.

▲ Plan an ongoing involvement campaign, possibly including a special newsletter.

▲ Consider running legacy clinics if you can. Test them first.

▲ Start a one-per-cent club.

DONOR PROFILE

Alice Jenks

'Drat!'

The peacefulness of Alice Jenks' Friday afternoon reading by the fireside had been sharply interrupted by the front gate banging. It had startled her and caused her to drop her glasses on the floor. 'Drat!' she exclaimed again.

Alice could hear her granddaughters shouting and laughing as they came running up the drive. She felt around her chair for the lost glasses. There was no way she could make it to the front door without them.

The shouting and general melée at the door increased, punctuated by the occasional anxious call through the letter-box from her daughter Geraldine, who was mildly attempting to establish order on the doorstep.

'Got them!' Triumph mixed with relief as Alice's fingers felt the familiar frames. With the loudest voice she could summon she implored her guests to wait – she was just coming.

Geraldine's worried face met Alice at the door. 'How ghastly you look,' they both thought as Geraldine brushed past her mother to flap and fuss on the inside. The girls stampeded upstairs to make even more noise on the landing. Alice flopped back into her easy chair.

Eventually Geraldine calmed down enough to make Alice a cup of tea and that worked wonders. Geraldine remembered why she had come. 'I've got you that booklet you wanted – you know, the one on how to make a will.'

'Thank you, my dear,' said Alice, taking it and putting it to one side without a glance. She'd read it later when her tiresome daughter and equally tiresome grandchildren had gone.

If she had known what was in her mother's mind perhaps the dutiful daughter wouldn't have been so helpful. Alice had decided she wanted to do some good in the world. That meant doing something more useful with all her worldly goods than leaving them all to Geraldine and her family, who were dependants no longer. They were well established and, Alice reasoned, would be quite unable to appreciate the benefits of granny Alice's estate.

So Alice was going to make some changes. All sorts of things were possible, she now realised, if she were to change her will ...

12

The future

'Still thou art blessed compared wi' me
The present only toucheth thee
But och, I backward cast my e'e
On prospects drear
And forward, though I canna see
I guess, and fear.'

Robert Burns
To a mouse

Crystal ball gazing is usually a pretty futile exercise. Life seems to have a habit of proving all our predictions wrong, just for the hell of it. Most people, I suspect, would prefer not to know what's in store for them in this world, for if they did they'd just get even more depressed, rather like Burns' Ayrshire farmer. We humans are inclined to be naturally negative.

The exception to this inherent human condition, of course, is the relationship fundraiser. He or she has got much to look forward to. It's a great time to be a fundraiser. Not only is he or she part of one of the greatest growth industries to be found anywhere, he or she is also part of this industry at a time of fundamental and very positive change. Fundraising, I believe, is definitely on the up.

But it pays to temper enthusiasm and optimism with some carefully balanced negatives. To consider just

Fundraisers will require the vision to see the long term and the courage to resist the clamouring demands for short-term signs of gain.

where this fundraising 'up' might lead, I think it is worth examining some of the problems of crisis dimensions fundraisers now face. For although future prospects for our profession are very good, the eventual outcome still depends on how these problems will be addressed. And that, I'm pleased to say, lies fairly, squarely and entirely in the hands of fundraisers themselves.

Short-term thinking

'The bottom line matters most' – so says our commercial culture. All commercial organisations naturally think and behave short term and charities are no different. They are, after all, commercial organisations and it is a mistake to think of them otherwise. They have objectives, targets, budgets, plans and goals. As in other commercial organisations the people in charge are usually obsessed with meeting this month's target to the exclusion of all other concerns. So they neglect to lay the foundations for longer-term income, they neglect to sow the seeds that will bring them rich harvests beyond measure in years to come. They'd rather eat the seeds now and in eating their seed corn, ultimately, they destroy themselves.

Yet fundraising is unquestionably a long-term activity and relationship fundraising demands that at intervals throughout that long relationship the fundraising organisation will be required to invest in the relationship with no immediate prospect of financial return. In the future fundraisers will require the vision to see the long term and the courage to resist the clamouring demands for short-term signs of gain. Perhaps in the future the people who surround fundraisers will also come to see that the organisation's interests are best served by those prepared to wait.

Of course, I am not advocating that if your

Survival may be the only possible strategy in the short term, but after a while it becomes something of a strain.

organisation is about to go under from immediate lack of funds you should be investing resources you haven't got in a legacy marketing programme. Fundraisers always have to keep their short-, medium- and long-term aims in balance. Survival may be the only possible strategy in the short term, but after a while it becomes something of a strain.

A programme of relationship fundraising, of course, is every fundraiser's ready answer to short-termism.

Consumerism

The proposed EEC directives and the restrictive clauses contained in Britain's 1991 Charities Bill are both signs of a growth in central government intervention in charities' affairs, prompted, no doubt, by strongly held beliefs that consumers are in need of statutory protection from unscrupulous fundraisers or their agents. However threatening or damaging these initiatives might be for fundraisers, they are likely to grow both in number and in the restrictions they herald. Nor is this movement of consumerism restricted to the UK or, indeed, to Europe.

Of course, consumers have a right to know the full story behind their charitable donations. If they wish to know the precise background to any specific point that information should not be withheld. But they don't need to have every aspect of their transaction spelled out in detail every time: that sort of background technical minutiae is hardly likely to enhance the emotional message in any fundraising appeal and is unlikely to be either in the interest of the charity or interesting to the donor.

But before externally imposed restrictions become intolerable and unworkable, fundraisers must start to show that, in general, the public have no need for protection from them and that specific offenders will be quickly dealt with *within the profession.*

'This is a great idea, but how on earth can I get it past my board?'

Public attention is now on fundraisers. We have to react both with care and reassurance. If we show we can be trusted then all will be well. If not, the forces that would restrict our enterprise need only the slightest further encouragement to pounce, so we had better not allow any more mistakes.

How to change your board

A further problem facing fundraisers is the increasingly important question of how to deal with the board.

This may not seem to be a legitimate aspect of relationship fundraising, but it would be silly to pretend that their relationship with the board isn't one of the most difficult and problematical areas for most fundraisers today. The problem consistently emerges at workshops as fundraisers' biggest worry.

'This is a great idea', the fundraiser will say, 'but how on earth can I get it past my board? They come in once every three months, they skim-read their background briefing papers on the train on their way to the meeting, then spend just two minutes specifically discussing our entire overseas programmes and too long dissecting the performance of the Grimsby gift shop. They haven't a clue why we're here and what we do.'

Another standard fundraiser's tale of woe concerns the board's premature panic in the early stages of a big gift or direct mail campaign, when money is flowing out to cover start-up costs but no money as yet is flowing in. However much fundraisers do to warn their boards that this is natural, even desirable, it seems almost inevitable that individually or collectively they will lose their nerve, just when they need it most.

These are familiar stories. Many charities complain that the people in real need of training and developing are the board itself, and they're the very ones who either

Unfortunately boards appoint fundraisers, not the other way round.

think they know it all already, haven't got the time, or haven't got the commitment.

Of course, not all board members are like that and many charities are fortunate enough to be served by truly exceptional individuals as board members. But generally these are the exceptions that prove the rule. Our trustee system, the very system of institutionalised trust that British charities are built upon, has an in-built flaw. There is no system for ensuring the quality and ability of trustees.

This has to change.

As professionalism increases amongst fundraisers it becomes ever more apparent that charity management is not the legitimate province of the well-intentioned amateur. It probably never was, but the increasing complexity and sophistication of the modern voluntary organisation means that well-meaning incompetents can now do considerable harm as well as waste copious amounts of time and money.

Charities don't want or need more names for their letterhead. They do need experienced, imaginative and available senior practitioners who understand their role and are prepared to undertake the task of supporting and guiding the full-time salaried staff. But even if standards and codes of practice could be established for charity boards, it is still hard to see how they could be implemented by any but the most brave or most foolish senior management teams. Unfortunately boards appoint fundraisers, not the other way round.

The tragedy is that those board members who are aware of how much charities have changed over the past two decades and of the implications and potential of that change are precisely the ones who fundraisers *don't* need to convert. The rest remain in blissful ignorance – it's nothing to do with them.

The best way to disarm an enemy is to make friends.

'Never did like that computer thing, you know.'

'My wife got some direct mail once. Hates it, positively hates it.'

'Yes, I think Grimsby would be a good place for a charity shop, you know. It's got a jolly good station hotel.'

'I think our fundraising department is really quite adequate – two people and a secretary.'

'What an appalling idea, that big gift thing. Next we know, you'll be asking me for money, what?!'

Similar phrases are familiar fare to fundraisers who've sat through successions of old-style board meetings that seem as interminable as they are unstructured and unproductive.

If you have difficulty with your board, perhaps a useful starting point towards effecting change might be to give them a copy of this book.

There is often a lot the fundraiser can do to bring relationship fundraising to the board. Involve them in planning your strategy, prepare special materials and presentations to keep them informed and involved, don't take them for granted. The best way to disarm an enemy is to make friends.

Persuade your board to meet donors, to visit projects, to go to workshops and seminars.

The technique takeover

Most fundraisers are coming to realise there is a proper limit to technique. Technique can only take us so far. Yet some still rigidly adhere to the formulae that worked so well a few years ago but are now showing increasing signs of tiredness. They are the minority.

The old formulae are now being challenged. Fundraisers are becoming increasingly aware that donors are not sitting targets; they are not easily fooled.

The future, as always, will belong to the innovator and those who are close behind.

What worked today won't necessarily work tomorrow. The future, as always, will belong to the innovator and those who are close behind.

The technique takeover is one crisis that I think is passing and indeed is almost past now. It is only a matter of time. We are not going to become an industry of soulless money-making machines. The embrace of the cut-throat world of commerce has left most fundraisers rather cold although the experience has not been entirely worthless. It has taught us quite a lot.

Technique, thankfully, will not be taking over. It will perhaps be taking its rightful place, as a valued assistant.

The lack of committed talent

The final epic problem facing fundraisers worldwide is the need to attract new people, the right people, into this business. We also have to find ways to retain the good people we have got and to reverse the current disastrous trend of high staff turnover as people leave the fundraising business after a few short years because it simply doesn't offer enough to make staying worthwhile. We need talented, resourceful, energetic, well-qualified and experienced personnel at all levels who really want to make a career in fundraising. Above all we need people who are committed, or are capable of becoming committed to the work they are going to do. Remember the difference between bacon and eggs.

We need pigs, not hens.

A happy ending

One thing I am sure of is that Theodore Levitt (see page 47) was right. The future for marketing professionals will indeed be one of more and more intensified relationships with customers in every field, from car buyers to magazine readers, from ice-cream addicts to

When it comes to relationship building, to developing and maximising the potential benefits of a long-standing customer relationship, fundraisers have the edge on all other marketing areas.

footwear freaks, from holidaymakers to home-owners, from gardeners and golfers to givers to charitable causes. That gives me a great deal of cause for optimism. Because when it comes to relationship building, to developing and maximising the potential benefits of a long-standing customer relationship, fundraisers have the edge on all other marketing areas. So if that is the future it seems to be going our way.

As this book, quite properly, comes to a close it makes sense to end on a few positive notes. There follows some of the good things I predict will happen for fundraisers in the near future and some of the not so good things that I confidently believe won't happen.

We will see
- More research.
- Better training and recruitment resulting in a regular supply of 'career' fundraisers.
- An enhanced image of our profession and improved understanding of what we do.
- Better leadership from trustees.
- An end to the absurd notion of fixed cost:income ratios for charities. How can a full service child care charity expect to run its organisation on the same expense ratio as one that merely allocates grants? And why should they be judged as the same?

Instead we will see better educating of donors as to what running a large voluntary organisation really involves and what it costs. The emphasis then will clearly be on *value for money* which will benefit both the donor and the cause.

We will not see
- The decline of print as a key medium of communicating with donors – *whatever* technology may bring.

- The increasing commercialism of charities as exemplified by sweepstake mailings, lotteries and so forth. Charities can sometimes ride piggyback on these devices but in the long run they only harm themselves if they take part in this kind of promotion.
- The restriction of personal data to such an extent that we can't accurately target who *not* to send appeals to.
- The disappearance of donors as the baby boomers grow older and the 'unimaginative' TV generation reaches maturity. I just don't believe these people will be able to resist a good fundraising appeal any more than their parents could.

That's what I expect to see and what I expect not to see. After that perhaps I might be allowed some wishful thinking.

What I'd really like to see
- More imaginative and courageous communications from charities. After all, fundraisers have the most dramatic and moving stories in the world to tell.
- Better leadership and motivation for volunteers and for staff at all levels and a less haphazard approach to the development of people – fundraising's greatest asset.
- More collaboration between charities, both on research and on promotion.
- Fundraising to become established in our schools and universities as a viable and rewarding career opportunity.
- A better image for fundraisers and charities generally.
- Encouragement of a more positive view of donors among fundraising professionals. If we can elevate the status of donors we can promote giving generally.
- Real teeth for our professional associations in regulating and controlling junk marketing and other unprofessional conduct from fundraisers.

... if people know you and like you they are far more likely to want to do business with you.

• Somebody to discover a practical alternative to the standard salutation 'dear friend'. It has all the sincerity and warmth of 'have a nice day' yet we seem to be stuck with it.

• Another name change I'd really like to see is a better word or phrase to describe the sector in society that fundraisers operate within. It's called the voluntary sector, or the not-for-profit sector and neither of these terms means very much to most people or adequately represents the importance and contribution of the organisations they purport to encompass.

Peter Drucker called it the human change sector, because its products are changed human beings. I see what he's getting at but the term seems as incomplete as the others and equally, if not more, ambiguous.

I don't have a valid suggestion of my own. It's no easy task. If any reader would care to venture their idea of a suitable catch-all word or phrase to describe our industry, please let me know.

• I'd really like to see dedicated donor service departments, set up to handle all contact with donors including all mail and telephone calls, making use of all the information donors provide so that donors can have one coordinated point of contact in one central place.

Maybe a lot of this is just wishful thinking, pie in the sky, but if these last wishes could come true, the future for fundraisers would not just be brilliant and full of promise, it would be guaranteed even greater success.

In the future fundraisers will pay increasing attention to the simple fact that is the core of this book: if people know you and like you they are far more likely to want to do business with you. For fundraisers the future will certainly be one of more and more intensified relationships.

ACTION POINTS

▲ Combat short-term thinking whenever and wherever it occurs in your organisation.

▲ Encourage management and subordinates to think long term and to set targets in short, medium and long terms.

▲ Encourage your board members to get involved; to understand your objectives and your problems. Persuade them to go on appropriate training courses.

▲ Organise presentations, training sessions and visits to projects for your board.

▲ Involve your board by encouraging them to meet donors at your functions or in the donors' own homes.

▲ Buy extra copies of this book to give as presents to your board of management (you may detect a mild tinge of vested interest here).

▲ See what you can do to encourage some of the positive developments that might be round the corner for fundraising.

DONOR PROFILE

Mr and Mrs Christisen

'Who was it?'

'Oh, nobody,' answered Mr Christisen wearily as he hung up. 'Just someone wanting to ask us some questions over the phone. I told them Milady wasn't home.'

'Couldn't you just have said we're not interested?' said Mrs Christisen irritably. 'They'll only ring back.'

'I don't think so,' replied her husband with a chuckle. 'I told him she'd gone up the Irrawaddy to pacify the natives and won't be back until after the big monsoon. He seemed thrown by that and rang off.'

Mr Christisen sat down by the fireside.

'I wish I could take these people seriously, you know. From where I sit there seem to be more problems in the world than ever before. Yet all these people can do is make facile phone calls and send me puerile and phoney begging letters.'

'What people, dear?' said Mrs Christisen patiently. 'And where exactly do you sit?'

'Where indeed!' Her husband was becoming just a bit indignant. 'It's all these worthy causes. I'm as generous as the next man but they're just not reaching me, not at all. When are they going to get their act together and start convincing me that they *can* make a difference in this mess of a world?'

Mrs Christisen put down her book and began to put on her cardigan.

'You could always join the Friends of Wetherfield Hospital or sponsor a duck or have your head shaved for charity. It's not them that's short of ideas, you know. It's you.' Mrs Christisen turned as she put on her coat. 'You really are an old skinflint, you know. You've got pots of money and you never do anything useful with it.'

'I'm not convinced it won't just be frittered away,' said Mr Christisen with some resignation. 'When they show me it'll do some good, they'll not find me ungenerous. Where are you going?'

'I've got a Greenpeace meeting tonight,' his wife replied, picking up her wet suit in the holdall behind the door. 'We're blocking the sewage outlet beside the harbour and hanging a 'Stop the dumping' banner across the town hall. I should be back by nine, though.'

The phone rang again just as Mrs Christisen closed the door behind her. 'Not again', thought Mr Christisen, wondering what to tell them this time.

Bibliography

Bayley, Ted D *The Fund Raiser's Guide to Successful Campaigns* McGraw-Hill, New York, 1988.

*Bird, Drayton *Commonsense Direct Marketing* The Printed Shop, London, 1982.

Burnett, Ken *Charity Annual Reports. The Complete Guide to Planning and Production* The Directory of Social Change, London, 1987.

Burnett, Ken (editor) *Advertising by Charities*. The Directory of Social Change, London, 1986.

Crouch, Sunny *Marketing Research for Managers* Pan Books/Heinemann, London, 1984.

Di Sciullo, Jean *Marketing et Communication des Associations* Editions Juris-Service, Lyon, 1988.

Drucker, Peter F *Managing the Non-profit Organization* Butterworth-Heinemann, Oxford, 1990.

Evans, Harold *Pictures on a Page* Heinemann, London, 1982.

Fraser-Robinson, John *Total Quality Marketing* Kogan Page, London, 1991.

Fraser-Robinson, John *The Secrets of Effective Direct Mail* McGraw-Hill, London, 1989.

Gordon Lewis, Herschell *How to Write Powerful Fund Raising Letters* Pluribus Press, Chicago, 1989.

Kobs, Jim *Profitable Direct Marketing* NTC Business Books, Lincolnwood, Illinois, 1988.

Kotler, Philip and Andreasen, Alan *Strategic Marketing for Nonprofit Organizations* Prentice Hall, New Jersey, 1991.

*Leiderman, Robert *The Telephone Book* McGraw-Hill, London, 1990.

Levitt, Theodore *The Marketing Imagination* The Free Press, New York, 1986.

Lord, James Gregory *The Raising of Money* Third Sector Press, Cleveland, Ohio, 1990.

Makens, James C *The 12-day Marketing Plan* Thorsons Publishers, Wellingborough, Northamptonshire, 1989.

McCorkell, Graeme *Advertising that Pulls Response* McGraw-Hill, London, 1990.

McDonald, Malcolm *Marketing Plans. How to Prepare Them. How to Use Them* Heinemann, London, 1984.

McDonald, Malcolm and Morris, Peter *The Marketing Plan. A Pictorial Guide for Managers* Heinemann Professional Publishing, Oxford, 1989.

McDonald, Malcolm and Leppard, John *The Marketing Audit* Butterworth-Heinemann, Oxford, 1991.

McQuillan, Judith (editor) *Charity Trends* Charities Aid Foundation, Tonbridge, Kent, 1991.

Mullin, Redmond *The Fundraising Cycle* Redmond Mullin Ltd, London, 1989.

Nash, Edward L *The Direct Marketing Handbook* McGraw-Hill, New York, 1984.

*Nichols, Judith E *Changing Demographics: Fund Raising in the 1990s* Bonus Books, Chicago, 1990.

*Ogilvy, David *Confessions of an Advertising Man* Pan Books, London, 1987.

*Ogilvy, David *Ogilvy on Advertising* Pan Books, London, 1984.

Panas, Jerold *Born to Raise* Pluribus Press, Chicago, 1988.

Rapp, Stan and Collins, Tom *MaxiMarketing* McGraw-Hill, New York, 1976.

Weber, Nathan (editor) *Giving USA* AAFRC Trust for Philanthropy, New York, 1990.

Williams, Ian *The Alms Trade. Charities, Past, Present and Future* Unwin Hyman, London, 1989.

* Author's particular recommendation.

Glossary

A/B split copy
Newspapers which are printed on more than one press often offer the facility to test different advertisements by printing alternate copies of their paper with either advertisement A or advertisement B. It is a very effective way to test different concepts. The term has now been widened to include any equally accurate test whether in newspapers or elsewhere and even if multiple approaches are being simultaneously tested.

Baby boomer
Someone born during the baby boom after the Second World War, between 1948 and 1964.

Beneficiaries
People who benefit from a will.

Codicil
A further document making a change, or adding to, an existing will. It must comply with the same formalities as the will.

Executor
Person appointed to carry out the terms of a will.

Data Protection Act
The Data Protection Act 1984 enables the UK Government to comply with the European Convention

on data protection and to meet growing concern about the use of personal data. The act applies to those who automatically process personal data.

Data Protection Registrar

All data users and computer bureaux must register with the Data Protection Registrar who provides guidance on principles of data protection and administers the terms of the Act, including instigating appropriate legal action if the terms of the Act are breached.

De-duplication programme

Running two lists together to identify exact duplicates one of which can be removed to avoid double mailing.

Estate

The total of what is left in a will including all property and money.

Guard book

A permanent record of your promotional results, either loose-leaf or bound. A copy of each promotion should be pasted into the book with all salient details including date, competitive activity, relevant events (eg weather, world headlines), tests, costs and all results.

Intestate

Someone dies intestate if they have not made a will.

Johnson box

The typed rectangle of punchy copy that appears in direct mail letters usually at the top above the salutation. It acts as an extended headline. Presumably someone called Johnson achieved immortality by inventing it.

Legacy/bequest

A gift left in a will.

Legatee
The recipient of a legacy.

Legator
Person leaving a legacy.

Lift letter
The second letter in a mailing pack designed to 'lift' response.

Mailsort
Mailsort is a trademark of the Royal Mail covering a range of services for large volume mailings, including discounts and terms and conditions for sorting and delivery of different types of mail. The mailsort symbol is a distinctive letter M where the stamps usually are.

Mailing Preference Service
The UK's register of individuals who have expressed the wish to be excluded from certain mailings.

Proved will
A will that has been established to be genuine and valid.

Pecuniary bequest
A gift of a fixed amount left in a will.

Reciprocal mailings
One charity mails another charity's donors and, in turn, allows that charity to mail its material to a similar segment of its own donors.

Residue
What is left of an estate after all debts, tax, costs and specific and pecuniary bequests have been paid.

Residuary bequest
The gift of all or part of the residue of an estate.

Reversionary bequest
A named person has access to the value of the estate which only reverts to another beneficiary on the death of the named person.

Index